When Mayors
Take Charge

When Mayors Take Charge

School Governance in the City

Joseph P. Viteritti

Editor

BROOKINGS INSTITUTION PRESS
Washington, D.C.

ABOUT BROOKINGS
The Brookings Institution is a private nonprofit organization devoted to research, education, and publication on important issues of domestic and foreign policy. Its principal purpose is to bring the highest quality independent research and analysis to bear on current and emerging policy problems. Interpretations or conclusions in Brookings publications should be understood to be solely those of the authors.

Library of Congress Cataloging-in-Publication Data
When mayors take charge : school governance in the city / [edited by] Joseph P. Viteritti.
       p.   cm.
   Includes bibliographical references and index.
   Summary: "Assesses the results of mayoral control nationwide, detailing the experience in three key cities: Boston and Chicago, the major prototypes for mayoral control, and Detroit, where mayoral control was not successful. Also provides the first in-depth examination of New York City, where the law installing mayoral control sunsets in 2009"—Provided by publisher.
   ISBN 978-0-8157-9044-0 (cloth : alk. paper) —
   ISBN 978-0-8157-9043-3 (pbk. : alk. paper)
   1. School districts—United States—Administration—Case studies. 2. Urban schools—United States—Administration—Case studies. 3. Public schools—United States—Administration—Case studies. I. Viteritti, Joseph P., 1946– II. Title.
   LB2817.3.W47 2009
   379.1'530973—dc22   2008045221

9 8 7 6 5 4 3 2 1

The paper used in this publication meets minimum requirements of the American National Standard for Information Sciences—Permanence of Paper for Printed Library Materials: ANSI Z39.48-1992.

Typeset in Minion

Composition by Cynthia Stock
Silver Spring, Maryland

Printed by R. R. Donnelley
Harrisonburg, Virginia

Contents

Acknowledgments

This book would not have been possible had Betsy Gotbaum not stepped up to the plate and taken on a project that many said was politically untouchable. Steve Aiello exercised skillful leadership as chair, keeping us focused on our mission and undeterred by political winds. Our panel, whose members offered a diversity of perspectives, shared a common commitment to produce a quality report. Tomas Hunt was a full partner in the project from beginning to end. Lauralie Ezra and Mariah Fraser provided excellent backup. Tracy Munford and Allan Goldfarb performed beyond the call of duty. At Brookings, Chris Kelaher was a supportive editor, while Mary Kwak, Janet Walker, and Susan Woollen saw to it that the manuscript pages were converted into a book. Katherine Kimball did a superb job copyediting the chapters. Maria Sese Paul of Sese/Paul Design performed her usual magic to produce a catchy cover. Each chapter, including those by the editor, represents the views of its author and not necessarily those of the Commission on School Governance, its members as a whole, or the Public Advocate for the City of New York. The project was supported by a generous gift from an anonymous donor.

LETTER FROM BETSY GOTBAUM

Public Advocate for the City of New York

Dear Reader:

In 2002 New York state law eliminated elected school boards and gave control of the New York City schools to the mayor. This law expires in June 2009. If the state legislature allows the law to sunset, the school system will revert back to the former structure. Anticipating the need for legislative action, Catherine Nolan, chair of the Education Committee of the State Assembly, asked me, as public advocate for the city of New York, to appoint a panel that would study the issue of mayoral control and make recommendations to the state legislature.

My professional interest in education policy began when I served as an assistant to Mayor John Lindsay. Earlier, upon graduating from college, I taught school in Brazil and subsequently received a graduate degree from Teachers College, Columbia University. Since becoming public advocate in 2002, I have focused on the issue of education, and my office has prepared many reports on the school system and its policies. Often these reports have been critical.

As defined by the New York City charter, the public advocate is "the watchdog" over the delivery of city services and the policies of the administration. In this sense, my office is uniquely positioned to evaluate school governance in New York City, but the political realities of this city demanded something independent and objective. To meet this need, I convened a commission comprising individuals who are truly independent, well respected, and well versed in the world of education.

I was delighted when Steve Aiello agreed to serve as chair of the commission. Steve, currently of Hill & Knowlton, is one of the leading public relations executives in New York. Before putting together an impressive resume of public service, he started out as a New York City public school teacher. Immediately before leaving New York in 1979 to work in the White House as a special assistant to President Jimmy Carter, he served as president of the New York City Board of Education and has been deeply involved in education and public policy issues ever since.

Steve's leadership has been bolstered by two distinguished cochairs on the commission. Lilliam Barrios-Paoli, a cultural anthropologist by training, has spent most of her career in public service. Before becoming president and chief executive officer of Safe Space NYC, Lilliam headed up a wide array of agencies and organizations in New York in the areas of employment, personnel, housing, health, and social services and chaired the Education Policy Committee of the New York City Partnership. David Jones has been president and chief executive officer of the Community Service Society of New York since 1986. Before that, he served as executive director to the Youth Services Bureau in New York City, as a special adviser to Mayor Edward Koch, and as chairman of the board of the Carver Federal Savings Bank.

The other members of the commission bring a diversity of perspectives. Journalist Clara Hemphill, also a contributor to this volume, is the principal author of three books that the *New York Times* has called the "most definitive guides" to public schools in New York City. Joan McKeever-Thomas has spent most of her career as an advocate for parents and teachers and is a former member of the citywide Panel for Educational Policy. Bert Pogrebin, an attorney with Littler Mendelson, spent fifteen years as the chief labor negotiator for the New York City Board of Education. Jeany Persaud is former chair of the Chancellor's Parent Advisory Council. Kim Sweet, former associate general counsel of New York Lawyers for the Public Interest, is executive director of Advocates for Children. Jacqueline Wayans is an education writer, journalist, and parent advocate.

The executive director of the commission, Joe Viteritti, was one of the first people I engaged when the idea of this commission occurred. It was his idea to solicit the fine papers that have been edited for inclusion in this volume. It was his job to accumulate all the evidence collected by the commission, present it to the members, and work with them to prepare a report. The report speaks for itself. It can be found on the website of the Public Advocate for the City of New York (http://pubadvocate.nyc.gov/documents/CSGFINAL REPORT9-4-08.pdf).

For nearly a year, the commissioners put in long hours toward this effort, and I am proud of the work they have done. I am confident that the commission's findings and recommendations will aid the state legislature in its deliberations to create an improved school governance structure for New York City.

BETSY GOTBAUM
Public Advocate for the City of New York

STEPHEN R. AIELLO

Prologue

When Betsy Gotbaum approached me about serving as chair of the Commission on School Governance, I was knee deep in the crisis of a client, which tends to be the nature of my business. Nevertheless, I agreed without a moment's hesitation. As Betsy has already explained, education has always been close to my heart. The assignment could have a significant impact on the future of the New York City public schools and, more important, on the children who attend them. Beyond that, the project gave me an opportunity to work with individuals I have known, liked, and respected for many years.

Some of my friends in New York had told me that taking up the governance question would be like opening a can of worms. But the can had already been left wide open by the state legislature, when it had the good sense to insert a sunset provision in the 2002 governance law requiring a review and creating an opportunity for revision. I speak from experience when I say that education policymaking in New York is messy; but democracy is messy, as it was meant to be. In the course of its work, the commission heard from more than one hundred individuals in New York, including public officials, labor leaders, community organizers, public school parents, and business representatives, not to mention Deputy Mayor Dennis Walcott and the schools chancellor, Joel Klein. We met with individual stakeholders, conducted parent forums in each of the five city boroughs, held three days of public hearings, and set up a website where people could get information on the work of the commission and submit their viewpoints on the governance issue.

One of the great challenges faced by commission members was to separate our (and others') assessment of the governance structure from our assessment of the incumbent administration in New York, which was not part of our mandate to consider. To focus our attention on the governance issue, we solicited papers from leading researchers who had studied governance and the experience with mayoral control in other major cities as well as New York. These papers helped us, and we hope others, understand common themes, considerations, and problems that had emerged in other places and put our own experience in New York in a broader analytic perspective.

These excellent papers have now been edited and updated for inclusion in this volume. The collection also includes two new chapters and a postscript by Joseph Viteritti, our executive director and the editor of the book. Drawing on his own considerable expertise, Joe has positioned our work in New York in a wider historical and political context.

If you have an interest in learning more about the governance of urban schools and the role that mayors can play in running these schools, this book is a wonderful place to start.

When Mayors Take Charge

JOSEPH P. VITERITTI

1

Why Governance Matters

Governance is an institutional arrangement that assigns power to public officials and defines the mechanisms for holding them accountable. In big-city school districts, good governance is the progeny of an uneasy marriage between democratic and managerial ideals. Like all large organizations, urban school districts require the skillful coordination of human and material resources; yet they are public institutions. Whereas democracy is based on a commitment to wide participation and deliberation in decisionmaking, management is energized by a determination to get things done efficiently and effectively. Democracy can be awkward, slow moving, and cumbersome, while managers need to be bold, agile, and sometimes obstinate. In one sphere patience is a virtue; in the other it can be seen as a disability.

Striking the proper balance between democratic and managerial expectations in the design of a governance system is no easy task. It is neither a science nor an art. It is itself a political process in the best sense. To have legitimacy, a governance system must be designed to involve those who have a stake in its functioning, or at least their duly chosen delegates. It must be carefully adapted to the political and institutional environment in which it is expected to thrive. It must not only create opportunities for leadership but also allow for representation, responsiveness, and transparency. The governance question goes to the heart of an American conversation that began in a small room in Philadelphia during the summer of 1787 and continues today throughout the land on multiple levels.

Roots and Branches

Americans have always been suspicious of concentrated power. Their system of government is based on the principle of checks and balances, according to which authority is shared among institutions. It is purposely clumsy. The power of local government is further circumscribed under American federalism. As a matter of law, local government is a "creature of the state." Even in states that honor the principle of home rule—a domain of authority the states assign to city governments on local issues—the amount of discretion appropriated to city governments is determined by the state legislature, which in most places enjoys "plenary power."[1] At the municipal level, mayors are expected to share power with a city council and in some places a city manager. Because of the distinct nature of local government—which more than any sphere in the public sector is responsible for the daily delivery of services to people and communities—local executives are granted wide latitude in administration. It is their job to make sure the buses run on time, get the trash collected, oversee the police, supervise emergency services, operate parks and recreation programs, and administer health and social services for the poor.

Education, on which more state and local dollars are spent than any other public service, has historically been treated as a special case. For more than a century and a half, local school boards have been elected so that schools can function separate and apart from the municipality, even though there are not many scholars remaining who share the notion once held by Progressive Era reformers that this separation will insulate schools from politics. That claim seems utterly naïve to anybody who has ever witnessed the rough-and-tumble of school politics, writ large or small. Nevertheless, the traditional model for governance endures in most places.

Separating education from an array of municipal services that are geared toward the needs of young people makes it more difficult to integrate these same services with what goes on in schools where children and young people congregate daily. In big cities, where disadvantaged students are especially dependent on support services to be ready for school, the need for service integration is more pronounced. Big-city school districts, for the past fifty years, have been the great disappointment in American education.[2] When we speak of the learning gap between the races in this country—which continues to be about four years in reading and mathematics—we are generally referring to the failure of urban schools, which are responsible for teaching a disproportionate number of students from African American and Latino communities.

It should come as no surprise that this national frustration with urban schools has led to demands for accountability and leadership. Nor should it be a surprise that opinion leaders at the local level turned to popularly elected mayors to answer the call. Somebody had to take charge. Somebody had to be held responsible. Somebody had to grasp this stubborn bull of a bureaucracy by the horns and show that urban school systems could be managed. A strong executive might fill the bill. Why not let the mayor run the schools in the same way that he or she runs other city agencies?

There was a new theory of democracy embedded in the call for mayoral control. Ironically, the idea was also borrowed from Progressive Era reformers who gave us independent school boards. When these nineteenth-century reformers got fed up with the corrupt shenanigans of their city councils, they turned to a strong-mayor model, which they called good government.[3] The mayor would be a more visible public figure, so they thought, more easily scrutinized by voters. The position itself would attract a higher caliber of personnel than that typically found in the council—a business leader, perhaps, who was above politics. He (and the mayor was most surely a "he" in those days) was more likely to clean up the mess that machine politicians had created in the corrupt recesses of the government, or so it was thought.

This new notion of municipal democracy was somewhat revolutionary for a generation brought up according to the precepts of Jeffersonian localism and Jacksonian populism. Decentralized grassroots democracy, epitomized in local legislatures, was considered to be closer to the people. The spoils system had allowed common folk to penetrate a class-based government controlled by wealthy gentlemen. In the earliest iterations of the office, American mayors were chosen by the city council. This was far more democratic than the previous arrangement, in which state governors selected city mayors, often from a rival party unsympathetic to local interests—themselves an improvement over the colonial governors who preceded them. Yes, the council, it could be argued, was close to the people. Sometimes, though, it got too close, and the grass roots of city politics had a way of burying its practitioners in deep layers of political soil. Popularly elected mayors were supposed to save us from all that as the nineteenth century turned into the twentieth.

There is a corollary theory of democracy implicit in the recent demands for mayoral control of the schools, of which I admittedly have been an early and consistent proponent.[4] Like contests for local legislatures, school board elections are characterized by low voter interest. Like members of city councils, members of school boards are not usually high-profile political personages in their local communities, especially in big cities. Certainly they were not so visible as mayors, and therefore they could be less subject to popular review. Visibility was supposed to promise accountability.

The introduction of the mass media into politics and government further changed the terms of conducting business in the public sector and turned the axiom of Jeffersonian localism on its head. Access to government, or at least knowledge about it, was no longer a function of geographic proximity, as it was in Jefferson's time. Citizens now seem to know less about officials who emerge from their own neighborhood institutions than about those who rule from the high towers of the government. The faces of government executives are more likely to be plastered on the front pages and flashed across video screens. That is true today from the president of the United States on down to the most remote official on the local planning or school board. Executives in government are more familiar to the average person. This does not automatically translate into greater accountability, but it is a start.

Elected school boards, especially those in large urban areas, brought their own problems as governing institutions. Those that were elected at large tended to underrepresent minority populations because minorities could be outvoted in citywide contests.[5] Those who were elected through single-member districts that represented discrete geographic communities tended to provoke, feed, and accentuate neighborhood animosities, which were often defined by race, ethnicity, and class.[6] Mayoral control, it was hoped, would bring peace and stability. The city of Boston, which tried both types of school boards before putting the mayor in charge of its schools, illustrates this point nicely. Desegregation battles in Boston, fought out on the local school board as well as in federal court, had brought racial animosity to an unprecedented level in the North. Mayoral control in Boston has engendered continuity in leadership and a new focus on learning. The Boston story is important because the Boston experience became an impetus behind contemporary demands for mayoral control of the schools in other cities, numbering nearly a dozen to date.[7]

Coinciding with enhanced federal and state roles brought on in education by more regulation, proficiency standards, and interventionist courts, the appearance of education mayors in big cities has led some scholars to speculate whether school boards, notably elected boards, are an endangered species.[8] A recent article in the *Atlantic Monthly* appearing under the title "First, Kill All the School Boards" actually argues the case along these lines rather strongly. The author, Matt Miller, quotes Mark Twain, who once said, "In the first place, God made idiots.... This was for practice. Then he made School Boards." The article approvingly cites the emergence of mayoral control in Boston and New

York and concludes that in an ideal world, we would "scrap" school boards, "especially in big cities, where most poor children live."[9]

Patterns of Mayoral Control

Not all forms of mayoral control are the same. In Boston the mayor picks a seven-member school committee from a list of names nominated by a screening panel, and then the committee chooses the superintendent. In Washington, D.C., the mayor selects the chancellor (superintendent) and four of nine board members, who must be confirmed by the city council (the other five members are elected). In New York the mayor selects eight of thirteen school board members, including the schools chancellor, who serves as superintendent of schools and chair of the board. As a result, each of these mayors enjoys different powers and prerogatives with regard to education policy and administration. In all cases the term *mayoral control* is an exaggeration, since all local chief executives are forced to share authority on municipal matters with other state, local, and federal officials. Education is no exception.

As several of our authors explain more fully in later chapters, the involvement of mayors in education, especially in large cities, where school districts depend on municipal officials for local funding, is not a new phenomenon.[10] From 1955 to 1976 Mayor Richard J. Daley appointed all members of the Chicago school board, as did all of his successors at city hall until 1995, when his son, Mayor Richard M. Daley, took over the schools. Although as mayor the elder Daley did not have formal authority to appoint the school superintendent, as the powerful Cook County boss of the Democratic Party he was able to effectively oversee educational affairs in much the way he ruled over all governmental matters in Chicago and its environs. But the two mayors functioned differently. The father operated according to a political model for governing; the son operates more as a manager.

The new model for governing carries different expectations for the present-day "education mayor." The elder Daley was preoccupied with keeping the political peace and maintaining control. This might have involved careful attention to the distribution of jobs to constituent groups that produced winning coalitions at the polls or making sure that African American students were kept out of schools in white neighborhoods where they were unwanted. It rarely involved a focus on improved instruction. Nor would current demands for the efficient management of resources have jibed well with the reward system that kept the political machinery of old Chicago humming. It is not accidental that the incumbent school chief in Chicago is called a chief executive officer or that the younger Daley chose his former budget director, Paul Vallas, to be the first individual to hold that office. Chicago's corporate model may be the purest form of managerialism that exists in American education; it is also a loose paradigm for the new type of school administrator installed by contemporary education mayors.

Never before were school organizations appended so closely to the institutional apparatus of the municipal government. Despite the promise of better service integration, some critics would wonder out loud whether schools really are like other city agencies. Actually, they are not. Each school is a unique community with its own culture. Each school requires intimate levels of cooperation from administrators, teachers, students, parents, and neighborhood actors in order to thrive.[11] No other local service requires this kind of collaboration. Schools are different.

Then again, no two agencies in city government are alike. Ask any police officer, firefighter, hospital nurse, or pothole filler. Moreover, if the integration of education into the governance structure of municipalities raises anxieties among school people, we should be reminded that the old-style education bureaucracies overseen by traditional school boards were notoriously inept, wasteful, and obstructive. Their failure to bring a majority of students to an acceptable level of academic achievement was a major reason behind calls for mayoral control. The old system did not work for most inner-city children.

Empowering mayors with such authority, nonetheless, introduced new risks. Although these innovative arrangements may allow the mayor to hold professional educators more accountable, not everybody is convinced that the voting booth is an adequate instrument for holding the mayor accountable. An up-or-down vote every four years may not be enough. The problem is exacerbated in jurisdictions that have term limits, in which an incumbent mayor might be required to stand for reelection only once in eight years. In other cases, it can turn the schools or their test scores into campaign props. Some commentators, however, hold that these are empty concerns since the electoral process seems to work in other policy domains locally and nationally. Or does it?

Although the city council, which has power to approve the local budget, should serve as an institutional check on local chief executives, the record of local legislatures is mixed, at best. As an institution, the council, especially in big cities, has had a difficult time shaking off its nineteenth-century reputation for cronyism, pettiness, and incompetence, much of it well deserved. While the high visibility of media mayors has increased opportunities for public scrutiny, it has also created a more formidable bully pulpit, which empowers skilled incumbents to manipulate coverage and sway public opinion. This was not as much a problem with Progressive Era mayors, who did not have access to electronic communications.

Accountability can be especially challenging now, when the mayor's press office has control over the very data by which the incumbent might be judged. It places an enormous responsibility on reporters to read beyond press releases and investigate the evidence behind a story. The passage of the No Child Left Behind Act and the imposition of reporting requirements by state education agencies have facilitated this role somewhat, but investigative news gathering still requires digging by the press. Not all reporters have the time, resources, and expertise to meet the challenge.

A reading of the professional literature, in these pages and elsewhere, reveals certain patterns that are evident in the politics of school governance. Whenever and wherever mayoral control of the schools was implemented, it was usually done with the strong support of business leaders. The latter have a clear stake in education. Good schools are a prerequisite for a business-friendly environment. An educated population is essential for a skilled workforce. There is a natural affinity between the corporate organizational culture and a managerial model that fixes responsibility in the hands of a strong executive who is expected to manage tax-generated resources wisely. In Boston the productive engagement of the business community proved to be of strategic importance in building a coalition for school improvement. As Dorothy Shipps warns in her study of Chicago, however, an overreliance on the business model for public schools can undermine democratic norms and leave ordinary people on the sidelines of school politics.

The implementation of mayoral control is usually a source of anxiety in African American and Latino communities, whose children constitute a majority of the students who attend urban schools. The centralization of power and authority at city hall can remove decisionmaking from community-based institutions, including schools themselves, where parents tend to have better access. Unlike business leaders, most parents do not have the political clout that is needed to get a call through to the mayor's office. Nor does mayoral control provide parents with the same kinds of local connections that are possible when a neighborhood gets to elect its own representative to a school board. Notwithstanding the messy politics associated with school boards, mayoral control replaces a governance structure designed on the basis of single-member representation at the community level with leadership that is chosen on an at-large citywide basis.

There is nothing necessarily illegal or unfair about the new arrangements, unlike certain types of electoral systems that systematically penalized minority voters; yet it is understandable why the more centralized system is greeted with caution and even suspicion by people who already see themselves as being powerless.[12] A lack of confidence in a governing arrangement, the widespread perception that it is unfair or rigged to favor one group over another, can ultimately bring it down. The Detroit experience, which ended with the termination of mayoral control in 2005, demonstrates the point rather dramatically. Legitimacy is indispensable to the health of any democratic institution. As Wilbur Rich adroitly explains in his chapter 7, the political tensions that surrounded the Detroit schools were multilayered, involving racial, partisan, and regional animosities. City residents had little confidence in the capacity of the system to treat them or their concerns seriously.

To be honest, school politics in the city, whether played out in Detroit or elsewhere, was never a beacon of robust democracy. Those who need to derive the most from the system in terms of instructional and support services usually are among the least empowered to demand it. As noted earlier, school board elections have historically been characterized by low turnout rates when compared with other political contests. Low turnout favors organized groups, which do not always represent populations in the schools. Consider the case of New York City. Before the 2002 implementation of mayoral control, New York had one of the most ambitious systems of political decentralization in the country. Yet for more than thirty years, turnout rates in community school board elections had not exceeded 10 percent of the eligible voters and were usually much lower. Candidates were largely anonymous. Although there is some dissatisfaction with the current arrangement in New York, there is no overwhelming public outcry for a return to the old system of elected school boards.

Of course, political scientists have known for some time now that the factors that give people a sense of political efficacy go well beyond structure. The ability of an individual or group to exercise influence is tied to a host of interconnected social variables such as income, class, and race. Prominent among the characteristics associated with political and civic involvement is education.[13] This basic fact of political life needs to be acknowledged in the current discussion. No matter what governance plans are put into place, if young people do not get a decent education, their chances of becoming engaged citizens as adults are greatly reduced. Indeed, their chances of living healthy and productive lives are greatly reduced. No local or municipal service is so clearly tied to their future as education. Schools not only need to be governed well, they need to succeed at what they were meant to do; they need to educate.

Crafting a System

Established tools are available for determining whether a school or school district is effectively educating students. Scores on standardized tests, notwithstanding their limitations, are the most common barometers. When combined with other measures such as graduation, dropout and attendance rates, and school safety data, test scores can be useful in judging the success of schools. Assessing the performance of a governance arrangement is a more complex proposition. Not only is there the problem of separating the structural arrangement from the existing leadership, both of which can affect performance, but also there is no reliable way to demonstrate a causal relationship between the success of a system over time and its institutional architecture. At best one can establish correlations or associations. Even this can be problematic for the careful researcher.

Kenneth Wong and his colleagues have designed one of the most sophisticated models imaginable for measuring the impact of mayoral control on school performance.[14] The model suggests that cities that have put the mayor in charge of education have managed (no pun intended) to improve student achievement better than other cities have. This is good news to be sure. Jeffrey Henig's more rudimentary analysis, in chapter 2, of scores from the National Assessment of Educational Progress, the so-called nation's report card, tells a different story, however. It indicates that cities in which the mayor was put in charge of schools do worse—perhaps, as he adds, because mayors have been asked to take charge of some of the worst school districts. So what are we to make of this? Does governance really matter? How are we to know?

The bottom line for any education plan adopted is that it should eventually produce results in the classroom. If students do not learn, then there is no point to any of this. But making a direct connection between structure and results is difficult, maybe impossible. Structure is not a solution; it is an enabler. It creates possibilities for the kind of bold leadership needed to turn around failing school districts. The New York City school system, for example, has undergone more change in the past seven years under the Bloomberg-Klein administration than over any similar time frame in its entire history. Most informed observers, whether or not they agree with the administration's changes, believe that this would not have been possible under the previous governance arrangement in New York. But those who are unhappy with many of the policies also feel that the present system does not provide for a sufficient level of public input or accountability. Structure should, after all, also create opportunities for democratic engagement and participation.

Governance does matter. It appropriates power, authority, and access, and it apportions these precious political commodities among those who govern and those who are governed. Striking the proper balance between the managerial and democratic imperatives required for running a city school district is the fundamental challenge of good municipal governance. The appropriate balance might change from time to time in a given city—at one point demanding a powerful executive capable of disrupting the status quo, at another requiring a consensus builder who can bring cooperation and stability.

The more power we give an executive to manage efficiently and effectively, the more diligent we need to be about checking that power so that the operative system is representative, responsive, and transparent. There is no single "best system" for achieving these goals. The final arrangement must be carefully embedded in the history and culture of the local environment. It must be fitted together by an assortment of diverse actors who have a stake in its success. The participants in this design process should study and learn from other people and other places. But in the end, what matters most is what works for them in their particular place and in their particular time.

What Follows

As Betsy Gotbaum and Steve Aiello have noted, the chapters in this volume were commissioned as part of a larger review that took place in New York City concerning the future of mayoral control in the schools. Although most of the inquiry conducted by the Commission on School Governance was focused on developments in New York, the panel also examined governance arrangements and their effects in other cities. The commission's approach in this regard was rather straightforward: identify the country's best scholars on the subject at hand and ask them to write about what they know. That same formula served us well in putting together this book. The contributions are thoughtful, well informed, and diverse in their perspectives.

The collection is organized into three sections. The first three chapters, by Jeffrey Henig, Michael Kirst, and Kenneth Wong, provide general overviews of the subject. Henig and Kirst have written as much on the subject of mayoral control nationally as any other researchers around, and Wong's recent book has attracted a great deal of attention from people interested in the issue. Henig is the most cautious of the three in estimating what can be learned from studying different cities or what might actually be achieved by altering governing structures. He warns us to move slowly and carefully. Kirst is more pragmatic. He sees the selection of a governance plan as a series of trade-offs among competing values that institutional planners want to fulfill. He reminds us that no system of governance is perfect and advises us when making a choice to just ask whether the system in place or under consideration is better than the alternatives. Kenneth Wong is the most enthusiastic supporter of mayoral control among the contributors. Drawing on data gathered for his earlier book and updated for this one, he finds that cities in which mayors are in charge of education not only improve student achievement but also manage their resources more effectively.

In addition to sharing their own perspectives on the general experience with mayoral control across the country, Henig and Kirst give some attention to Cleveland, in which it might be said that mayoral control is proceeding without much direct involvement by the mayor, at least compared with other cities such as Boston, Chicago, and New York, where the mayor seems to have a strong sense of ownership in the schools. Although he was an enthusiastic supporter of school reform, Mayor Michael White never saw himself as the personification of education in Cleveland, nor would doing so have been appreciated by his high-profile school superintendent, Barbara Byrd-Bennett. White's successor, Jane Campbell, insisted on a larger presence in education; but the present mayor, Frank Jackson, has played a rather passive role in school matters so far.

The next three chapters, written by John Portz and Robert Schwartz, Dorothy Shipps, and Wilbur Rich, provide in-depth case studies of Boston, Chicago, and Detroit, respectively. The three cities studied here are prototypes of big cities that have tried mayoral control of their schools. In Boston the mayor worked in close collaboration with education professionals to achieve reform; in Chicago the mayor often worked around school administrators or worked without them. In Detroit, it might be said that mayoral control went forward without the public or its support, but not for very long.

John Portz has followed mayoral control in Boston more carefully than any other researcher. His collaboration with Bob Schwartz allows the addition of historical insights from one who has closely observed education in Boston for more than three decades. In answer to Mike Kirst's question about whether things are getting better as a result of a governance change, Portz and Schwartz generally would answer affirmatively in reviewing the Boston experience, although a reading of their chapter suggests that a number of cautionary caveats are in order when one makes generalizations that might be transposed elsewhere.

Writing on Chicago for many years after having served as codirector of the Consortium for Chicago School Research there, Dorothy Shipps has generally been less positive in her assessment of mayoral control. Shipps has persistently raised concerns with what she sees as the outsized role assumed by the business community and the diminution of community influence in policymaking since the mayor took over the schools.[15] Here she steps back from the situation a bit and, acknowledging some progress in academic performance, addresses the institutional capacities that are needed to make mayoral control of the schools work best in large American cities.

Wilbur Rich's chapter on Detroit is a study of mayoral control undone and what can happen when a system of governance lacks legitimacy among the people who are being governed. Drawing on a concept developed in his previous research on urban school systems, Rich sees a "public school cartel" at work that instinctively opposed changes to the status quo ante in order to protect long-standing interests that do not necessarily coincide with the welfare of students and schools.[16] Rich has written extensively on race, urban education, city mayors, and Detroit politics, but this is his first in-depth assessment of the experience with mayoral control in the Motor City.

The last three chapters of the book are the first systematic examination of mayoral control in New York City to date. Here I find myself in fine company. Diane Ravitch is the premier historian of education in New York; Clara Hemphill's series of books on the city's schools are widely considered essential reading for any parent with school-age children in the Big Apple. In her historical essay, Ravitch explains that mayors have always had a large influence over education in New York, but she finds that the amount of authority given to the mayor under the current plan is unprecedented and problematic. Hemphill, focusing her attention at the community level, finds that the elimination of elected local school boards, while not to be regretted, has left a rather confused and confusing array of institutions in place for parents and other activists who want to have a say in their schools or who just want to be informed.

My chapter places the institutional arrangement of the schools in the larger framework of municipal government, an approach I would commend to students of school governance in other cities. Here I draw not only on the findings and recommendations of the Commission on School Governance, for which I had the privilege to serve as executive director, but also on my past experience as an adviser to the charter commission that wrote the present city charter. Throughout its history, New York City has attempted to balance a tradition of having both strong mayors and strong communities. The balance began to lean more heavily toward the mayor with the adoption of the 1989 charter, and it probably tipped too far when the mayor took over the schools in 2002. The recommendations made by the Commission on School Governance are designed to correct that imbalance without undermining the goal of having the mayor play a central leadership role in education. I trust that these findings and recommendations will be of interest to scholars, students, and practitioners in other cities, in the same way that developments around the country informed the project in New York. In the short postscript at the end of this volume, I share some final thoughts on the benefits, difficulties, and pitfalls of studying governance and its possible improvement.

There is some overlap among the chapters, especially between the introductory chapters, which provide general overviews, and the remaining chapters, which penetrate more deeply into specific cities. This could not be avoided in soliciting such comprehensive reviews of the topic. As editor I wanted to give all the authors free rein in saying what they had to say, which I believe in all cases is quite valuable for anyone interested in the subject. Readers will find agreement, disagreement, and an invitation to draw their own conclusions.

I should also emphasize that while the central topic of this book is mayoral control, school governance, even in cities where the role of the municipal executive has been greatly enlarged, is not just about the power of these mayors. School governance does and should involve many players and institutions, as becomes apparent in the forthcoming pages.

There is an excellent and burgeoning literature on the subject of mayoral control, much of it written by the contributors to this volume.[17] I suspect and hope that there is more to come on this important topic. The idea and its implementation are works in progress in need of ongoing study. This book is a marker on that journey.

Notes

1. See Anwar Hussain Syed, *The Political Theory of American Local Government* (Random House, 1966); Gerald E. Frug, "The City as a Legal Concept," *Harvard Law Review* 93 (April 1980): 1057–154; Joseph P. Viteritti and Gerald J. Russello, "Community and American Federalism: Images Romantic and Real," *Virginia Journal of Social Policy and the Law* 4 (Spring 1997): 683–742.

2. See Charles M. Payne, *So Much Reform, So Little Change: The Persistence of Failure in Urban Schools* (Harvard Education Press, 2008).

3. Joseph P. Viteritti, "The City and the Constitution: A Historical Analysis of Institutional Evolution and Adaptation," *Journal of Urban Affairs* 12, no. 3 (1990): 221–36.

4. Joseph P. Viteritti, *Across the River: Politics and Education in the City* (New York: Holmes and Meier, 1983); Joseph P. Viteritti, "The Urban School District: Toward an

Open Systems Approach to Leadership and Governance," *Urban Education* 21 (October 1986): 228–53; Joseph P. Viteritti, "Urban Governance and the Idea of a Service Community," in *Caring for America's Children,* edited by Frank J. Macchiarola and Alan Gartner (New York: Academy of Political Science, 1989), pp. 110–21; Joseph P. Viteritti, "Abolish the Board of Education," *New York Times,* January 6, 2002, p. A13.

5. See Kenneth J. Meier and Robert E. England, "Black Representation and Educational Policy: Are They Related?" *American Political Science Review* 78 (June 1984): 392–403; Theodore Robinson and Robert E. England, "Black Representation on Central City School Boards Revisited," *Social Science Quarterly* 62 (September 1981): 495–502; Joseph P. Viteritti, "Unapportioned Justice: Local Elections, Social Science, and the Evolution of the Voting Rights Act," *Cornell Journal of Law and Public Policy* 4 (Fall 1994): 199–271.

6. Donald R. McAdam, *Fighting to Save Our Urban Schools—and Winning: Lessons from Houston* (Teachers College Press, 2000).

7. The cities are Boston, Chicago, New York, Cleveland, Providence, Harrisburg, Hartford, Trenton, New Haven, and Washington, D.C.

8. William G. Howell, ed., *Besieged: School Boards and the Future of Education Politics* (Brookings, 2005); Noel Epstein, ed., *Who's in Charge Here? The Tangled Web of School Governance and Policy* (Brookings, 2006).

9. Matt Miller, "First, Kill All the School Boards," *Atlantic Monthly,* January–February 2008, pp. 92–94, 96–97, quotations on 94, 97.

10. Marion Orr, *Black Social Capital: The Politics of School Reform in Baltimore* (University Press of Kansas, 1998).

11. Nicholas V. Longo, *Why Community Matters: Connecting Education with Civic Life* (State University of New York Press, 2007); Clarence Stone and others, *Building Civic Capacity: The Politics of Reforming Urban Schools* (University Press of Kansas, 2001); Robert D. Putnam, "Community-Based Social Capital and Educational Performance," in *Making Good Citizens: Education and Civil Society,* edited by Diane Ravitch and Joseph P. Viteritti (Yale University Press, 2001), pp. 58–95.

12. See Stefanie Chambers, *Mayors and Schools: Minority Voices and Democratic Transitions in Urban Education* (Temple University Press, 2006).

13. Norman H. Nie, Jane Junn, and Kenneth Stehlik-Barry, *Education and Democratic Citizenship in America* (University of Chicago Press, 1996); David E. Campbell, *Why We Vote: How Schools and Communities Shape Our Civic Life* (Princeton University Press, 2006); Peter Levine, *The Future of Democracy: Developing the Next Generation of American Citizens* (University Press of New England, 2007); Ravitch and Viteritti, *Making Good Citizens.*

14. Kenneth K. Wong and others, *The Education Mayor: Improving America's Schools* (Georgetown University Press, 2007). See also my review, "The Education Mayor: Improving America's Schools," in *Teachers College Record,* March 11, 2008 (www.tcrecord.org/content.asp?contentid=15094).

15. Dorothy Shipps, *School Reform, Corporate Style: Chicago, 1880–2000* (University Press of Kansas, 2006).

16. Wilbur C. Rich, *Black Mayors and School Politics: The Failure of Reform in Detroit, Gary, and Newark* (New York: Garland Press, 1996).

17. See, especially, Jeffrey R. Henig and Wilbur C. Rich, eds., *Mayors in the Middle: Politics, Race, and Mayoral Control of Urban Schools* (Princeton University Press, 2002); John Portz, Lana Stein, and Robin Jones, *City Schools and City Politics: Institutions and Leadership in Pittsburgh, Boston, and St. Louis* (University Press of Kansas, 1999); Alexander Russo, ed., *School Reform in Chicago: Lessons in Policy and Practice* (Harvard Education Press, 2004); Shipps, *School Reform, Corporate Style;* Chambers, *Mayors and Schools;* Wong and others, *The Education Mayor;* S. Paul Reville, ed., *A Decade of Urban School Reform: Persistence and Progress in the Boston Public Schools* (Harvard Education Press, 2007); Larry Cuban and Michael Usdan, eds., *Powerful Reforms with Shallow Roots: Improving America's Urban Schools* (Teachers College Press, 2003); Michael W. Kirst and Fritz Edelstein, "The Maturing Mayoral Role in Education," *Harvard Educational Review* 76 (Summer 2006): 152–64; Frederick M. Hess, "Assessing the Case for Mayoral Control of Urban School Systems," *American Journal of Education* 114 (May 2008): 219–45.

General Overviews

PART

I

JEFFREY R. HENIG

2

Mayoral Control: What We Can and Cannot Learn from Other Cities

Fashions in education governance come and go. At one time in American history, mayoral control of schools was the norm in large cities.[1] Education was a department within municipal government, in much the same way as might be policing, fire protection, or public works. The Progressive Era reformers of the early twentieth century deemed that arrangement a failure. Mayors, it was decided, were too much creatures of the political machines that often dominated local politics. They used their position of authority to turn the public schools into a source of patronage: teacher jobs were payoffs for party workers; contracts to build new schools were allocated to businesses that provided campaign support or kickbacks. Progressive reformers pushed hard to separate the education system from general-purpose government. They did this by creating separate school districts, each with its own decisionmakers, often elected on a special election day and often with dedicated revenue streams.

Today, tides are shifting in the other direction. When the state legislature, in 2002, gave New York City mayor Michael Bloomberg the authority he had requested for taking control of the school system, the city joined what was then still a fairly small and as yet unproven countermovement. Boston and Chicago had led the way, instituting mayoral control in 1991 and 1995, respectively.[2] Although their efforts were garnering generally positive reviews, there was at that point no compelling evidence that the changes undertaken in those cities were making a real difference in what happened within classrooms or within students' minds. Moreover, some of the places that beat New York to the punch—cities such as Cleveland (1998), Detroit (1999), and

Washington, D.C. (partially, in 2000)—were having a start rocky enough to signal to the attentive that mayoral control is not an automatic and universal cure-all.

New York City's high visibility, combined with the generally positive exposure it has received, gave the nascent movement added momentum.[3] Newly elected mayors Antonio Villaraigosa of Los Angeles and Adrian Fenty of Washington, D.C., each visited New York in well-publicized sojourns to gain insights into how to shape their own efforts to take over the schools. Whereas Villaraigosa gained only a stunted version of the control he sought, Fenty won approval for a strong version that essentially eliminated the locally elected board and gave him power to appoint his own superintendent.

Although the full impact of mayoral control in these cities is still to be determined, what is clear is that a number of cities—as well as state legislatures considering taking an affirmative role in restructuring school governance—will be looking closely at the mayoral control model for years to come. Even places that have taken the plunge will be reexamining their choices at times. Under the terms of its original grant of authority to Mayor Bloomberg, the New York state legislature required that the decision be revisited and reaffirmed if it were to extend beyond June 2009.

What should citizens and responsible policymakers consider when making judgments about whether and how to alter the system by which their schools are governed? In particular, what can they learn from the experience of other cities, and how should the lessons from other places be interpreted in light of local opportunities and needs? Using the impending reassessment of mayoral control in New York City as a focal point, this chapter considers these questions and draws some broader conclusions about how evidence about the consequences of structural reforms should and should not be employed.

Why Should We Care about Other Cities?

"What does it matter how mayoral control is working in other cities?" a reasonable citizen or policymaker, faced with assessing governance structure, might ask. "Isn't the relevant question how it is working here, and aren't we in the best position to make that judgment just by observing what is going on in our own community?" Cities and school systems can differ in important ways relating to political culture, bureaucratic capacity, fiscal health, student characteristics, local leadership, the power of key interest groups, and the like. Because local context matters, it does make sense to weigh local experience heavily in assessing whether particular policies or institutional arrangements are or are not a "good fit." We all know stories of ballplayers who have been all-stars in one city only to perform poorly after moving to another team, as well as tales of journeymen players who have suddenly blossomed after a mid-career trade. What works well for public schooling in Boston might not travel well to New York; what falls apart in the Motor City might work wonderfully in the Big Apple.

There are, though, at least three reasons why experiences in other places provide important grist for decisions even in places like New York, which has the advantage of having a track record of mayoral control of its own. The first has to do with the passage of time. New York's version of mayoral control is still newly minted. Most serious observers recognize that it can take a minimum of four to five years to even begin to see serious results from major structural reform in education. A new administration, even if it gets out of the gate immediately, needs time to get its programs announced, to hire the right people and to train those already in place. The best instructional techniques, introduced into an existing organizational setting, might take even more years to generate compounded and substantial changes in test scores.

New York's schools chancellor, Joel Klein, has said that "eight years would be a minimal amount of time" to transform a large urban school system. Drawing conclusions earlier than that can be tragic, he argues, observing that he believes this was the case in San Diego, where schools superintendent Alan Bersin, a leader Klein admired and has sought to emulate, "served for six-plus years, and I think he would've—if he had stayed three or four more years—completed the critical work that he needed. It pains me to see him gone."[4] By that schedule it may be still too early to accurately gauge the consequences of mayoral control in New York, a possibility underscored by the fact that some of the most dramatic changes relating to empowering schools and establishing school partnerships with private school support organizations were only getting into the field well into the mayor's second term.

A second reason that experiences in other cities can be useful is that they help disentangle the general issue of whether mayoral control is good from the relevant, but distinct, question of whether one likes or dislikes the policies and practices of a particular regime. Mayoral control is a governance and administrative arrangement, not an identifiable and consistent package of pedagogical and reform strategies. The argument in its favor is that, over time, a district under mayoral control will be more likely to find and adopt the right policies or that, in general, if implementing the same policies, it will do so with greater efficiency and effectiveness than school systems with more traditional school boards. The proof of that pudding depends on how the institutional form operates when different drivers are behind the wheel. That cannot yet be determined in New York—in which, so far, mayoral control and the Bloomberg-Klein approach are one and the same—but careful observation of what has happened across various mayoral control systems can yield better inferences about what the range of likely possibilities might be.

The third reason to study the experiences of other cities is that New Yorkers might want to consider maintaining mayoral control but altering it in some respects. As commonly used, the term *mayoral control* is a loose label that encompasses a variety of institutional particulars. The various places that have adopted it allow consideration of variations in the form mayoral control can take, with an eye toward adjustments that might open options more attractive than a stark selection between the current arrangements and reversion to earlier ones.

Scanning the Landscape: Forms of Mayoral Control

Nationally, discussion about mayoral control has been powerfully influenced by three cases. Boston and Chicago, as mentioned, were early adopters and have received the most attention. Although New Yorkers might think of their experience as relatively new and still in the testing stage, elsewhere it is widely discussed—usually in positive terms—and now rivals the other two cities as a prominent poster child of the genre. When new mayors in other cities make their pitch for gaining authority over the schools, they are as likely, or more so, to name New York as their model as the other cities. Yet a number of other cities have mayoral control of some form or another in place, and some of them have experience with mayoral control that spans a much longer time.

Table 2-1 lists some of the examples along with basic information about when mayoral control was initiated and key elements of its form in each city. Several points can be made right away. First, we know very little about most of these. If we are serious about wanting to know whether the form itself has predictable consequences, there is quite a bit of serious research yet to be done. Second, several of the existing cases of mayoral control are historical remnants of the period before the Progressive Era rather than fully contemporary adoptions; indeed, in Baltimore and Philadelphia, two of the cases frequently cited as recent examples of mayoral control, the contemporary changes actually weakened the mayors' powers. Third, no one cites most of these cases as examples to emulate; while the big three of Boston, Chicago, and New York are highly touted, most other cities in which mayoral control is in place have yet to generate accolades or even much public notice. Fourth, the particular details of mayoral control vary in some important respects, including the size

Table 2-1. *Major Examples of Mayoral Control*

City	When initiated	Important changes	Specific features
Baltimore	Historical, 1899	Changed to weaker form, 1997	Mayor and governor jointly appoint board.
Boston	1992	1996	Mayor appoints all of board, which appoints superintendent.
Chicago	Historical; augmented, 1995		Mayor appoints all of board, which appoints superintendent (CEO).
Cleveland	1998	Reaffirmed by referendum, 2002	Mayor appoints all of board, which appoints superintendent. (Mayor had the appointment power at first, but the initial legislation provided for this to revert to the appointed board after thirty months.)
Detroit	1999	Reverted, 2004	While board was in place, mayor appointed six of its seven members, which appointed the CEO.
Harrisburg	2000		Mayor appoints a board of control, which appoints superintendent.
Hartford	2005		Mayor appoints majority of board, which then selects superintendent (five of nine). Mayor named himself to the board in December 2005.
Jackson, Miss.	Historical		Mayor appoints the board, with approval by city council.
New Haven	Historical		Mayor appoints board.
New York City	2002		Mayor appoints majority, with others appointed by borough presidents. Mayor appoints the superintendent (chancellor).
Oakland	2000	Fiscal problems led to state intervention, 2003	Mayor appoints three of the ten members; others are elected.
Philadelphia	Historical	State converted to partnership arrangement, 2001	Mayor appoints two and governor three members to School Reform Committee.
Providence	2003		Mayor appoints all of board, which appoints superintendent.
Trenton	1978		Mayor appoints board, which hires superintendent.
Washington, D.C.	Partial, 2000; full, 2007		Mayor appoints chancellor. Former local board now to function as a state board.

Sources: Stefanie Chambers, *Mayors and Schools: Minority Voices and Democratic Tensions in Urban Education* (Temple University Press, 2006); Martha T. Moore, "More Mayors Move to Take Over Schools," *USA Today,* March 20, 2007 (www.usatoday.com/news/education/2007-03-20-cover-mayors-schools_N.htm); Kenneth K. Wong and others, *The Education Mayor: Improving America's Schools* (Georgetown University Press, 2007).

of the board, the proportion of board members appointed by the mayor, whether the mayor can directly appoint the superintendent, and the relative involvement of the state.[5]

The discussion of consequences can be separated into three broad categories: impacts on management and administration, impacts on democracy and public involvement, and impacts on student learning. Little is known with certainty about any of these things and progressively less about each of the three categories. As a social scientist accustomed to fretting about inferences of causality and the need for accumulation of systematic studies using different methodologies and examining the phenomenon under different conditions and contexts, I am acutely aware of the tentativeness of our knowledge base right now. Policy decisions often must be made on the best available evidence rather than established certainties, however, and in that spirit I have done my best to distill and present informed judgments rather than definitive and consensual findings. I follow that distillation of what seems to be known with an explicit discussion of what is definitely not known. In particular, there is little systematic information on how mayoral control may evolve over successive administrations or how particular aspects of mayoral control designs might make important differences in the outcomes they produce. Recognizing the limits of certain knowledge is not an excuse for paralysis or for resorting to what feels right, but it does underscore the risks of sharp institutional change and the importance of building in mechanisms for self-correction over time.

Getting Things Done: Mayors, Management, and Change

A sense of frustration and a desire to shake up the decisionmaking, as much as the specific arguments for mayoral control, account for a good deal of the support for governance reform. School reform has been on the national agenda for at least twenty-five years, since the famous 1983 report, *A Nation at Risk,*[6] warned Americans that a mediocre educational system was making us vulnerable in an increasingly competitive global economy. Despite much public hand-wringing, it appears to many that performance has been stagnant at best. Worse, to some it has seemed that key actors within the education system have been giving only lip service to the seriousness of the problem, blaming failure on insufficient funding or insurmountable challenges associated with concentrated poverty while blithely proceeding as if there were nothing they could do. This is the same kind of frustration and desire for change that is fueling a range of other proposed solutions, among them vouchers, charter schools, private management, high-stakes testing, and the mandates of the No Child Left Behind Act.

There are both theoretical and practical reasons for thinking that a shift to mayoral control can leverage change even in the face of historically lethargic or resistant bureaucracies. Theories about public administration and civic capacity suggest that mayors may be better able than elected school boards to mobilize a broad range of public resources, force various other agencies dealing with families and youth to coordinate with schools and their missions, and draw on a wider array of management and administrative expertise resident throughout local government. Mayors, arguably, also are in better position to link issues of schooling to those of economic development and to pull into the discussion a corporate sector that might otherwise sit on the sidelines during what are often volatile discussions about children and schools. Mayors, chosen citywide in elections that engage a broad array of groups and interests, are structurally less dependent than school board members on teachers unions, which can wield tremendous influence in the generally low-visibility, low-turnout elections that typically select school boards. That, in theory, gives them a freer hand to engage in a range of administrative strategies that many believe are conducive to more efficient and effective use of government resources—including closing schools, contracting out for key functions, and bargaining more aggressively to limit teacher work rules and tenure protections.

Theory aside, in many of the places that have adopted mayoral control, state legislators and civic leaders have simply concluded that the school boards they have tried to work with are amateurish, made up of micromanagers and political grandstanders, and hopelessly paralyzed by internal rifts. The breadth and depth of these perceptions is captured in the title of a recent volume on American school boards, which characterizes them as "besieged."[7] In the meantime, particular mayors in office or on the horizon appear to many of these reform-oriented groups to be more eager and open to new ideas.

At least initially, there are some signs that shifting to mayoral control can make a difference in some areas and activities that are generally presumed to be precursors of improvements in learning. When the mayors involved care about education and are willing to devote time and attention to school reform, there is evidence that they may be better able to keep the issue visible and raise its priority on the local agenda. John Portz and Robert Schwartz, in chapter 5 of this volume, provide evidence of a sharp increase in the tendency of the Boston mayor, following reform, to use public speeches as a way to highlight the importance of schools in the local agenda. This may be evidence that mayors can convert their visibility into the broad public engagement that many argue is necessary if reform initiatives are to be substantial and sustained.[8]

Mayors without formal authority over schools are also able to use their bully pulpit to promote a reform agenda, and there are some high-profile cases of mayors who are doing just that. Michael Kirst and Fritz Edelstein highlight Long Beach, California, as a "prime example of how mayoral involvement in education need not rely on formal changes to governance." The city's mayor, Beverly O'Neill, has worked closely with the superintendent's office in a partnership that appears to have provided much of the multiagency coordination and public support that proponents of mayoral control talk about. Long Beach won the Broad Prize for Urban Education in 2003.[9] Francis Shlay, as mayor of St. Louis, made up for a lack of appointment power by backing a slate of reform-oriented school board candidates and helping them all get elected.[10] Kenneth Wong and his colleagues cite Douglas Wilder, the mayor of Richmond, Virginia, as an example of a politically skillful mayor who used his informal power and authority to hold the superintendent accountable to him even when there was no formal line of authority to call upon.[11]

In at least some cases, though, mayors who start out using their informal resources to champion school reform end up feeling they need more, suggesting that, in their view at least, informal power may not be enough to do the trick. Albuquerque's mayor Martin Chavez has made education reform a prominent theme in his administration but has continued to argue that he needs more formal authority if he is to realize his vision. Anthony Williams, when he was mayor, won a difficult battle to gain the right to appoint some members of the District of Columbia school board.[12] "My biggest regret is not being able to get further with the schools," he says now, indicating that his failure to gain a stronger formal role was an important factor in his decision not to run for a third term in office.[13]

In what is the most systematic study to date, including urban school districts both with mayoral control and with traditional governance arrangements, Wong and colleagues have found at least some evidence that formal power makes a difference in management and accountability. Analyzing eighty-seven State of the City speeches made by mayors in multiple cities, they find that mayors in general are talking quite a bit about education, with more than half emphasizing it as a priority for the city, about one in three discussing ways the city can directly manage the school system, and about one in four specifically mentioning accountability measures.[14] In the same study, mayors with formal control were somewhat more likely to take a public stance than those without formal power.

But formal power may not be sufficient to move matters from talking to action. According to Wong and colleagues' findings, even for mayors with formal authority it can be difficult to move from public cheerleading to focusing on more specific accountability tools. When looking for specific emphasis on accountability, test scores, standards, and the importance of building public confidence in the schools, the authors find no difference between mayors with formal authority and those who lacked it. "The language of leadership may more easily allow for generalization without firm commitments, whereas discussions of accountability systems and in particular standards and achievement tests are less amenable to mere platitudes," they speculate.[15]

That a formal role is no guarantee of management and administrative success is also suggested by the cases of Baltimore and Philadelphia, cities in which mayors had a long-standing role in selecting boards only to see state legislatures attenuate that control owing to their dissatisfaction with local leadership. In his 1987 campaign for mayor, Kurt Schmoke ran heavily on his desire to be the education mayor of Baltimore. His predecessor, William Donald Schaefer, had possessed formal powers, but other than taking advantage of them as a source of patronage, he largely left the schools to their own devices while focusing much more attention on downtown development. Schmoke's efforts to experiment with the use of private providers to run some public schools—one of the nation's earliest efforts to pursue the kind of contracting-out arrangements that are now commonly associated with mayoral control regimes—backfired, contributing to an erosion of his constituency and making it easier for the Maryland legislature to forcefully step in, in 1997, establishing an arrangement in which the mayor must share power with the state.[16] In October 2001, the Pennsylvania governor announced a plan to eliminate Philadelphia's mayor-appointed school board and turn over most of the administrative functions to a private company. In the face of intense local resistance, the state backed down from this extreme plan, instead handing oversight to a school reform committee to which both the mayor and governor made appointments.[17]

There is also reasonably good evidence that the move to a stronger mayoral role can lead to improved financial oversight and better management systems. For the most part, the reports have been anecdotal and disproportionately focused on the high-visibility cases of Boston, Chicago, and New York City. Mayoral control is frequently initiated precisely when there is a broadly shared sense that the existing school board and central office lack the capacity or will to deal effectively with corruption, waste, and handling of the most basic services relating to textbook purchase, deteriorating facilities, school security, and the like. Starting at a low point, new mayor-led efforts have the opportunity to draw on expertise from other agencies, the local business community, or private contractors.

Fairly typical is the recent experience in Washington, D.C. Adrian Fenty, the newly elected mayor, made gaining control over the schools his signature effort, and shortly after midnight on the day he accomplished this goal he fired the sitting superintendent and hired Michelle Rhee. Fenty and Rhee announced ambitious goals for radically changing the local organization and culture. What initially gained the most attention, though, involved the relatively prosaic issue of getting textbooks into the classrooms in time for the beginning of the school year. In early August 2007, Rhee made headlines when she announced that, because of flaws in the system she inherited, as many as half of all classrooms might not have their textbooks when schools opened for the new academic year. After jointly touring a warehouse full of dusty and incompletely labeled boxes filled with books, she and the mayor pledged to do their best to kick the operation into high gear. Although the first day of school had a number of glitches, local coverage indicated that many schools and principals thought things went much better than in previous years. "When I see the fire department pulling up to deliver copy paper, I know we're on to something," one principal reported, in what could be construed as a perfect advertisement for the notion that mayoral control can produce, in the form of interagency collaboration.[18]

That said, there are indications that the Fenty-Rhee regime might not yet have management issues totally in their control. On September 27, 2007, Victor Reinosa, D.C.'s deputy mayor for education, had to tell the city council that his office would miss an established deadline to provide a full report on the textbook situation.[19] The textbook incident highlights one of the challenges to school reform that even mayoral control regimes may find difficult to surmount. Not long after the story about the undistributed textbooks hit the front page, it was revealed that the manager of the district's textbook operation had been fired by former schools superintendent Arlene Ackerman in 1998 after books were not delivered on time for that school year. After he fought his dismissal, the textbook manager was rehired with back pay and an additional monetary settlement. Michelle Rhee has indicated her desire to be freed from personnel laws that constrain her expressed desire to fire potentially a large number of senior employees, but it remains to be seen whether she will succeed in gaining that authority.[20]

Kenneth Wong and his colleagues have gone the furthest in attempting to systematically analyze the impact of mayoral control on management issues. In their multicity longitudinal analysis, summarized in chapter 4 of this book, they expected to find that districts with mayoral control tended to spend more per student than cities under traditional governance arrangements, especially on direct instruction, student support services, and school administration services, the areas they argue most directly affect teaching and learning. They also expected to see evidence of an association between mayoral control and reallocation of spending to provide more staff at the school and classroom level and less on central administration. Although they find that mayoral control cities were not spending more, they did find evidence that they were spending differently. There is some evidence as well that mayoral control may lead to less administrative spending, some shift toward greater instruction support, and a decline in outstanding debt. Funding was driven far more, however, by factors relating to the character of the students (race, ethnicity, poverty, special needs), the size of the district, and competitive pressure from private schools.

Overall, it appears that mayoral control, if it systematically leads to greater administrative efficiency, does so modestly and slowly and in ways that are not easily captured by the kinds of simple budgetary accounting systems we have available to monitor such things across places and over time.

Doing It Right: Mayors, Pluralistic Values, and Democracy

As in New York City, the experience in other cities suggests the importance of distinguishing between getting things done and the particular processes relied upon to choose which things to do. When control has been handed to activist mayors with strong political resources and generally supportive relationships with state and federal officials (and during periods of general fiscal expansion, or at least in solid postindustrial economies), the switch seems to generate momentum and reform. Things happen under mayoral control, and when measured against a backdrop of political and bureaucratic stalemate this sense of movement is often welcomed in and of itself. Much of the apprehension at the outset, as well as much of the criticism after implementation, has focused instead on the issue of how the agenda for change is shaped. Although mayoral control has the potential to broaden participation and debate, at least some groups in some of the major cities have complained of being frozen out. They argue that what is done—and how that is decided upon—are as important as the fact that something is being done.

The most important complaints have come from racial minorities, parents, and teachers. Although the concept is presented in race-neutral language, mayoral control has sparked racially defined responses in a number of cities. There are several reasons for this. Public schools and school systems have played an important historical role in the economic, social, and political advancement of African American families and communities. Jobs, including good jobs, opened to blacks within public schools during periods in which discrimination ran rampant in the private sector and other public bureaucracies. As large urban centers began to experience black in-migration and white suburbanization, blacks made political inroads by gaining positions on school boards and at the upper reaches of school administration earlier than they did, for instance, in the police and fire departments.[21] This historical role gives added emotional and symbolic importance to the issue of governance of schools. Giving immediacy and a more concrete manifestation to these theoretical and symbolically based concerns is the belief among many in the African American community that mayoral control is a precursor to the imposition of a cluster of specific policies—school closings, contracting out to private providers, erosion of tenure and other protections to teacher independence, and institution of special programs designed to attract white and wealthier households—that they believe will be implemented in a way that will hit directly at their jobs and valued community institutions.[22]

It is possible that the racially defined reactions against mayoral control have been knee-jerk suspicions that will ebb over time. Boston and Cleveland both revisited the issue of mayoral control after having had a chance to watch it in action, and in both cases the public endorsed retaining the change. Portz and Schwartz provide details on the Boston case in this volume. Although the 1996 margin of victory for retention of the appointed board was more than two to one, there continued to be a strong racial pattern, with two of the city's politically active predominantly black wards voting to return to the elected board and with the degree of support and opposition across all precincts strongly correlated with the size of the black and white populations.[23] In Cleveland, initial concern that mayoral control was being promoted by a racially hostile state legislature appears to have eased over time. When Michael White, the African American mayor who first took the reins, announced his decision not to run again and was succeeded by a white woman, the potential certainly was there for resistance to mayoral control to grow. But that seemingly has not been the case. Cleveland voters in 2002 voted to retain mayoral control, and the reform remains in place, even as the city has moved into its third-generation mayoral administration at the helm.[24]

Stefanie Chambers has looked most closely at whether mayoral control results in reduced influence by minority parents and community organizations. She interviewed forty-six community activists, parents, school and city officials, and researchers in Chicago between 1998 and 2002 and thirty-seven in Cleveland from 2000 to 2002. This research indicates that parent and community activists felt they had lost access, although the findings were less stark in Cleveland than in Chicago. Chambers concludes that there may be fundamental tension between the emphasis on test scores that often accompanies mayoral control and the kinds of broader involvement that she feels is important if schools are to fulfill "their democratic responsibility of giving people the skills they need for success in our democratic system."[25]

In addition to race, another point of cleavage has tended to arise between mayoral control regimes on the one side and teacher and parent activists on the other. It is possible that some reduction in access by parents, activists, and minority organizations is an inevitable by-product of the greater focus, coherence, and sustainability promised by the advocates of mayoral control. It is also possible that some of the discontent uncovered by Chambers in Cleveland and Chicago, and frequently voiced in New York City as well, is unreliable as an indicator that democracy has somehow been compromised and should be viewed more as predictable resentment by particular groups that had previously had privileged access (teachers, vocal and middle-class parents) and now find themselves forced to compete with a broader range of legitimate stakeholders. But the alienation of interests that are in some ways closest to the ground and with the most directly at stake is of legitimate concern.

Even if bypassing some of the previous stakeholder groups is useful as a strategy for jump-starting needed reforms, there are at least five reasons to be concerned if mayoral control comes at the cost of limiting access by organizations representing minorities, teachers, and parents. First, despite majoritarian principles that public policies toward schools should be shaped by all citizens, there are long-standing American beliefs that parents, because they have more at stake, and teachers, because they have more expertise, should have more say in setting education policy than the average voter in mayoral elections. Second, parents and teachers at ground level may have valuable information about what is and is not working—information that may not be readily accessible to central administrators even when they are armed with sophisticated data systems. Third, when considered against the backdrop of a history of painful battles over racial exclusion and fairness in public schools, resilient racial patterning might raise questions about the legitimacy of mayoral control as a governance approach. Fourth, if the sense of marginalization on the part of parents, teachers, and minorities reflects a narrowing of the range of voices being heard by those with the authority to shape school policies, there is a societal price that might be paid as divergent and pluralistic ideas and values are screened out of public debate. Fifth, a fairly extensive literature on coproduction of urban services, community empowerment, social capital, and civic capacity suggests that even the best-designed and most effectively managed policy initiatives may founder if they fail to engage the participation and political support of recipients and other stakeholders.

The counterargument—that restraining influence by these traditional stakeholders is a price we have to pay for clear progress—would be most persuasive, and could conceivably trump these concerns, if there were compelling evidence that strong mayoral control leads to clearly better results. To the extent that research so far finds a mixed picture, in which formal mayoral authority is only sometimes associated with clear gains and mayors without formal control can sometimes do just as well, this counterargument loses some bite.

Mayors at the Bottom Line: Test Scores and Other Important Outcomes

It is tempting to evaluate mayoral control by going directly to the conventionally defined bottom line: changes in student proficiency and educational gaps as measured by standardized test scores in reading and mathematics. The past twenty-five years have witnessed a steady shift in the terms of the national education debate, from one centered largely around equity in inputs (equalizing resources, equalizing access) to one centered on educational outcomes, measurable changes in what children actually learn. The 2001 enactment of the federal No Child Left Behind legislation, with its explicit goal of making all children proficient by 2014 and its ladder of steps to keep the pressure on schools and districts to reach that goal, represents the apotheosis of this approach. For some of the most enthusiastic proponents of the accountability movement, attention to anything other than test scores is diversion: claims that good things are happening should be treated with skepticism if they do not get translated into measurable gains.

There is much to be said for the directness, focus, and tough-mindedness of the accountability-for-outcomes approach, but there are a number of reasons to be cautious about relying too exclusively on test-score outcomes as barometers for judging whether mayoral control should be extended, abandoned, or reconfigured. One, as alluded to earlier, is that too immediate and exclusive a focus on test scores could lead to premature decisions that mayoral control is not working. Frederick Hess has argued that urban school reform often fails to have impact because it takes the form of "spinning wheels," cycling through superficial changes without taking the time to make the deeper reforms that are needed.[26] Failure to give a new reform structure like mayoral control time to unfold and take root risks hasty abandonment of a structural change that may be working in the right direction.

This has been a concern in Harrisburg, Pennsylvania, where mayoral control has yet to generate the kinds of outcomes that reformers hoped to see. Discussing test scores that led the *Pittsburgh Business Times* to rank Harrisburg as the worst district in the state, the local newspaper tried to find the balance between righteous indignation and recognition of the need to give the existing leadership more time. Suggesting that characterizing the schools' test performance as poor was too mild—"in some cases, 'appalling' would be a more apt description"—the editorial writers argue that the mayor and superintendent should not be blamed. Part of the problem, they suggest, was a decline in state support, and part was the need to give mayoral control, initiated in 2000, still more time.[27]

Judging mayoral control based on test scores in the immediate aftermath of its institution could also work in the other direction, leading policymakers and citizens to misattribute gains to initiatives that may have been put into place before mayoral control. Just as New York City's chancellor Klein argues that reforms he is instituting now might take years to show their true value, some argue that at least some of the recent improvements in the city's test scores may be more properly attributable to reforms, like the since-abandoned Chancellor's District program, initiated by his predecessors.[28]

Looking at cities that have had mayoral control in place for a longer time can help somewhat in addressing such concerns. Table 2-2 presents some basic data on test scores for those urban districts that participate in the National Assessment of Educational Progress Trial Urban District Assessment.[29] The cities that take part in this assessment were not specifically chosen for the purpose of evaluating mayoral control, but they do provide a chance to compare, using the same test instrument, five districts with full or partial mayoral control with six districts that have more traditional school governance arrangements.[30] The table presents average scores for students at the low end (10th percentile), the median (50th percentile), and high end (90th percentile) and also the change from 2003 to 2005 (in percentage points) in the score of the median student. The low and high scorers provide us with information that would be lost if we looked, as is common, simply at

Table 2-2. *Average NAEP Test Scores under Mayoral Control and Traditional Urban School Systems, 2003–05*[a]

School system	Mayoral control in place before 2003	Low scores (10th percentile)	Median (50th percentile)	Top scores (90th percentile)	Ratio 90th to 10th percentiles	Change in median score, 2003 to 2005
Reading						
National		166.77	219.12	261.95	1.57	0.64
Atlanta	No	153.99	199.77	251.14	*1.63*	**4.49**
Austin	No	**169.76**	**217.80**	**261.27**	1.54	n.a.
Charlotte	No	**174.93**	**222.23**	**266.47**	1.52	1.13
Houston	No	166.87	209.79	**255.44**	1.53	**3.13**
Los Angeles	No	*146.38*	*194.45*	246.35	*1.68*	*–0.21*
San Diego	No	157.44	209.18	254.41	1.62	*–0.08*
District of Columbia	Partial	*141.00*	*190.58*	*240.77*	*1.71*	1.86
Boston	Yes	166.35	208.38	247.11	1.49	1.73
Chicago	Yes	*152.48*	198.67	*244.35*	1.60	*–0.05*
Cleveland	Yes	155.99	*197.62*	*237.82*	1.52	1.65
New York City	Yes	**168.63**	**213.17**	254.54	**1.51**	**2.86**
Mathematics						
National		199.39	238.62	272.45	1.37	3.40
Atlanta	No	184.55	*218.65*	259.92	1.41	*4.70*
Austin	No	**207.62**	**242.17**	**276.44**	1.33	n.a.
Charlotte	No	**208.29**	**244.76**	**280.71**	1.35	*2.52*
Houston	No	**199.72**	233.13	266.46	1.33	**6.83**
Los Angeles	No	*179.95*	220.64	260.26	*1.45*	5.25
San Diego	No	193.91	**234.03**	**268.94**	1.39	**7.70**
District of Columbia	Partial	*175.02*	*209.97*	*248.10*	*1.42*	6.16
Boston	Yes	195.98	229.55	263.44	**1.34**	**10.39**
Chicago	Yes	*177.72*	*215.25*	*253.76*	*1.43*	*1.15*
Cleveland	Yes	186.61	220.80	*252.40*	1.35	6.29
New York City	Yes	194.37	231.11	265.53	1.37	4.85

Source: Data from National Center for Education Statistics, Institute of Education Sciences, July 6, 2007 (nces.ed.gov/nationsreportcard/reading/tuda.asp; nces.ed.gov/nationsreportcard/mathematics/tuda.asp).

n.a. Not available.

a. The top three scores in each category are shown in bold, the bottom three in italics.

averages or medians. Some critics of mayoral control, for example, have argued that mayoral regimes, in an effort to hold and attract more affluent families, might focus attention on the median student and above to the detriment of those who have the greatest need. In the table, I have highlighted the highest and the lowest three scores in each column.

Of the five mayoral control schools, only Boston and New York make it into the top three on more than one of the dimensions; Chicago and the District of Columbia, relative to the others, do poorly almost across the board. Cleveland is in the bottom three in reading for the median- and top-scoring students. That it does well in the equity measure (a lower ratio of 90th percentile to 10th percentile) is hardly something to brag about, since that finding is fully attributable to the fact that its top students do so poorly, not—as would be desirable—that its poorer students are doing unusually well. In general, the six more traditionally governed districts do better. Two—Austin and Houston— are among the top three on at least five dimensions and never in the bottom three; Charlotte is consistently a high scorer, falling into the bottom three only on change from 2003 to 2005; San Diego does well on math for median and top scorers and is second only to Boston in improvement in math from 2003 to 2005.

Table 2-2 has limitations as a window into the causal relationship between mayoral control and test scores. One possibility is that schools under mayoral control do worse because they have to deal with tougher populations. This is credible since Austin, Charlotte, and San Diego have the highest family incomes among this group and Cleveland has the lowest. Figures 2-1 and 2-2 take the income dimension into account. The diagonal line in each of those figures shows the test score that would be predicted based on the city's income level, with cities that fall above the line doing somewhat better than would be expected and those below somewhat worse. The first thing to note is that family income is a powerful predictor of test scores, as the empirical literature in the field would lead one to expect.[31] But some cities do better than others in beating the scores that would be predicted based on their level of affluence. New York City, while scoring only in the middle of the pack on reading, is actually doing quite a bit better than would be expected given its median family income; Washington, D.C., in contrast, is doing much worse.

These figures do not satisfactorily take into account all the student characteristics that should be used to assess performance, but as a rough approximation they do suggest that the lackluster performance of mayoral control cities is not easily dismissed as simply a consequence of different economic conditions.

Figure 2-1. *Reading by Income*

Median score

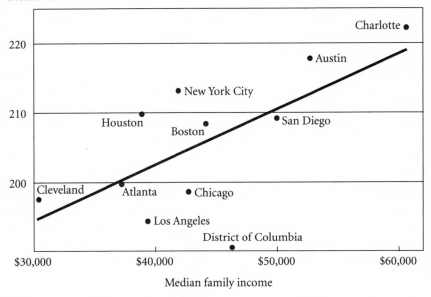

Median family income

Source: Author's analysis based on 2005 test score data from the National Center for Education Statistics, "2005 Trial Urban District Assessment in Reading" (http://nces.ed.gov/nationsreportcard/ reading/tuda.asp) and income data downloaded from individual district profiles from NCES, "School District Demographics System" (http://nces.ed.gov/surveys/sdds/).

Houston, a traditionally governed city, does markedly better when we control for income; the District of Columbia and Chicago, two mayor-controlled cities, look even worse when median income level is taken into account.

A second reason to be wary of relying too heavily on the data in table 2-2 is that mayoral control cities may have low scores because they started from an unusually low level. This makes sense, for example, if cities are more likely to adopt (or have imposed upon them) mayoral control precisely because their schools are underperforming. If lower average scores for mayoral control cities is simply a factor of a lower starting point because the transition tends to come during a crisis, that should presumably be associated with great improvement from 2003 to 2005. Yet as indicated in table 2-2, among the mayor-controlled districts, only those in New York (in reading) and Boston (in math) were leaders in upward movement.

Wong and his colleagues, in this volume, report on their analysis of changes in test performance over the period 1999–2003 for 101 districts, 10 of which have some form of mayoral control. The authors offer an upbeat assessment of

Figure 2-2. *Math by Income*

Median score

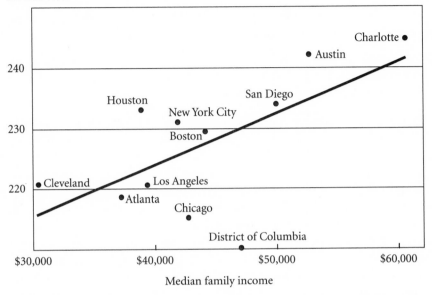

Median family income

Source: Author's analysis based on 2005 test score data from the National Center for Education Statistics, "2005 Trial Urban District Assessment in Mathematics"(http://nces.ed.gov/nationsreport card/mathematics/tuda.asp) and income data downloaded from individual district profiles from NCES, "School District Demographics System" (http://nces.ed.gov/surveys/sdds/).

their results. "Does mayoral control raise student achievement?" they ask. "The answer, simply put, is *yes*."[32] That is because their overall measure of mayoral control is positively correlated with gains in reading and math scores when calculated with a two-year lag. As they move on to provide an answer expressed with more nuance, however, the story gets quite a bit murkier. Giving mayors power to appoint the majority of a school board is quite consistently associated with gains, but giving the mayor even more power (the power to appoint board members without oversight from a nominating committee) actually has a negative effect. More important, when they look at the test scores in high-performing compared with low-performing schools, they find evidence that mayoral control is associated with an expansion of the achievement gap.

Mayors, they speculate, may need to focus initially on high-performing schools in order to stem a brain drain of more-advantaged students to private schools, charter schools, or surrounding communities. This suggests the possibility that, when faced with a choice between focusing on families with greater need and those with greater economic and political resources, mayors may be more likely than elected school boards to aim at the high end, at least initially. Overall, Wong and colleagues find that other factors that mayors inherit—including composition of the student body, previous achievement level, and private school competition—all weigh more heavily in determining perform-ance than does the simple on-off switching of the mayoral control option.

What Is Not Known: The Uncertain Terrain of Second-and Third-Generation Mayoral Control

Mayoral control does not spring forth randomly. It tends to emerge in districts with certain characteristics: central city, high poverty, substantial minority population, struggling schools, a dysfunctional school board, a mobilized and concerned business community, and an attentive state legislature. Almost always, mayoral control has been initiated by cities led by a mayor who has run as a reformer, has identified schools as a transcendent priority, and has the confidence of civic leaders and state officials.

What happens in a mayoral control city when the stars are differently aligned? What happens if key stakeholders become complacent, if the state is hostile, if the sitting mayor's interests lie in other policy matters, or if the mayor is under pressure from constituencies more interested in developing the downtown area, cutting taxes, building tourism, fighting terrorism, and fighting crime?

As already mentioned, the nation's experience with mayoral control in the nineteenth and early twentieth centuries was not entirely favorable and led to the establishment of education as a largely separate decisionmaking structure, deliberately buffered from intrusion by general purpose government. Propo-nents of the contemporary movement to reabsorb education into general purpose government argue that things have changed. Today's "new, improved" mayors, attentive as they are to the pressures of global economic competition and the need to support strong public schools to hold and attract business, will never flag in their allegiance to schools, according to this optimistic view.[33] The nation's experience with the new manifestations of mayoral control, how-ever, is almost exclusively with first-generation mayors controlling the city's education, who may not be emblematic of all mayors to come.

The most visible and influential examples of mayoral control provide almost no insights into the issue of succession. Boston's mayoral control ini-tiative originated with Mayor Raymond Flynn; Flynn, though, was quickly succeeded by Thomas Menino, who was elected in 1993 and is currently serv-ing his fourth term. Chicago's mayors have held the power to appoint the school board since the 1830s, but the city's experience with its augmented form of mayoral control has been exclusively under Mayor Richard M. Daley, who has been serving since 1989. In Providence, Hartford, and Philadelphia, the current governance arrangements have been in place under a single mayor or one so recently elected that it is too early to say what direction the new regime might take. Washington, D.C., had experience with partial mayoral control only under Mayor Anthony Williams; its current, stronger form of mayoral control has coincided with the first term of Mayor Adrian Fenty.

The cases in which mayoral control has extended beyond the first generation offer a mixed picture. Dennis Archer was mayor of Detroit in 1999, when mayoral control was first put in place. But Archer did not run for another term. Despite the fact that his successor, Kwame Kilpatrick, wanted to retain formal control of the schools, in 2004 voters opted to return to an elected school board, defeating by a margin of more than two to one a proposition that would have extended mayoral control.

The case of Baltimore raises at least some questions about the premise that second- and third-generation mayors can be counted on to retain a laser-like focus on school reform. Kurt Schmoke did fit the model of the new-style mayor in attempting to use Baltimore's long-standing strong mayoral structure to raise educational performance. His effort ended with a whimper, however. Under the partnership arrangement imposed by the state, Martin O'Malley retained some joint authority over the school system, but, like Baltimore mayors before Schmoke, he put more of his attention on other issues. In 1999–2000, for instance, only 6 percent of O'Malley's press releases focused on education, compared with 19 percent on public safety and crime, 17 percent on economic development, 12 percent on public works, and 11.5 on general government operations.[34]

Of the urban districts that adopted mayoral control in the contemporary era, Cleveland has had the most experience with the issue of mayoral succession. Michael White, an African American, was in office when mayoral control was initiated in 1998. White had been actively involved with school issues during his two terms of office before mayoral control was instituted, and besides building his own knowledge of the issue he had taken steps to build grassroots support for education reform by organizing a series of citywide summits bringing various stakeholders together and backing reform-oriented candidates in school board elections.[35] Initially ambivalent about mayoral control, White gradually came to the conclusion that he needed power to appoint a board if the city were to make substantial progress. The state legislation granting him the power to appoint the board also gave him authority to appoint a superintendent (chief executive officer [CEO]).[36] His selection, Barbara Byrd-Bennett, a seasoned and respected education leader who was also African American, set about instituting a series of reforms, taking the lead role, with White backing her up as needed while allowing her room to shape policy and avoiding any inclination to micromanage.[37] Enthusiasm for the new regime was running high. White, to the surprise of many, chose not to run for reelection, however.

Mayoral control was not a key issue in the 2001 race to succeed White. The two leading candidates both pledged to support mayoral control. Jane Campbell, the victor, who was white, avoided some potential racial backlash by aligning herself with Byrd-Bennett, a move that Stefanie Chambers describes as a political "master stroke."[38]

Much of the positive momentum established under the White–Byrd-Bennett regime initially seemed to carry over into the Campbell–Byrd-Bennett era. According to *Catalyst,* a Cleveland newspaper that focuses exclusively on education, "New teachers and instructional coaches were brought in; under-performing principals were taken out. Professional development became more embedded in the daily lives of faculty."[39] Moreover, the efforts seemed to pay off—test scores and graduation rates rose. In 2002 a major bond issue passed, and in July 2003 the school board awarded Byrd-Bennett a $54,000 bonus. A mark of the general level and breadth of enthusiasm is that both the mayor and the teachers union reacted positively to the school board's decision to reward Byrd-Bennett. "The real question is, did she earn it?" said Richard Decolibus, president of the Cleveland Teachers Union. "We think, for the most part she's been a good CEO." Mayor Campbell, who signed off on the bonus, praised Byrd-Bennett's performance in bringing up test scores and attendance rates in the 72,700-student district. "In this town we pay athletes millions of dollars," Campbell said. "What matters most is the education of our children. I want her paid as the most valuable player she is."[40]

The high times did not last, however. Over time, the relationship between the mayor and the CEO she had inherited became somewhat fraught, with at least some local observers concluding that Campbell was insisting on more hands-on involvement than her predecessor had or than Byrd-Bennett felt was appropriate. Corporate and foundation funders who had been providing the district with additional resources began to feel frustrated that change was not more dramatic, and this sense of disillusionment was fed somewhat by media revelations that Byrd-Bennett had used some of the discretionary funds raised by donors to fly first class. The CEO had always seemed a bit imperial to some, but people were willing to look the other way when they believed things were moving in the right direction. Now, with test scores stagnating, some foundations succumbed to what is sometimes referred to as donor fatigue, and the electorate's support for a growing school budget declined.[41] In the summer of 2005, voters rejected a major levy that Byrd-Bennett had campaigned for, and almost immediately thereafter she announced her intention to resign.

In November 2005, Jane Campbell was defeated. Her successor, Frank Jackson, became Cleveland's third-generation mayor under the mayoral control structure. He appears to have a different style and working relationship with Eugene Sanders, Byrd-Bennett's replacement, from that characterizing either of the two previous regimes. Rather than a highly visible cheerleader and tone setter, as White had been, Jackson appears to be more comfortable in a background role. As one local leader I spoke with commented, if there is a major issue confronting the CEO or an important event or school board meeting at which Sanders is speaking, Mayor Jackson "is quite likely to be in the audience ... but he does not, at this stage anyway, stand up and say, 'I'm the mayor, this is what I think, this is what we're going to do, this is what I've requested the district to do.'" Some in the Cleveland school reform community are concerned that stronger leadership is required, but for the time being the jury is out on whether Cleveland will regain the momentum it seemed to have lost.

Mayoral control has been launched largely in response to short-term alignments and particular personalities. This runs counter to an important tradition in American political thought, which conceives of governance institutions at least in part as a tool for reducing dependence on individuals. The American allegiance to the idea of checks and balances reflects the belief that institutional forms should be chosen with an eye toward the future and with an appreciation for the fact that today's popular leaders will be replaced and that under some future scenarios their offices might be held by individuals less admirable, less able, or with different values or philosophies. This is the Achilles' heel of the contemporary movement for mayoral control, and at this point, not enough is known to confidently judge whether this vulnerability will prove to be a tragic one.

All or Nothing? Or Something in Between?

In addition to the general ignorance about the possible directions of second- and third-generation mayoral control, there is also a lack of knowledge about the way variations in the details of mayoral control institutions affect how they play out. The term *mayoral control* is a large umbrella under which are included formal and informal governance arrangements that differ in their particulars. In some places, the mayor appoints a minority of school board members, in some a majority, and in some all. In some places the mayor appoints the superintendent, in others the mayor shares that responsibility, and in still others the school board plays that critical role. Cities with mayoral control over schools can differ in other ways as well: in the extent to which revenues for the schools come from earmarked taxes or must be assigned from general revenues; in the extent to which there are formal channels for parents and citizens to have input, apart from their role as voters in school board or general elections; in the presence or absence of organizations with data access and research capacity to provide independent information on school performance; and in the extent to which the state legislature, governor, or state board of education retains active oversight and the will and capacity to intervene.

Currently, there is only sketchy information about the range of these institutional differences and almost none at all about whether these are differences that matter. The important cross-city work conducted by Wong and colleagues differentiates among three dimensions of mayoral control.[42] Their empirical work suggests that these differences do matter. The particular patterns of their findings, however, are somewhat puzzling and, absent additional research or new and better theories, do not provide a comprehensible guide to jurisdictions that might be looking to pick and choose among options to maximize a range of possible values. What does seem consistent with what is known at this point is that cities have maneuvering room not only in their decision about whether to have mayoral control but also in devising specific parameters that constitute the particular form that mayoral control will take.

Final Thoughts

Governance structures do not hire, pay, or train teachers. They do not make sure children go to school ready to learn. They do not devise curriculums, draw up lesson plans, look children in the eye and understand what motivates them, or stand in front of a class and guide it through the learning process. If governance arrangements are relevant it is because of the things they either facilitate or undermine.

For struggling and complex urban school systems, what matters are vision, capacity, and sustained political support. A central question, then, has to be whether mayoral control is more likely to augment or undermine these.

Structural reform should not be done willy-nilly. Governance arrangements are part of the basic rules of the game upon which communities build their political and civic lives. Change is often a good thing, but changes in the basic rules of democratic decisionmaking are different from policy changes initiated within those basic rules. Imagine the Giants or Jets being handed a new rulebook every game night that altered the number of yards required for a first down, the length and height of the goalposts, the shape of the ball. Rational planning, negotiations over priorities and compromises, and proper sequencing of short- and long-term strategies all depend upon some consistency in the institutional parameters.

Change in the structure of governance is especially risky if it is based just on short-term factors and particular personalities. The New York state legislature was unwilling to enact mayoral control when Rudy Giuliani was mayor and asked for that power but was willing to do so when the mayor was Michael Bloomberg. The citizens of the District of Columbia and a majority of members within Congress currently are encouraged by the style and energy of Adrian Fenty. But it takes no stretch of the imagination to predict how Congress would have reacted to a proposal to give control of the District of Columbia's schools to Marion Barry. Structures are designed to last—need to last—whereas individual leaders and administrations come and go. The next man or woman in the office may be less devoted to education, less skilled, or less wise.

Notes

1. Fritz Edelstein, *Mayoral Leadership and Involvement in Education: An Action Guide for Success* (Washington: U.S. Conference of Mayors, 2006).

2. In Chicago's case, 1995 marked the strengthening of what had always been a strong mayoral role in education.

3. Notably, in 2007 the city won the prestigious Broad Prize for Urban Education, awarded annually to a district that has demonstrated the best performance in raising overall achievement and reducing gaps in education.

4. Joel Klein, interview by Hedrick Smith, *Making Schools Work,* PBS, October 5, 2005 (www.pbs.org/makingschoolswork/dwr/ny/klein.html).

5. Other differences may be important, too; for example, the degree to which education is funded from earmarked revenue sources or must compete with other agencies for general revenue.

6. National Commission on Excellence in Education, *A Nation at Risk: The Imperative for Educational Reform; A Report to the Nation and the Secretary of Education, United States Department. of Education* (U.S. Government Printing Office, 1983).

7. William G. Howell, ed., *Besieged: School Boards and the Future of Education Politics* (Brookings, 2005).

8. Clarence N. Stone and others, *Building Civic Capacity: The Politics of Reforming Urban Schools* (University Press of Kansas, 2001).

9. Michael W. Kirst and Fritz Edelstein, "The Maturing Mayoral Role in Education," *Harvard Educational Review* 76 (Summer 2006): 159.

10. Edelstein, *Mayoral Leadership and Involvement in Education*.

11. Kenneth K. Wong and others, *The Education Mayor: Improving America's Schools* (Georgetown University Press, 2007). The Richmond story took an odd turn in September 2007. The mayor had instructed the school board to move its offices out of City Hall to make room for his economic development department. Backed by the council, the school board refused, and Wilder evicted them in the middle of the night, dismantling their offices and moving the contents into moving vans. A school board member attributed Wilder's act to his resentment of the board's refusal of his request that they cede to him power to hire and fire the superintendent. Lisa A. Bacon, "Famous Mayor under Fire in Virginia," *New York Times*, October 21, 2006, p. 25.

12. Jeffrey R. Henig, "Washington, D.C.: Race, Issue Definition, and School Board Restructuring," in *Mayors in the Middle: Politics, Race, and Mayoral Control of Urban Schools*, edited by Jeffrey R. Henig and Wilbur C. Rich (Princeton University Press, 2004), pp. 191–220.

13. Quoted in Yolanda Woodlee, "Williams Muses on Life in and after Office," *Washington Post*, September 12, 2007, p. 4.

14. Wong and others, *The Education Mayor*, p. 183.

15. Ibid., p. 182.

16. Marion Orr, "Baltimore: The Limits of Mayoral Control," in *Mayors in the Middle*, edited by Henig and Rich, pp. 27–58.

17. Eva Gold, Jolley Bruce Christman, and Benjamin Herold, "Blurring the Boundaries: A Case Study of Private Sector Involvement in Philadelphia Public Schools," *American Journal of Education* 113 (February 2007): 181–212.

18. Quoted in Theola Labb, "Opening with Optimism: Fresh Paint in Some; Schedule Mix-Ups, Other Issues Elsewhere," *Washington Post*, August 28, 2007, p. B2.

19. Theola Labb, "Lew Seeks Control of Maintaining Schools: Chief of Upgrades Testifies; 'Gridlock' in System Cited," *Washington Post*, September 28, 2007, p. B1.

20. Gary Emerling, "D.C. Textbook Chief Appealed Firing," *Washington Times*, September 5, 2007, p. A1.

21. Jeffrey R. Henig and others, *The Color of School Reform* (Princeton University Press, 1999); Marion Orr, *Black Social Capital: The Politics of School Reform in Baltimore, 1986–1998* (University Press of Kansas, 2000).

22. Henig, "Washington, D.C."

23. Boston has had a particularly rocky history of race relations around school integration, and it is possible that this contributed to the pattern. See also John Portz, "Boston: Agenda Setting and School Reform," in *Mayors in the Middle*, edited by Henig and Rich, pp. 96–119. Various chapters in *Mayors in the Middle*, however, suggest that the racial framing is common, at least in the early stages (see, especially, Henig, "Washington. D.C."). Portz finds no patterned relationship in the Boston vote between opposition to mayoral control and the proportion of the precincts that were Hispanic.

24. Stefanie Chambers, *Mayors and Schools: Minority Voices and Democratic Tensions in Urban Education* (Temple University Press, 2006), p. 85.

25. Ibid., p. 196.

26. Frederick M. Hess, *Spinning Wheels: The Politics of Urban School Reform* (Brookings, 1998).

27. *Pittsburgh Patriot-News,* "Test Scores: It Takes a Long Time to Bring a Failing District Up to Standards," editorial, September 4, 2007.

28. Deinya Phenix and others, "A Forced March for Failing Schools: Lessons from the New York City Chancellor's District," *Education Policy Analysis Archives* 13 (September 2005) (epaa.asu.edu/epaa/v13n40/). See also Diane Ravitch, "Why I Resigned," *New York Sun,* February 15, 2008 (www.nysun.com/opinion/why-i-resigned/71390/).

29. The District of Columbia does not formally participate in the Trial Urban District Assessment, but it has a sufficient sample because it is normally included in the National Assessment of Educational Progress samples for states.

30. District of Columbia schools were only partially under mayoral control at the time the data were collected.

31. On the importance of family and student characteristics, see Richard Rothstein, *Class and Schools: Using Social, Economic, and Educational Reform to Close the Black-White Achievement Gap* (Teachers College Press, 2004).

32. Wong and others, *The Education Mayor,* p. 83; emphasis in the original.

33. Michael Kirst and Katrina Bulkley, "'New, Improved' Mayors Take Over City Schools," *Phi Delta Kappan* 80 (March 2000): 538–46.

34. Orr, "Baltimore," p. 50.

35. Wilbur C. Rich and Stefanie Chambers, "Cleveland: Takeovers and Makeovers Are Not the Same," in *Mayors in the Middle,* edited by Henig and Rich, pp. 159–90.

36. This was transitional. After thirty months, the primary power to appoint a superintendent would revert to the board, with the mayor's concurrence required.

37. For Byrd-Bennett's reforms, see Michael Kirst's chapter 3 in this volume.

38. Chambers, *Mayors and Schools,* p. 84.

39. *Catalyst Cleveland,* "A New Chief, a New Chance," June 2006 (www.catalyst-cleveland.org/archives/06-06/0606story1.htm).

40. "Byrd-Bennett 'Delighted' about $54,000 Bonus: Schools CEO Also Gets 3 Percent Pay Raise," News Channel 5, Cleveland, July 31, 2003 (www.newsnet5.com/education/2371297/detail.html).

41. With respect to donor fatigue, foundations typically prefer to circulate their funding over time in order to move on to new projects rather than let just one or two initiatives dominate their portfolio of giving, although there are exceptions, of course.

42. Those dimensions (addressed in chapter 4 of this volume) are whether the mayoral control arrangements are "new style" or are the result of long-standing institutional reforms from an earlier era; whether the mayor appoints the majority of the school board; and whether the mayor has full appointment power or is, rather, restricted.

MICHAEL W. KIRST

3

Mayoral Control of Schools: Politics, Trade-offs, and Outcomes

In the early 1990s, after many decades of a limited role in education, mayors in some cities began to take control of their schools. Boston initiated this changed mayoral role in 1991, followed by Chicago in 1995, Cleveland in 1998, Harrisburg, Pennsylvania, in 2000, New York City in 2002, and the District of Columbia in 2007. Baltimore and Philadelphia had considerable mayoral control in the 1990s, but most of it later reverted back to the state. Oakland, California, the District of Columbia, and Detroit initiated partial mayoral control, which failed and was subsequently abandoned. This pattern suggests that the local context is crucial in determining the characteristics and sustenance of mayoral control of schools. Los Angeles, Fresno, and Albuquerque mayors, for example, have all been frustrated in their attempts to take charge of schools, in part because their school districts extend beyond the city boundary.

A basic rationale for mayoral control has been the assumed link between improved schools, city economic development, and retention of middle-class families. An implicit policy assumption is that mayors are better equipped than school boards to highlight school problems and mobilize the personnel and resources needed to solve them. Larry Cuban and Michael Usdan posit a three-pronged theory for why mayoral control might succeed: First, linking urban school governance to existing political structures (including the business community) will produce organizational effectiveness, which will improve teaching and learning as measured by standardized test scores and enhanced coordination with city-provided offerings in recreation, the arts, and medical and social services. Second, better management will make urban school systems more efficient and effective by tightly aligning organizational goals, curriculum, rewards and sanctions, professional development of teachers and principals, and classroom instruction to academic achievement. Third, when noneducators who lead urban districts are connected openly to existing state and local political structures, the chances of improving and sustaining students' academic achievement will increase.[1]

Another theory of action places greater emphasis on enhancement of accountability. Success is partly based on streamlining governance so that fewer people are held accountable by more voters. A single person, the mayor, is accountable rather than several board members elected by subdistricts in staggered elections. In these theories of action, the basic hypothesis is that mayors are better able than school boards to spotlight attention on problems in their districts and increase resources to address those problems.

However, most policy analysts would doubt whether governance changes in and of themselves can directly improve classroom teaching and learning.[2] There is a complex multidirectional flow of influence and resources from government to students. But without new central governance many urban districts cannot adopt major reforms or improvements.[3] Mayors can influence classrooms in many ways by adopting curriculum standards, hiring better teachers, and providing high-quality instructional materials.

Trade-offs among Conflictual Values

Herbert Kaufman has provided an insightful analysis of the evolution of local governance.[4] He demonstrates that historically city governance has been characterized by a search for accommodation among three competing governance objectives: representative democracy, centralized executive leadership, and technical nonpartisan competence. Control by a large subdistrict-elected school board such as that in New York in 1970 would exemplify the first; mayoral control of education, as in New York City, the second; and the third, the civil service system in 1950 that empowered trained and qualified nonpolitical civil servants who made decisions based upon technical and professional considerations.[5] At various stages of New York City's history each of these three governance objectives has been ascendant. The objectives compete and cannot all be maximized simultaneously. The crucial decision at any given time is which one objective should be traded off to make another ascendant. This could depend on the specific conditions and context of the city at a particular time.

The reaction to Tammany Hall spurred the creation of the city's board of education, housed at 110 Livingston Street in Brooklyn, at the beginning of the twentieth century. Nothing exemplifies the goal of professional civil service teacher hiring in the 1950s more than the New York City Board of Examiners, which licensed teachers and principals. The civil rights movement was an important impetus for the decentralized elected boards in 1970. In the 1990s, the shortcomings of the New York City schools' performance and dissatisfaction with the "community-controlled" boards encouraged mayoral takeover. The excessive emphasis on one of the three objectives tends to set in motion demands for redressing the balance. For example, a July 26, 2007, poll conducted by Quinnipiac University indicates that New York public opinion favors more representative democracy with shared control by the next mayor and with a board of education. The same poll, however, concludes that most voters think Mayor Bloomberg's takeover of the public schools has been a success.[6]

Theoretically, one could diminish the need for trade-offs by trying to emphasize all three objectives at once. Mayoral control could be mitigated through decentralized school-site councils like Chicago had in 1992. More decisions could be delegated to professional educators with graduate degrees and selected through civil service examinations. But this fight-power-with-other-power approach would likely lead to stalemates, so choices need to made among the three values and the right balance crafted for a particular local context. This decision can be informed by a review of mayoral control in other cities.

How can one evaluate the arguments favoring redistribution of power from school boards to mayors? One useful concept, called "institutional choice," focuses on the crucial policy decision, of which an alternative institution should be the decisionmaker. For example, courts in the 1960s were reluctant to delegate civil rights protection to local school boards in Alabama. Another type of institutional choice is whether to place various functions in the hands of markets (for example, parental choice of schools) or politics (for example, school board elections). Both of these institutional choices could be problematic. Some parents may not have many good schools to choose from, but turnout for many big-city school elections is less than 15 percent of the district's registered voters. The recent state accountability movement included an institutional choice to enhance the curricular and testing roles of state government by overriding local decisions on what to teach.

Two general characteristics help guide institutional choice in making decisions: agreement on substantive goals and the capacity to achieve them. Substantive goals are crucial because of the need to ensure support for a policy. Courts may be more supportive of civil rights than some school boards, but the courts' substantive goals must be buttressed by a capacity to implement its decisions in the local school context. Courts cannot run school districts very well.

So which institution should be chosen to control the schools? A method for choosing can be called "comparative institutional advantage," that is,

> the distrust directed at one decision-maker [e.g., a school board] must be carefully weighed against the advantages of that decision-maker. Both the advantages and disadvantages of an alternative decision-maker [e.g., the mayor] also must be carefully analyzed. The logic of comparative institutional advantage implies the futility of seeking a perfect or ideal decision-maker or implementation of a policy favored by local citizens. The real world offers a least-worst choice of imperfect institutions to make and implement policy.[7]

Governance and Improved Education

Education research does not provide many clues about this connection. For example, in 2002 Deborah Land reviewed research published since 1980 on the role and effectiveness of school boards. Her comprehensive analysis stresses "the limited number of data-based studies."[8] Land finds conjecture and scattered case studies as the only basis for evaluating the effectiveness of appointed as opposed to elected school boards. In 2007 Frederick Hess surveyed four hundred books, articles, and papers that addressed appointed school boards and mayoral control. He concludes that "fewer than a dozen explicitly considered the impact of board reelection on local school reforms in more than a cursory fashion. Most of the research is the work of a small group of scholars replicating and repurposing a small number of case studies. In the end, there were not even a handful of rigorous, systematic studies that examined the effect on some dimension of school improvement."[9] Even in case studies that find some impact upon test scores from mayoral takeover, the trade-off issue is highlighted. Stefanie Chambers asserts that test scores increased in Chicago and Cleveland, but the cost was fewer opportunities for grassroots participation in the school system by minorities.[10]

Although the overwhelming weight of the evidence is inconclusive, a 2007 book by Kenneth Wong and others (summarized in the next chapter) contends that integrated governance by mayors "will lead to statistically significant, positive gains in reading and math, relative to other districts in the state."[11] Wong also claims that mayoral districts focus on fiscal discipline by containing labor costs and reducing bureaucratic spending and are more likely to stress outcome performance goals. These bold assertions that the governance structure is crucial should be reanalyzed to make sure that the multiple correlation statistical techniques are sufficient and controlled adequately for alternative explanations. For example, a new curriculum could be the cause of test score increases, and Wong cannot control for many education initiatives that differ between the cities. Moreover, the achievement score increases Wong and his colleagues find are small.

Wong is somewhat more convincing concerning the positive impact of mayoral control upon new policy and administrative coherence, continuity, and civic support compared with the prior regimes. The research summary by Hess also ends on a positive note because mayoral control

> does provide good reason to think that replacing an elected board . . . is a promising way to jump-start coherent and sustained school improvement. The experience of cities like Boston and Chicago illustrates that sustained mayoral leadership can make a difference. An appointed school board may be less susceptible to narrow demands and better able to summon the focus, patience, and unity to support tough minded reform. Moreover, replacing an ineffective board atop a dysfunctional system offers an opportunity to "reshuffle the deck," upend routines and political understandings that can hinder improvement, and create the opportunity for focused and responsible governance.[12]

But even this conclusion may imply that mayoral control should be a temporary arrangement that jolts the system, then reverts back to a higher priority for representative democracy or professional neutral competence.

Local Context Matters: Boston and Chicago Adopt Different Strategies

A closer examination of two cities demonstrates the importance of local context in balancing the three competing values discussed above. Boston put more emphasis on technical expertise under an experienced city superintendent who had a traditional education and professional background. Chicago chose a city administrator with no prior top-level experience in education administration. The two cities' initial change strategies were different. But both cities featured executive centralization under a mayor as its prime value with scant attention to representative democracy. The new powers granted to mayors in Chicago and Boston resulted in fundamental changes in the governance of the large urban education systems in these two cities. These changes could easily be labeled "regime changes."

Chicago has 450,000 students enrolled in six hundred schools with a $6.7 billion budget, while Boston has 58,000 students with a $73.4 million budget. The systems in both cities are now governed by leaders closely affiliated with the mayors and largely answerable to them. Boston now has a school policy committee appointed by the mayor; in Chicago a corporate-style board, also mayor appointed, oversees the city's schools. Out of these governance changes have emerged significant policy changes that have, for the most part, received considerable public support compared with previous governance systems. This analysis encompasses the initial years of mayoral takeover in both cities.

Despite similarities in the changing shape of governance in Boston and Chicago, the mayors and the leaders of the school systems opted for substantially different styles of school reform. School districts in both cities had been fiscally dependent before takeover, but the mayors did not have full control of the school board process. The Chicago superintendent, Thomas Payzant, and Boston's mayor, Thomas Menino, focused on a "professional" model of reform, aligning education standards and building teacher and administrator capacity. In Chicago, on the other hand, the mayor, Richard Daley, and the chief executive officer of the public school system, Paul Vallas, emphasized a top-down model (layered over a previous school-site decentralization reform model) in which the managers create a vision with clear accountability mechanisms and both schools and students receive sanctions if the achievement goals are not met.

Formal governance changes enhancing the role of the mayor were introduced in Boston and Chicago in the late 1980s and the early 1990s. In Boston, a series of decisions between 1989 and 1996, both legislative and electoral, gave the mayor the power to appoint the Boston School Committee. Up until this time, the school committee had been directly elected in some form. This change gave the mayor a much stronger role in the operations of the school system and created a direct line of authority to him.

Boston's mayor Raymond Flynn spearheaded the charge to alter the governance structure of the Boston public schools. He was supported by the state legislature, which was becoming increasingly concerned with the Boston schools, and by the business community. Much of the African American community was skeptical of eliminating an elected school committee, and the Irish of South Boston (who had long held power on the elected committee) also opposed the change.

In Chicago, the governance changes of 1995 granting an enhanced role to the mayor were layered over earlier reforms instituted in 1988. That reform, which was supported by state Democrats and civic activists, shifted power from the district to local school councils. In this legislative change, the mayor's ability to appoint the city's school board was decreased. However, the impetus for this decentralization was not a desire to increase the influence of educators. Rather, Dorothy Shipps argues, it was designed to enhance the influence of parents and community members; she comments that "educators were blamed for the problems and their discretion curtailed."[13] At first there were many candidates for the local-site councils, but over time fewer ran, and competition decreased. Moreover, the system lost considerable central direction, so that over time the value of democratic representation became less urgent, and a stronger executive at the center became a higher priority.

Whereas the 1988 reforms pushed control toward the local schools, the legislation passed in 1995 shifted power up the ladder to the mayor. These changes gave the Chicago mayor more authority than any mayor since before the Progressive Era, effectively turning the education system into a department of city government. Specifically, the 1995 legislation eliminated the school board nominating committee, which had effectively minimized the mayor's ability to select school board members, and replaced the traditional board with an advisory board to the mayor. In this new structure, only one of the five members was to be focused on education (through the chief education officer), and the mayor appointed all members. The legislation also temporarily limited the right of the unions to strike and reduced the number of issues subject to union bargaining.

In both cities, the primary initiators of governance changes granting more power to the mayors were the business community, the mayor (especially in Boston), and state legislators. Local groups, such as community activists and minority group representatives, were not directly involved, and educator organizations including the teacher unions were also peripheral to the debates or opposed the change. Reformers in the two cities had similar reasons for supporting these governance changes. The primary goal in both cases was to establish clearer lines of political authority and responsibility, making the city's mayor ultimately accountable for the progress (or lack thereof) of the public schools.

Although the goals of those who pushed through the governance changes in Boston and Chicago had certain similarities, there were also some important differences. In Chicago, there was a strong emphasis on improving the effectiveness and efficiency of the public schools—particularly the fiscal efficiency of the district. Although improved efficiency was also a factor in Boston, it was not nearly as central to the discussion in that city as was improved classroom instruction.

Another difference between the reforms in these two cities involved the role and purpose of the district's "leader." Reflecting the focus on efficiency, the Chicago Public Schools were to be led by a business-style chief executive officer , rather than a traditional superintendent. In Boston, on the other hand, both Flynn and Menino explicitly wanted a strong educator-leader at the head of the school system. Although Mayor Flynn wanted to be held accountable for the state of the Boston public schools, he claimed he was not interested in being directly involved with the district's operations. Mayor Menino made Tom Payzant a member of his cabinet, but the mayor often spoke for the school system at contentious community meetings. Before coming to Boston, Payzant had been school superintendent in San Diego and Oklahoma City.

Finally, the view of city and state leaders about the capacity of educators to reform education was rather different. In Chicago, there was continual skepticism about the ability (and motivation) of educators to improve schools—both the 1988 reforms, which shifted power toward parents and community members and the 1995 reforms, which granted additional power to the mayor, moved control away from educators. Boston leaders shared some of these concerns, but they were still interested in vesting considerable authority in public education professionals.

Boston and Chicago: Similar but Different

In Chicago, Paul Vallas, a former budget director for the city, moved to the new position of chief executive officer of the Chicago public schools. The selection of Vallas supported the business and other community interests in having someone from outside traditional public education at the helm of the city's schools. In this top-down change model, management creates a vision and defines clear sanctions for individuals and schools that do not make progress toward that vision.

In Boston, Payzant was a much more traditional choice for a district leader, and his selection reflected the mayor's interest in having a professional educator who would stay away (at least to some extent) from the political issues that had consumed much of the time of previous superintendents. Payzant's approach was much more within the framework of traditional education reform, and his primary focus reflected a professional education model involving higher standards and professional educator capacity building through extensive staff development. In short, Boston's local context valued the technical nonpartisan competence of educators much more highly than did Chicago, but both cities moved to trade off representative democracy for more-centralized mayoral leadership.

In 1996 roughly one hundred Chicago City Hall employees came to work in the central office, displacing more traditional education staff. While school-site councils still exist at all the Chicago public schools, their influence has been minimized, and the new central office leaders have increased their role in the functioning of the city's schools. Owing to the combination of no budget crises, no strikes, and a generally positive view among the public of the reforms that Mayor Daly instituted, the legitimacy of the school system improved.

The direct impact of the governance changes on the actual governance structure of the public schools has not been as marked in Boston as in Chicago. The most notable change has been the elimination of the bitter battles within the Boston School Committee and between the committee and the mayor—a logical outcome of the school committee's being appointed rather than elected. As in Chicago, labor relations, particularly with the teachers union, have improved in recent years. Also similar to Chicago, some of the most blatant education budget problems in Boston have disappeared. While the Boston mayor has always influenced the amount of money spent by the public school system, governance changes have allowed him to also influence how those dollars are spent. Unlike Chicago, however, Boston saw no dramatic changes in the structure or staffing of the school district's central office brought about by the installation of city employees in key units.

The style and substance of the education reforms that are taking place in the context of these governance changes are quite different in the two cities. Although accountability measures in Chicago have generally focused on minimal standards and on raising the educational outcomes of the worst-faring students in the city's schools, there have also been changes for those students at the upper end of the performance spectrum. For example, Chicago created alternatives such as magnet schools, accelerated programs such as International Baccalaureate options, and charter schools. Alongside efforts to remove "troublesome or slow-learning students" from regular public schools to other settings such as transition centers and alternative high schools, the push for more "upper-end" options is linked with the goal of bringing middle-class families back into the Chicago public schools.

One hope for increased mayoral control of schools was that mayors would be more able to link together currently fragmented programs designed to support students and families. In Chicago, Mayor Daley has been able to help schools through support from a variety of other city agencies. But there has not been as much integration between schools and children's services as some had wanted.

Overall, two assumptions were part of the initial Chicago strategy. The first is that much of the capacity necessary to improve performance was already available within the public school system and that incentives and sanctions were necessary to draw out this preexisting capacity. Thus there has been less emphasis in Chicago than in Boston on building additional classroom instructional capacity through professional development. The second is that test scores, though perhaps not a perfect measure, are the most logical means of assessing progress in the provision of quality education.

The style of the education reforms being undertaken in Boston, while arising out of a similar governance change, is quite different than in Chicago. Payzant emphasized his long-term commitment to a decade of steady, resolute progress through central district staff training, new materials, and high standards. Chicago left choices about reading curriculum to each school and provided options. Some of the methods Payzant has used include leadership development, whole-school change, diagnostic classroom testing, and creation of a reorganization plan directed at student performance. His focus on teaching and learning issues has included a reliance to some extent on professional educator norms, rather than sanctions, as a means to increase performance. Boston, unlike Chicago, has seen little change in the tenure of administrators or teachers and no talk of radical reconstitution of failing schools.

The different directions taken by leaders in Boston and Chicago were not simply the whims of individual mayors and school district chiefs. Rather, they reflected to some extent the different historical and political contexts of these two cities, especially the desires of powerful constituencies within these cities and states. In particular, the regime changes in both cities reflect the different emphases of the business communities. For example, owing to the role of the business community and Republican legislative leaders in initiating the 1995 reform in Chicago, it is not surprising that a business-style leader like Vallas was initially brought in to direct the school system. Initially, the Boston business community was concerned with fiscal issues, but after mayoral takeover it tended to focus more on issues of curriculum, school quality, and teacher improvement.

In 2005 the Aspen Institute commissioned a team of experienced researchers and educators to evaluate the Boston experience.[14] The study, mostly positive, points out that there is still a long way to go. Boston has a clear theory of instructional improvement and educator capacity building. It has strong central leadership and some noteworthy test score and college transition gains. But graduation rates are low, and the achievement gap by race and ethnicity remains. Stronger central executive leadership has been greatly enhanced, but Boston struggles with how to provide grassroots representation and its impact on school policy.

The Boston Parent Organizing Network, formed by a diverse group of parents, activists, and community members, began to advocate for improvement in the Boston public schools. The parent organization helped create a new position, deputy superintendent for family and community engagement, and a reorganization of the public schools' Family Resource Center. Parents continue to express concerns about the uneven quality of Boston schools and about the quality of instruction for English learners and handicapped students. The Aspen Institute has noted that "from parents and community groups we also heard concerns about inclusiveness. There is a sense that the city's elites—the political leadership, the business community, and the universities—have greater access to decision-making authority than other groups. . . . But many city residents and grassroots groups feel left out. They feel they have opportunities for input but are not at the table when decisions are made."[15]

The Boston school board before mayoral takeover was considered to be fractious and ineffective, so reinstituting that form of democratic representation has been rejected in a voter referendum. However, the newer mayor-appointed seven-member school committee takes two hours for its meetings twice a month. Nonpolicy matters such as contract, personnel, and day-to-day operations are delegated to the superintendent. The mayor handles much of the external politics for the Boston public schools.

The Cleveland Case

The evolution of Cleveland's education system under mayoral control highlights the difficulties and complexity in assessing the impact of mayoral control.[16] Fifty-five thousand students are enrolled in Cleveland public schools in 2007–08, with a budget of $700 million. The city's mayor, Michael White, appointed Barbara Byrd-Bennett from the New York City school system in 1998, and she stayed through 2006. She was clearly in command of the district, with the school board and the mayor in the background. She assumed leadership of a deeply troubled system, staggering under the weight of a $150 million debt, that recently had been taken over by the state. Observers described the system as being in chaos and despair. Before her arrival in Cleveland, an operating tax increase had been approved by the city's voters in 1996, and Byrd-Bennett was able to gradually pay off the debt and had clean audits from 2001 until she left the post in 2006.

Byrd-Bennett focused on academic improvement using budget increases from state, local, and foundation resources. The elementary school day was increased thirty minutes, with eighty minutes specified for literacy. She recruited a large group of new young teachers along with instructional specialists in math, English, and technology. Teacher training, support services, and computers were added, along with summer schools. She reconfigured the grades into a K–8 structure. Cleveland's expenditures grew by 53 percent from 1998 to 2003, slightly more than the statewide average. There were significant gains in the proficiency pass rates for grades 4 and 6 on reading and math tests. In 2001 Cleveland passed a $335 million school repair bond. The continuation of mayoral control was approved by the voters in 2002 by a significant majority.

But in 2003 Cleveland's budget turned around and fell from $670 million in 2003 to $558 million in 2004. About twelve hundred teachers were cut; nearly all of them were young and had been hired after Byrd-Bennett tried to staff low-performing schools. Class sizes increased substantially, while assistant principals, social workers, and security officers were cut. In 2005 voters turned down a school operating tax by 55 to 45 percent, with white voters highly negative and black voters (who turned out at lower rates) more supportive of the tax increase. The district touted an increase in fourth- and sixth-grade reading scores since 1998 at a rate twice the state average since 1998.

Perhaps Byrd-Bennett stayed too long in the job (she thinks so, as she says in a 2006 newspaper interview).[17] Her compensation and some underpayments to the state created a whiff of scandal. But Cleveland is the poorest city in the nation, and by the time she left, falling property values resulted in a decline in local tax revenue of 17 percent between 1998 and 2006. Ohio's school finance system is not equalized and relies heavily on local property values. Enrollment has declined by 15 percent, and gains in achievement scores turned flat after 2004.

Although there is no groundswell to repeal mayoral control, there is rising criticism that the board is too much a rubber stamp for the administration. In July 2007, the new mayor, Frank Jackson, was criticized by the *Plain Dealer:*

[The terms of] five of the nine members expired June 30. It was bad enough that City Hall did such an abysmal job of publicizing the openings that only seven candidates initially applied. It is unforgivable that the mayor chose to reappoint four of the members, three of whom could be poster children for the term "ineffectual," and at the same time ousted John Moss. Rather than embrace a board member who is both articulate and engaged in a district business, Jackson instead rewarded members who question little and lead less.[18]

More citizens are turning to the city council for help, but because council members have no direct authority over the school system, they are uncertain about their role. Council members attend community meetings about school closures and reorganizations but cannot do much about citizen concerns. In an exit interview, Byrd-Bennett said that meaningful reform will not take place until community leaders address the deep-seated economic and social problems in city neighborhoods.[19] Early studies of mayoral control, however, have concluded that mayoral integration of children, youth, and family policies with schools has not been impressive.[20]

What can we conclude from this brief Cleveland history? Did mayoral takeover help create the initial student attainment gains? Did more and then less money make a difference in system performance? Is the balance between central executive leadership and democratic representation right? In 2005 an Aspen Institute report praised the Cleveland literacy system and observed that "by every measure, the Cleveland Municipal School District has made steady progress since 1998."[21] The report illustrated how Cleveland had aligned assessment, curriculum, and instruction. Cleveland created an extensive classroom formative assessment to provide early feedback. In order to provide more consistent classroom implementation, Cleveland received funds from the Stupski Foundation and the State of Ohio to integrate human and financial resources into a specific implementation plan. Teachers and principals were provided with pacing charts and standards specific to each grade, along with extensive professional development. Cleveland's instructional approach for standards alignment has significant research support. But other factors intervened, and its future is unclear. Cleveland also demonstrates how different mayors have different views about their role and the risks in basing mayoral control on the attributes of a single mayor. Frank Jackson, the present mayor, has been much less active and assertive than was Mayor White or Mayor Jane Campbell, who succeeded White.

The mayors who have served Cleveland since the institution of mayoral control have never been the public face of the school system. They have worked behind the scenes with a prominent superintendent. A nominating committee screens board candidates, and the mayor appoints them to four-year terms and selects a board president. The mayor and the board appoint the superintendent. This system began in 1998 and voters agreed to keep it in 2002. The board is not especially active in public engagement or public questioning of the superintendent's decisions. The public is allowed to speak at only one of the two board meetings a month. Board committee meetings are private.

The Impact of Mayoral Control

One city, Detroit, has retreated from mayoral influence over schools. The Detroit mayor, Dennis Archer, never wanted control, and the Republican legislature's inclusion of a state official on the Detroit board with a partial veto failed to gain much public legitimacy for the Detroit mayor's enhanced role. So it was no surprise that in 2005 the Detroit voters approved an eleven-member school board elected by subdistricts. Even though different city contexts are crucial, a variety of standards can be used to assess overall mayoral impact. A reasonable standard for success is the one used by Ronald Reagan in a 1980 televised debate with President Carter, "Are you better off now than you were four years ago?" Reagan knew the record of inflation, Iran hostages, and other issues inclined the voters to say no—as did Detroit voters in 2005 about mayoral control of the public schools.

Boston and Cleveland voters overwhelmingly reauthorized mayoral control, and the Illinois legislature voted by a large majority to continue the Chicago mayor's role. Partial control by the mayor in Oakland and Washington never worked and was eventually dropped. Jerry Brown, Oakland's mayor, added three members to a seven-person elected school board but decided it was ineffective, so he did not push for renewal. The District of Columbia hybrid model of four mayoral appointees and five elected members was characterized by former mayor Anthony Williams as "trying to drive a car with one pedal." The full control won by the district's mayor, Adrian Fenty, in 2007 has some new features, such as his appointment of an ombudsman for citizen complaints, and might be instructive for other cities.

In sum, none of the present mayor-controlled cities wants the old system back. Boston does not pine for the fractious and ineffective school committee; Cleveland's board was characterized by "nonstop confrontations, intrusions, chaos, and showmanship."[22] Chicago's fifteen-member school board was too large to operate effectively in 1994. New York's central school board, appointed by borough presidents and the mayor, was supplemented by thirty-two decentralized districts with considerable authority. There has been no widespread public support in New York to restore this pre-2002 complex decentralized system.

This does not imply that there is no dissatisfaction with mayoral takeover. One argument heard often is that the mayor cannot fundamentally improve classroom instruction and so ends up facilitating marginal changes in buildings, budgets, labor peace, textbooks, supplies, new teachers, and so on. Moreover, some analysts are disappointed in the mayors' progress in combining education with children and youth policies and services. There are no comprehensive studies of mayoral impact on unions and collective bargaining. Critics contend that mayoral control has been implemented in ways that overstress executive centralization without sufficient attention to representative democracy, citizen participation, or professional technical control.

Boston and Cleveland highlight the uncertain role of city councils in all the mayoral takeover cities. No city has a clear idea of what the council should be doing in terms of public representation and citizen complaints about the schools. The thirteen-member Boston City Council retains its approval of the entire amount of the school budget and holds hearings on school issues. But these council hearings are largely symbolic and theatrical. The council has scant impact on school policy or operations, except a few minor concessions by the mayor on the budget to get the total amount approved. The plan suggested by Los Angeles mayor Antonio Villaraigosa had no formal role for the city council, even though the council has major operational responsibilities for city departments. In sum, if there is no traditional school board, citizens turn to the city council for redress of complaints but with scant impact. The Richmond, Virginia, mayor proposed a role for the city council in nominating school board members and the superintendent in a new mayor-council school takeover plan. These types of divided power arrangements, however, like the partial mayor control structures in Oakland, Washington, and Detroit, raise questions about who is in charge.

Governance Options for Mayors

There are numerous options for mayoral involvement in schools. Complete takeover of school boards, authorization of charter schools, selecting slates of school board candidates, working in partnership with school districts on specific issues, and operating as a convener and facilitator to bring various stakeholders together for school reform. Again, the appearance in some cities of these options, and more, illustrates the importance of distinctive local contexts as an important determinant of the mayor's role.[23]

Governance is not a panacea for all the school systems' problems, and empirical data such as test scores cannot be the only indicator of progress. Choices among governance alternatives must be made, but no alternative will satisfy all demands that confront school systems. Governance choice is a pragmatic process that must set priorities among the three competing objectives outlined earlier: decentralized executive leadership, representative democracy, and technical nonpartisan competence. Chicago went through all of these priorities between 1987 and 1997. In 1987 the city had a powerful general superintendent of schools in charge of a large centralized bureaucracy.

In 1988 Chicago passed a law to devolve considerable decisionmaking discretion to each school site, including selection of the principal by an elected site council. The site council had significant influence over curriculum and some budget categories. The site councils were partially governed by a fifteen-member school board. In 1995, however, the Illinois legislature gave the mayor dominant power, and Mayor Richard M. Daly reasserted his control over many aspects of the school sites' former direction. Chicago's school-site councils lost many of their prerogatives through a complex array of problems such as fiscal deficits, low voter turnout, lack of support from teachers' and principals' organizations, business dissatisfaction, and some poorly performing councils.

One view is that strong centralized leadership by the mayor is needed to "jolt" a complacent and ossified school system. Election of two board members every two years cannot shake up the school system sufficiently. Mayor Fenty assumed control of the District of Columbia schools in summer 2007 and found dilapidated facilities; he saw responses to "urgent requests" being satisfied in 379 days, flags with forty-nine stars, and a backlog of ten thousand work orders.[24] Washington has had seven superintendents in the past ten years. Mayoral control has jolted the system by closing twenty-three schools, firing ninety-eight central office employees, creating an early retirement incentive for teachers, and overhauling twenty-seven underperforming schools.

This suggests a potentially useful longitudinal governance pattern. Centralized mayoral control to jolt the system could be followed by a new balance of mayoral control with democratic representation. The three competing governance objectives could be rebalanced as the city context changes. But the historical lessons of institutional choice also must be kept in mind: what governance array can best help accomplish the objectives of the school system, such as improving classroom instruction and pupil achievement? Moreover, the more divided school governance is, the more difficult it becomes to locate accountability. Some of the key determinants of the preferred governance arrangement depend on which of the three competing objectives (representative democracy, centralized executive leadership, technical nonpartisan competence) is most appropriate for a city at a specific time within a specific historical, political, and educational context.

Whatever its impact, there are political and geographic limits to the spread of mayoral control. Many cities are not contiguous with school districts. For example, San Jose, California, has twenty school districts within its boundary, and southern cities are part of county school districts. The decline in the number of teacher strikes has also removed a crucial trigger for mayoral takeover. But test scores in many cities have not risen sufficiently to offset state and local dissatisfaction. More efforts at mayoral takeover seem likely. And if the mayors do not succeed in cities like Chicago, Boston, and Cleveland, voucher advocates will have a stronger case—at least for the worst-performing big-city schools. Reformers will continue to use governance and organizational changes in an effort to improve the performance of students.

Notes

1. Larry Cuban and Michael Usdan, eds., *Powerful Reforms with Shallow Roots: Improving America's Urban Schools* (Teachers College Press, 2003).

2. Michael Kirst, *Mayoral Influence, New Regimes, and Public School Governance*, RR-049 (Philadelphia: University of Pennsylvania, Consortium for Policy Research in Education, 2002).

3. Donald McAdams, *What School Boards Can Do* (Teachers College Press, 2006).

4. Herbert Kaufman, *Politics and Policies in State and Local Government* (Englewood Cliffs, N.J.: Prentice-Hall, 1963).

5. David Rogers, *110 Livingston Street* (New York: Random House, 1969).

6. Quinnipiac University Polling Institute, "Congestion Pricing Is Bad, but Fare Hikes Are Worse, New York City Voters Tell Quinnipiac University Poll; Most Say Bring Back Board of Education" (www.quinnipiac.edu/x1302.xml?Release ID=1087).

7. William H. Clune, *Institutional Choice as a Theoretical Framework for Research on Education Policy* (Philadelphia: University of Pennsylvania, Consortium for Policy Research in Education, 1987), p. 4.

8. Deborah Land, "Local School Boards under Review," *Review of Educational Research* 72 no. 2 (2002): 229.

9. Frederick M. Hess, "Looking for Leadership: Assessing the Case for Mayoral Control of Urban School Systems," *Policy Study* 7 (St. Louis: Show-Me Institute, February 6, 2007), p. 7.

10. Stefanie Chambers, *Mayors and Schools: Minority Voices and Democratic Tensions in Urban Education* (Temple University Press, 2006).

11. Kenneth K. Wong and others, *The Education Mayor: Improving America's Schools* (Georgetown University Press, 2007).

12. Hess, *Looking for Leadership,* p. 21.

13. Dorothy Shipps, *School Reform, Corporate Style: Chicago, 1880–2000* (University Press of Kansas, 2006).

14. Aspen Institute, *Strong Foundation, Evolving Challenges: A Case Study to Support Leadership Transition in Boston Public Schools* (Washington, March 2006).

15. Ibid., p. 13.

16. The Cleveland analysis is based on review of interviews and articles in the *Cleveland Plain Dealer* and the *Cleveland Catalyst* and by publications of the Aspen Institute.

17. Lonnie Timmons, "An Exit Interview," *Cleveland Plain Dealer,* February 12, 2006.

18. *Cleveland Plain Dealer,* "A Nice, Compliant School Board," editorial, July 4, 2007.

19. Timmons, "An Exit Interview."

20. Cuban and Usdan, *Powerful Reforms.*

21. Helen W. Williams, "The Cleveland Literacy System: A Comprehensive Approach to Changing Instructional Practice in the Cleveland Municipal Schools," paper prepared for a meeting of the Urban Superintendent Network of the Aspen Institute Program on Education, Washington, June 10–12, 2005.

22. Joseph F. Wagner, "School Board Seats Filled Quietly," *Cleveland Plain Dealer,* June 24, 2007 (www.cleveland.com/clevelandschools/plaindealer/index.ssf?/cleve-landschools/more/1182686130140490.html).

23. United States Conference of Mayors, "Mayoral Leadership and Involvement in Education," Research Report (Washington, 2001).

24. Catherine Gewertz, "D.C. Schools Get School Repair Blitz," *Education Week,* September 15, 2007, p. 11.

KENNETH K. WONG

4

Does Mayoral Control Improve Performance in Urban Districts?

Mayoral appointment of school boards is gaining national prominence as a reform model. The public is paying growing attention to mayoral
control as an option to improve public school governance, as is indicated by
2006 and 2007 Gallup polls that surveyed the public's view on mayoral control in schools. In 2006 only 29 percent were in favor; in 2007 that number had
jumped to 39 percent, and among parent respondents, 42 percent were in favor.[1]
Such trends in public opinion, combined with growing media attention to
mayoral involvement in urban schools, elevate this topic in today's education
policy circles. The 2007 annual meeting of the National Conference of State
Legislatures drew a huge audience to the session on mayoral control and the
future of school boards. Currently, almost two-thirds of the states have passed
legislation authorizing either the city or the state to govern and manage school
districts that are underperforming. Appointed school boards now run the districts in New York, Philadelphia, Chicago, Boston, Baltimore, Cleveland, Providence, and Trenton, among others. Since summer 2007, the mayor in
Washington, D.C., has exercised complete control over the school system with
his appointment of the school chancellor and deputy mayor for education.

The growing public support for mayoral control suggests the promise of the
reform's core design—an integration of electoral accountability and education
performance at the system-wide level. The question is, does mayoral control
work to raise district performance? This chapter addresses this critical question with evidence on the effects of mayoral control on student achievement
and management performance. In the last several years, my colleagues and I

have conducted extensive analyses of the nation's 100 big-city school systems, which allow us to compare systems that are governed by elected boards and those that are under mayoral control. We have found that mayoral control has a statistically significant, positive effect on student achievement. Mayoral control also improves management and financial administration. However, mayoral control does not seem to be associated with a reduction in the achievement gap between the highest- and the lowest-performing schools

In essence, mayoral control allows the city's public, parents, and taxpayers to hold the mayor and his or her appointed school board ultimately accountable for school performance. This governance reform, which can be characterized as "integrated governance," is designed as a corrective to sprawling administrative and political subsystems with too much fragmentation.[2] Mayoral control, when properly designed and implemented, can enhance educational accountability. In light of the rising importance of this strand of reform, several issues that are critical to system-wide improvement demand attention: What are the effects of mayoral appointment of school boards on student achievement? Do institutional checks and balances account for district performance? Does mayoral control widen or narrow the achievement gap? Do mayors spend more money on administration? Does mayoral control provide more resources for teaching and learning? These issues of accountability and management form the basis for considering the future of mayoral control in urban districts.

Assessing Academic Performance

In a recently published book, *The Education Mayor: Improving America's Schools,* Francis Shen, Dorothea Anagnostopoulos, Stacey Rutledge, and I report on the most comprehensive empirical analysis to date of the effects of mayoral control on student outcomes and management performance.[3] We examine 104 big-city school systems located across forty states, and we synthesize standardized achievement data from thousands of schools. The study examines multiple years of data by using a mixed-methods approach, both applying statistical models and conducting in-depth case studies that connect the macro policy conditions to the micro-level practices in a sample of urban classrooms. The detailed research design and methodologies can be found in that book. Here, I highlight some of the study's key findings on student achievement as well as tables on school performance in the middle grades that are not part of the earlier book.

District-Level Performance

Because the mayor operates at the system-wide level and the enabling conditions at the district level may take some time to affect student achievement, our study looks at district-wide year-to-year performance across urban districts. We analyze student achievement over the period 1999 to 2003 in a purposeful sample of 101 urban districts for which we have school-level achievement data from the National Longitudinal School-Level State Assessment Score Database. We examine the core subjects of reading and math outcomes separately. The database lacks achievement results for some districts in some states for some years, especially the early years of 1999 and 2000. Accounting for these data constraints, for elementary achievement analysis we have 451 district-year observations for reading achievement and 449 observations for math achievement. These observations include the districts with some degree of mayoral appointment of school boards: Chicago, Boston, Baltimore, Cleveland, Detroit, Philadelphia, Oakland, New Haven, Jackson (Mississippi), New York, and Providence. Because the District of Columbia is a single-district state, it is not possible to standardize its performance against districts in other states. Our analysis does not include the small and midsize neighboring districts of Harrisburg, Hartford, and Trenton. For high school analysis, for which less data are available, we have 264 observations for reading and 268 observations for math. The smaller number of observations limits the inferences we can make about high school achievement.

The use of panel data allows us to look at two types of changes in governance. First, we have differences across districts: in a given year some districts have mayoral control, while others have elected school boards. Second, we observe changes within a district over the period 1999–2003. In Oakland, for instance, elements of mayoral control were introduced in 2000. In Philadelphia, governance changes were not put into place until 2001.

Value Added Function

In keeping with the social science approach to the relationship between education inputs and outputs, we estimate the value added function as measured in terms of standardized district achievement, relative to other districts within the same state. Standardized achievement is measured as the z-score of the district for a given year. We include a series of input and control variables, with greatest interest in the effect of governance arrangements on district output. Again, our methodological approach is discussed in greater detail in our earlier book.

Introducing the notion of value added through the use of a lagged achievement control variable enables us to better isolate the effects of governance changes as distinct from influences such as unobserved family background influences—parental involvement, for example. If the assumption holds that parental involvement is roughly the same from one year to another (for example, active parents in year $t - 1$ are still active in year t, and parents active in year t were also active the previous year), then those parental involvement factors will be captured by the lagged achievement variable. To the extent that new factors, which did not determine the previous year's achievement, enter into the present year's achievement production, our analysis has omitted variables.

Institutional Dimensions of Mayoral Control

Our analysis identifies three key dimensions on which mayoral control can be institutionalized: the presence of a mayor with a vision on education accountability (or what we characterized as a "new-style" mayor), formal authority for that mayor to appoint a majority of the school board, and the extent to which the mayor's appointive power is restricted. Because we are not sure which aspect of mayoral control may be most salient, we consider each aspect independently before summing them up into an index.

Based on these three dimensions, we create three dichotomous variables. Each variable measures a unique aspect of mayoral control. We use this method—a series of yes-or-no questions about mayors' formal powers—because of the complexity involved in specifying a mayor's precise level of formal control and informal influence. For instance, does giving the mayor formal powers, such as hiring the school district chief executive officer, actually empower the mayor relative to other interests in the city? Since the data that would allow us to accurately assess whether a mayor has a lot of influence or a little power are not readily available, we try to address this question by thinking about factors that are likely to be closely associated with mayoral power in the education realm. We consider three factors: *NEW STYLE* is a dichotomous variable, coded as 1 if the mayor has adopted a new style of governance integrating electoral accountability and school performance and 0 if the school system remains governed within a traditional regime. *MAJORITY* is a dichotomous variable, coded as 1 if the mayor has the power to appoint a majority of the school board and 0 if the mayor can appoint none or any submajority of the board. *FULL* is a dichotomous variable, coded as 1 if the mayor has full appointment power for the school board, with no requirement of the city council, nominating process, or other formal approval, and 0 otherwise.

Because the effectiveness of mayoral control may also depend on the cumulative effect of these powers, we add an additional index variable that sums over the three dimensions noted above. This index variable, labeled *MAYOR_INDEX*, has a low value of 0 and a high value of 3. As discussed in greater detail in our book, we run two sets of statistical models. In model A, we include the three measures of mayoral control independently. This allows us to test their relative contribution to student achievement and other outcomes. We then run model B, in which we replace the three individual measures with the composite mayor index.

Our data set allows us to look over many districts and across multiple years. This means that our unit of observation is not simply the district (as it would be if we had only data from one year) but the "district-year." The values of the mayoral control variables change over time within the same district. We also take into consideration a number of control variables, such as poverty, racial or ethnic composition of the student body, city governance, private school enrollment, revenues, and special education and English-language learner populations, among others.

A related issue concerns the duration of mayoral control, timing, and possible lag effects. It could be the case that mayors are not able to bring about changes in the school system until they have been able to establish a new management regime. To the extent that this is true, we would expect to see the effects of mayoral control not in the same year as the reform is implemented but in later years. Although our data constraints affect the extent to which we can evaluate lag effects, we run separate models in which we look at one-year and two-year lagged effects. In these models, we are looking at the effect of governance structure in year t on student performance in year $t + 1$ and year $t + 2$. With more years of data going forward in the near future, we may be in a better position to evaluate the long-term effects of mayoral control, beyond a one- or two-year window.

A variable that we are not able to measure across all districts is the extent to which the mayoral reform has become institutionalized through the multilayered policy organizational system. For instance, have management practices really changed after one year of mayoral involvement? That is, how long will it take for mayors' actions to affect teaching and learning in their city's schools? This is related to, but not the same as, the simple duration of the reform. Although a reform is likely to take deeper root the more years it has been in practice, it is not clear that just because a reform has been in place for multiple years it will necessarily be implemented widely. For instance, a mayor may be in power for three years, but if that mayor makes few systematic changes, the duration of the takeover will not accurately represent the low level of systemic implementation of the reform.

Elementary School Performance

With the details of the study design now laid out, we turn to the central question of our study: does mayoral control raise student achievement? Our study suggests that mayoral governance matters. More specifically, majority appointment power of school board members is an effective strategy for raising achievement. At the same time, a lack of oversight of the mayor's choices may actually work against this progress. Furthermore, mayoral control, like the traditional regime, still faces the challenge of poverty and other structural problems that hinder student achievement.

How does mayoral control relate to standardized elementary reading achievement? Our research indicates that giving the mayor power to appoint a majority of the city's school board is associated with a standard deviation increase of 0.14 in standardized elementary reading achievement. When we give the mayor two years and look at the two-year lag model, not only is there a positive association with majority appointment power but also for new-style mayors (those who focus on accountability) there is a 0.15 standard deviation increase as well. Driven by these two aspects of mayoral control, the composite mayoral control index is significantly and positively related to achievement in both the baseline and two-year lag models. At the same time, however, allowing the mayor full power to appoint school board members without oversight from a nominating committee is inversely related to elementary reading achievement.

A similar pattern emerges in elementary math achievement. The positive effects of new-style mayors are seen after two years. In the two-year lag model, the presence of a new-style mayor is associated with a 0.14 standard deviation increase in elementary math achievement on standardized tests. We observe the same inverse relationship between math achievement and allowing mayors full appointment power without committee oversight.

Putting the evidence from reading and math analyses together, it is clear that mayoral leadership has made a difference. It may take a couple of years, however, for that difference to be seen in aggregate, district-wide achievement results. At the same time, the absence of restrictions on whom the mayor appoints to the school board seems to dampen achievement levels. In light of these findings, a few policy implications are immediately evident. First, optimal systems should design mayoral control systems to include nominating committees that provide the mayor with a slate of candidates from which to choose school board members. Second, evaluation of mayoral control should recognize that improvements from mayoral control may take at least two years to become evident in aggregate statistics.

To develop a better understanding of these results, one needs to recognize the strong adverse effects of several structural and contextual variables in the urban system. The most important relationship is the strong predictive power of previous district achievement on current district achievement. This is true in both reading and math, and it suggests that it is difficult to change the absolute position of a district's achievement. If a mayor inherits a district that is performing near the bottom of the pack, no amount of skill on that mayor's part is likely to make the entire district leapfrog to the top within a short period of time. Instead, the more realistic goal is for the mayor to improve the trajectory of the district's performance. Our results are consistent with this pattern of tangible, persistent gains. When we look at where the districts start out, we see that a standard deviation increase of 0.15 will not rapidly move mayor-led districts above the mean in their state. It does, however, put the districts one important step closer to that goal.

A consistent finding across both elementary achievement models is a significant, inverse relationship between standardized achievement and the percentage of school-age children attending private school. This may be an indicator of brain drain, with some of the city's best students opting out of the public school system and into private options. Not surprisingly, the percentage of children in poverty in a district is inversely related to achievement. This is consistent with the long-standing finding that students from lower socioeconomic backgrounds perform less well in school.

Our study also finds significant, inverse relationships between achievement and the percentage of Hispanic and African American students. The magnitude of these effects is great, approximately three times as large as the effects of mayoral control. As discussed earlier, because our data are aggregated up from the school to the district level, we need to be wary of ecological inference issues. Nevertheless, in light of scholarship that has identified a persistent racial gap in American public education, these results may suggest that though changes in institutional governance can raise overall district performance, there is still much to be done to lift the achievement of all city students.

Progress in Lowest-Performing and Higher-Performing Schools

A promising effect of mayoral control is the academic improvement of the district's lowest-performing schools, such as schools in the lowest quartile. To be sure, these schools have a higher concentration of students eligible for free and

Table 4-1. *Proportion of Students Rated Proficient on State Assessment Tests in Lowest Quartile of Elementary Schools, Selected Districts, 1999–2003*[a]
Percent

District	Grade	Schools (n)	Reading					Math				
			1999	2000	2001	2002	2003	1999	2000	2001	2002	2003
Baltimore	3	27	5.6	11.2	11.1	9.5	32.7	1.6	4.8	13.5	8.2	34.9
Baltimore	5	27	5.9	13.9	15.9	13.8	41.8	3.1	10.2	18.1	14.8	26.1
Boston	4	20	0.0	3.1	17.6	22.2	22.6	2.5	8.4	6.6	8.7	7.1
Chicago	3	113	13.7	18.3	20.4	20.2	24.0	20.4	20.6	31.1	29.5	35.3
Chicago	5	112	19.1	19.1	21.9	22.9	26.1	10.4	13.5	18.2	18.9	27.5
Cleveland	4	21	19.6	19.3	22.1	26.6	n.a.	14.8	18.4	22.8	30.5	n.a.
Detroit	4	41	n.a.	n.a.	16.2	19.8	46.5	n.a.	n.a.	23.5	26.6	34.2
New Haven	4	7	6.6	10.9	12.4	10.8	13.7	11.0	19.6	21.6	26.8	31.9
New York	4	84	13.9	24.9	28.0	30.2	37.5	25.4	25.8	33.1	34.8	55.4
Oakland	3	17	14.2	18.6	21.8	23.7	16.5	16.5	22.5	27.6	23.3	24.7
Oakland	4	15	11.9	13.3	13.0	19.5	8.9	11.8	17.9	19.8	22.6	19.7
Philadelphia	5	48	3.8	9.4	9.6	12.2	n.a.	1.6	5.5	6.9	11.0	n.a.
Providence	4	6	27.4	25.1	34.7	32.3	29.2	0.4	2.3	10.4	16.5	14.0
Washington, D.C.	3	26	34.7	41.5	39.6	40.9	n.a.	35.6	45.8	48.1	47.3	n.a.
Washington, D.C.	4	29	35.4	41.2	42.6	43.0	39.5	34.4	42.0	43.6	45.3	42.2

Source: Data from U.S. Department of Education and American Institute for Research, National Longitudinal School-Level State Assessment Score Database (NLSLSASD), 1999–2003.

n.a. Not available.

a. Achievement can be compared year to year within a given district, but without proper statistical controls districts cannot be directly compared with one another because different tests are being used in each district. When within-district comparisons are not appropriate (for example, change of test from one year to next), we report a missing value. All achievement measures are percentage proficient, with two exceptions: the achievement measure in Detroit is percentage satisfactory and above, and the measure in Washington, D.C., is the normal curve equivalent.

reduced-price lunches. In most cases, these schools are also educating greater percentages of African American students than the overall district average. Despite these structural challenges, schools in the lowest quartile in mayor-controlled districts show steady progress. From 1999 to 2003 (where data are available), these schools made steady progress in the percentage of students who tested proficient in the state annual benchmarking grade assessment. As shown in table 4-1, the percentage of third-grade students in Baltimore's lowest-quartile schools who scored at proficiency level in reading rose from 5.6 percent to 32.7 percent. Proficiency in math for fifth-graders in Chicago's lowest-performing schools improved from 10.4 percent to 27.5 percent, and

Table 4-2. *Proportion of Students Rated Proficient on State Assessment Test in the Lowest Quartile of Middle Schools, Selected Districts, 1999–2003*[a]
Percent

District	Grade	Schools (n)	Reading					Math				
			1999	2000	2001	2002	2003	1999	2000	2001	2002	2003
Boston	8	9	1.0	2.2	5.1	4.7	8.6	11.1	18.6	27.1	n.a.	n.a.
Chicago	8	111	2.6	6.9	10.4	14.8	15.1	35.1	44.7	32.1	42.7	38.2
Cleveland	6	6	3.0	4.3	12.4	15.0	n.a.	6.8	7.7	9.3	8.3	n.a.
Detroit	7	17	n.a.	n.a.	15.2	15.1	20.6	n.a.	n.a.	n.a.	4.8	9.9
New York	8	31	5.3	8.8	7.2	18.4	24.1	14.5	16.9	16.7	14.8	19.3
Oakland	6	5	11.0	13.3	16.8	23.3	14.3	9.5	11.4	13.3	15.7	15.8
Oakland	8	5	4.2	8.8	12.0	19.5	14.8	14.2	11.5	16.0	16.6	16.0
Philadelphia	8	25	2.4	5.6	8.0	7.3	n.a.	5.0	9.7	11.3	14.6	n.a.
Washington, D.C.	6	24	41.4	48.4	47.3	47.4	n.a.	38.9	43.1	41.9	42.8	n.a.

Source: Data from U.S. Department of Education and American Institute for Research, National Longitudinal School-Level State Assessment Score Database (NLSLSASD), 1999–2003.
n.a. Not available.
a. Achievement can be compared year to year within a given district, but without proper statistical controls, districts cannot be directly compared with one another because different tests are being used in each district. When within-district comparisons are not appropriate (for example, change of test from one year to next), we report a missing value. All achievement measures are percentage proficient, with two exceptions: the achievement measure in Detroit is percentage satisfactory and above, and the measure in Washington, D.C., is the normal curve equivalent.

for Cleveland's fourth-graders, it rose from 14.8 percent to 30.5 percent from 1999 to 2002. Similar trends in middle grades are shown in table 4-2.

Although tracking low-performing schools by district serves as a useful first step in evaluating mayoral control, additional analytic steps are needed to specify the effects of mayoral control on the achievement gap. Specifically, we develop a measure that enables us to conduct comparisons across districts. For analytical purposes, we focus on the ratio of the top quarter of schools to the bottom quarter of schools. We refer to this as the "75-25 ratio," as it represents the average performance of schools in the 75th percentile and above divided by the average performance of schools in the 25th percentile and below. We use the 75-25 ratio as our dependent variable in our statistical analysis of the achievement gap.

To provide a sense of what these ratios look like, tables 4-3 and 4-4 present the inequality ratios for elementary grades in mayoral control districts. Most of the ratios hover around the value of 2, implying that schools in the top quarter of the district score twice as well on the state achievement test as their

Table 4-3. *Inequality Ratios of Mayoral Control Districts, Selected Elementary Grades, Selected Districts, 1999–2003*[a]

District	Grade	Reading					Math				
		1999	2000	2001	2002	2003	1999	2000	2001	2002	2003
Baltimore	3	2.5	2.6	2.4	2.2	1.6	4.0	4.2	3.8	3.6	1.6
Baltimore	5	2.3	2.5	2.1	2.6	1.4	3.6	3.3	2.8	3.5	1.8
Boston	4	3.7	5.5	1.9	2.5	2.8	3.3	3.7	4.5	4.6	4.3
Chicago	3	2.3	2.4	2.0	2.1	2.2	2.2	2.4	2.0	2.2	1.9
Chicago	5	1.8	2.0	1.9	2.1	1.9	2.3	2.6	2.4	2.7	2.1
Cleveland	4	1.8	2.1	1.9	2.2	n.a.	1.9	2.3	2.3	2.5	n.a.
Detroit	4	1.4	1.3	1.6	1.5	1.3	1.4	1.3	1.4	1.5	1.6
New Haven	4	3.5	2.8	2.2	2.4	1.9	2.7	2.4	2.5	1.9	1.6
New York	4	2.1	1.9	1.9	1.8	1.7	1.8	2.0	1.8	1.7	1.4
Oakland	3	2.4	2.5	2.6	2.6	2.5	2.0	2.6	2.3	2.3	2.0
Oakland	4	3.0	2.5	2.8	2.1	2.9	2.4	2.6	2.0	1.9	2.1
Philadelphia	5	3.5	2.9	3.4	3.0	n.a.	6.0	5.1	4.5	4.0	n.a.
Providence	4	1.4	1.7	1.4	1.4	1.3	3.5	4.0	2.5	1.9	2.1
Washington, D.C.	3	1.3	1.2	1.3	1.3	n.a.	1.4	1.3	1.3	1.3	n.a.
Washington, D.C.	4	1.3	1.3	1.3	1.3	1.3	1.3	1.3	1.3	1.3	1.3

Source: Data from U.S. Department of Education and American Institute for Research, National Longitudinal School-Level State Assessment Score Database (NLSLSASD), 1999–2003.

n.a. Not available.

a. The inequality ratio is represented as the average performance of schools in the 75th percentile and above divided by the average performance of schools in the 25th percentile and below (the 75-25 ratio). Ratios can be compared year to year within a given district, but without proper statistical controls, they cannot be directly compared to one another because different tests are being used in each district. When within-district comparisons are not appropriate (for example, change of test from one year to the next), we report a missing value. The ratio is the performance difference between the highest-performing and the lowest-performing quartile of schools in a school district for the specific subject and grade in a given year. All achievement measures are percent proficient, with two exceptions: achievement measure in Detroit is percent satisfactory and above, and the measure in Washington, D.C., is the normal curve equivalent.

counterparts in the bottom quartile. Looking over the time span of 1999–2003, it is difficult to make generalizations about trends across districts. Chicago's achievement gap during this period remains roughly the same for elementary reading and math.

Effect on the Achievement Inequality Ratio

To better understand what explains these inequality ratios, we turn to multivariate analysis similar to the analysis conducted for estimating the overall district-level performance. Here, the unit of analysis is the grade-district-year. For each year 1999 through 2003, we measure the 75-25 ratio as it is available for

Table 4-4. *Inequality Ratios of Mayoral Control Districts,*
Selected Middle Grades, Selected Districts, 1999–2003[a]

District	Grade	Reading					Math				
		1999	2000	2001	2002	2003	1999	2000	2001	2002	2003
Boston	8	2.3	2.4	1.5	n.a.	n.a.	5.5	5.5	3.0	2.4	3.5
Chicago	8	1.6	1.5	1.6	1.5	n.a.	3.4	3.4	3.4	2.9	2.8
Cleveland	6	2.1	2.0	3.1	3.1	n.a.	2.8	3.1	2.7	3.3	n.a.
Detroit	7	1.4	1.6	1.4	1.7	1.4	1.9	1.6	n.a.	1.7	1.7
New Haven	6	1.9	2.3	2.4	2.7	2.5	2.0	2.7	2.1	2.4	2.6
New Haven	8	2.1	2.5	1.9	2.3	2.2	3.6	4.3	2.2	2.5	3.1
New York	8	2.0	2.2	2.3	2.4	2.2	2.8	2.9	3.5	2.8	2.3
Oakland	7	2.6	2.7	2.2	2.5	2.4	3.3	2.5	2.6	2.9	2.9
Oakland	8	2.3	2.9	2.2	2.0	2.4	2.8	4.6	3.1	2.6	2.5
Philadelphia	8	3.4	2.8	3.0	2.5	n.a.	7.0	4.6	4.6	3.4	n.a.
Providence	8	1.3	3.3	1.4	1.5	1.3	1.8	7.0	1.9	1.7	1.4
Washington, D.C.	7	1.3	1.1	1.4	1.4	n.a.	1.2	1.3	1.4	1.3	n.a.
Washington, D.C.	8	1.2	1.4	1.2	1.3	1.2	1.2	1.3	1.3	1.4	1.3

Source: Data from U.S. Department of Education and American Institute for Research, National Longitudinal School-Level State Assessment Score Database (NLSLSASD), 1999–2003.

n.a. Not available.

a. The inequality ratio is represented as the average performance of schools in the 75th percentile and above divided by the average performance of schools in the 25th percentile and below (the 75-25 ratio). Ratios can be compared year to year within a given district, but without proper statistical controls, the ratios of separate districts cannot be directly compared with one another because different tests are being used in each district. When within-district comparisons are not appropriate (for example, change of test from one year to the next), we report a missing value. The ratio is the performance difference between the highest-performing and the lowest-performing quartile of schools in a school district for the specific subject and grade in a given year. All achievement measures are percentage proficient, with two exceptions: the achievement measure in Detroit is percentage satisfactory and above, and the measure in Washington, D.C., is the normal curve equivalent.

different grades across different districts. In this part of the analysis, we look at all 100 districts in the sample, not just those with mayoral control. Our data are school-level data, which means that as a prerequisite, a school district must have enough schools in a particular grade that the inequality spread between them can be considered. A district with only four schools, for instance, would be too prone to outliers for our purposes. Our decision rule was that, to be included in our analysis, a particular district-grade must have at least ten schools. Because school districts typically have more elementary schools than middle schools, and more middle schools than high schools, we separated out our regressions into elementary and middle school categories. The middle school category had only 107 district-grades with at least ten observations, and because of this skewed and reduced sample, we focus solely on the elementary grades.

Some districts have more than one grade's worth of data available, and consequently they supply more of the observations in our analysis. Because different grades are involved, we introduce the variable *GRADEi* to serve as an additional control. If certain grades are associated with lower inequality ratios, this control variable will capture that effect. Aside from this addition, however, we examine the relationship between the 75-25 ratio and various inputs using the same production function, state fixed-effects model as we did for the overall district achievement.

Having set up the analysis, we are ready to address the question, does mayoral control reduce the achievement gap? The answer seems to be no, at least in the short run. Although majority appointment power is inversely and significantly related to the reading achievement gap, the overall mayoral control index is positively and significantly related to inequality in both reading and math. There also is a positive relationship between new-style mayors and the achievement gap in elementary reading. These positive relationships may be a result of mayors' interests in maintaining high-performing schools in order to anchor middle-class communities in the city. We also find that districts with fewer board members elected district-wide are associated with wider achievement gaps in math, suggesting that this governance arrangement as well can lead to more stratification.

Other contextual factors influence the achievement gap. If one looks at the nongovernance control variables, there is clearly a strong predictive power of previous inequality on existing inequality in both reading and math. Although this result is not surprising, it serves as a reminder that reducing entrenched achievement inequality is an extremely difficult task. We also see that larger per pupil expenditures are inversely associated with the 75-25 ratio in math, suggesting that greater resources may be effective in reducing the math achievement gap. The only student background variable that is significantly related to the 75-25 ratio is the percentage of special-education students in the district. The magnitude of the effect of special education on the gap is quite large, suggesting that it is an important factor in explaining the achievement gap. Interestingly, the measures of minorities in the student body are not significant in our analysis. This may be explained by the fact that in districts with a high concentration of minority populations, both high- and low-performing schools are serving predominantly minority students.

Our cross-district analysis of 75-25 ratios finds a positive relationship between mayoral control and the ratio in both elementary reading and math.

A move from a traditional governance regime to a new-style governance is associated with roughly a 0.38 increase in the 75-25 ratio in elementary reading. The magnitude of this impact will depend on the baseline ratio in a particular city. In a school district that had about the same inequality as Chicago, the baseline would see the best 25 percent of schools outperform the lowest 25 percent by roughly 2 to 1. Our analysis suggests that in this district, the introduction of mayoral control would change that ratio to 2.38 to 1.

One way of interpreting the finding that mayors and achievement stratification are positively linked is that mayors, facing competition from both the suburbs and private schools, may need to invest resources into high-performing schools in order to stem brain drain. In metropolitan areas where districts are competing for high-performing schools, it is likely that the city's overall performance might significantly improve if two of every ten departing brain drain students could be kept. The appointed school boards in Chicago and Philadelphia, for example, have introduced more rigorous curricular programs, such as Advanced Placement and International Baccalaureate classes, as a strategy to attract well-prepared students. Another explanation may be the assessment structure itself: Chicago's first-wave accountability focused schools on the achievement of the top students as well as what is being called the "bubble" students (those on the cusp), whereas No Child Left Behind focuses on the bottom quartile. The data in our study capture only the first year of No Child Left Behind, when schools were just starting to adapt.

It may also be the case that the mayors see greater need to establish stronger schools for middle-class residents before tackling the greater problem of turning around the district's worst schools. High-performing schools serve as an anchor for middle-class families. In 2005 Mayor Daley used that imagery in evaluating his school reforms: "So how does government help build stronger neighborhoods? . . . You start by building what I call community anchors: schools, libraries, parks, and police and fire stations. *The most important anchor, by far, is the school.*"[4] Recognizing this link between citywide economic interest and education is important when one considers the relationship between redistribution and development. As Paul Peterson has argued, "In some cases redistribution may be economically beneficial [but] in the contemporary United States . . . it must be recognized that in most cases redistributive programs have negative economic effects" for the city as a whole.[5] In the realm of education, mayors may see a need to respond to corporate and civic interests that are demanding high-performing schools for the city's tax base.

To be sure, we do not go so far as Peterson in arguing that a focus on equality "comes at the expense of the development of the big-city economy."[6]

Nonetheless, we recognize that mayors are caught between competing interests. Certainly, turning around low-performing schools can have positive economic effects. Mayors need to be mindful of the development of a new, skilled labor force that draws on all sectors of the city. Redistributive programs can go hand in hand with citywide interest.

These results may provide some evidence to support the concerns of those who believe that mayoral control will lead to programs that favor business interests.[7] But it is important to recognize that although mayoral control is associated with higher 75-25 ratios, it does not appear that the lowest-performing schools are getting worse. Rather, they are not improving as fast as some of the highest-performing schools. In this view, mayoral control is a reform that improves student performance overall but, at least initially, improves student performance at a greater rate in the upper quartile of city schools.

These dual findings raise a question of trade-offs and citywide interest that are at the heart of most discussions on schools and inequality. Should the city focus on raising the floor of student achievement or focus primarily on closing the gap, even if that means dropping the ceiling? Clearly, this policy challenge poses trade-offs in terms of local policy priorities. Nonetheless, as many urban centers face increasing economic constraints, there is a need to maintain a strong, middle-class city population at the core. High-performing schools are necessary to attract and keep those residents in the city. A strong middle-class presence enables the city to build a broader political coalition for an intergovernmental lobby. The middle class also forms a strong voice with which to air concerns on education quality. In addressing the challenges of the lowest-performing schools, cities must also recognize that their mission may be made quite difficult by the levels of poverty and special-education needs of students in those schools. In this view, the most efficient use of resources may be to make simultaneous investments in both high-performing and low-performing schools, understanding that the overall 75-25 ratio may grow in the short run.

High School Performance

Before I discuss the high school results, it is worth emphasizing that the National Longitudinal School-Level State Assessment Score Database has less high school than elementary school data. Part of the problem is that states have less high school data readily available for analysis. Whatever the reasons, the consequences for our analysis are that we are left with a much smaller sample when we examine high school reading and math performance. Specifically, the database does not contain high school data from these states (for which we did have elementary school data): Alaska, Arkansas, Colorado, Connecticut, Louisiana, Maryland, Minnesota, Mississippi, New York, North Carolina, Oklahoma, South Carolina, and Tennessee. As a result of these dropped observations, we are left with no districts like New York City, where a mayor appoints a majority, but not all, of the board members. We therefore drop the "majority" category from the analysis. Clearly, better data collection and analysis at the high school level remain priorities for future research in this area. This data collection could cover both achievement scores and other indicators such as attendance, drop-out rates, or graduation rates. We will continue to work in this area, and we hope that others will as well. In light of this need for more data, we proceed cautiously in interpreting the high school results.

Data limitations aside, the high school results mirror the elementary results in that the power to appoint a majority of school board members is significantly, positively associated with higher reading and math achievement, whereas full appointment power without oversight is inversely related to achievement in both subjects. That the high school results mirror the elementary results gives us reason to think that they are credible. The same processes that lead to improvements in elementary achievement may also be operating for high school achievement. Many reforms, such as reducing central office bureaucracy, can be thought to be grade-level neutral. Less red tape in the central office will benefit all schools, regardless of the grades they serve.

The control variables in the high school statistical regressions are generally related to standardized achievement in the same way they were in the regression models on elementary achievement. Once again, a significant inverse relationship between standardized achievement and the percentage of Hispanic and African American students in the district remains statistically significant in the high school models as well. The magnitude of these effects at the high school level, however, is even more striking. In high school reading, a 1 unit point increase in the percentage of African American students has an impact on achievement more than five times greater than a governance switch to a majority mayor-appointed board. Although the conclusion remains that mayors can produce significant, positive change at the high school level, it is evident that deeper challenges remain for a school system hoping to overcome underperformance.

Effect of Governance Change on Student Achievement

Some skeptics believe that the large urban school districts in the United States face too many external obstacles ever to be effective. Our empirical analysis assesses the marginal effects that a change in institutional governance can have on student outcomes, even controlling for all of the socioeconomic challenges that many researchers have documented.

The results of our analysis suggest that a governance change that gives the mayor the power to appoint a majority of the school board will lead to a z-score improvement of 0.15 to 0.19 in elementary reading and math. To give these gains some context, we can consider again the starting points of the mayoral control districts, measured as their z-score in 1999. Practically every district has a negative z-score, and most z-scores are less than −1, meaning that every district in 1999 was performing below the state mean. Most districts had more than one standard deviation below the mean. If we were to go through the list of other districts (those not under mayoral control) in our total sample, most would have similar z-scores.

Our analysis predicts that two years after the introduction of a mayor-appointed school board, achievement will rise approximately 0.15 to 0.19 of a standard deviation. This is a significant improvement, even if it does not bring the district all the way back to the state average. The limited time span of our data prevents us from estimating long-term changes, but our look at two-year lag effects, where the relationship between mayoral control and achievement becomes even stronger, leads us to believe that the long-term effects could be an increase of at least 0.15, and perhaps more.

It also appears that mayors can have an impact in the context of high school achievement. Because of our smaller sample and more-limited data, we can not make general inferences as we can for elementary achievement. The indications are positive, however, that mayors may be able to have a similar positive impact on high school reading and math achievement.

Implications for Governance Change

Our study provides evidence that mayoral control has a positive effect on student achievement. More specifically, mayoral power to appoint a majority of the city's school board is associated with an improvement of about 0.15 to 0.19 of a standard deviation in standardized elementary achievement. However, a lack of oversight on the mayor's choices may slow this progress. Our analysis suggests that mayors have a positive effect on academic accountability, but they still face an enormous challenge in the context of concentrated poverty and disenfranchisement in urban school communities.

These findings suggest implications for governance redesign. First, depending on local context, it may make sense to include proper checks and balances in the institution of mayoral governance of schools. These mechanisms include nominating committees that provide the mayor with a slate of candidates from which to choose school board members. Second, evaluation of mayoral control should recognize that academic improvements may take at least two years to become evident in aggregate, district-level outcomes. Third, our achievement results are the marginal effects of mayoral control, holding all else constant. In other words, even if poverty levels remain the same, funding levels do not improve, and private school competition holds constant, our model predicts that a governance change leads to significant, positive improvements in overall district achievement. If mayors can work simultaneously to reduce poverty and increase funding, the overall effect of mayoral control may be even larger in the longer run.

The positive achievement findings may suggest the viability of a dual strategy that focuses on sanctions and support for failing schools in districts under mayoral control. At the urging of the mayor, much stricter grade promotion policies have been implemented in New York and Chicago. In Philadelphia, the appointed school board started implementing academic promotion policy in grades 3 to 9 during the 2003–04 school year. To be promoted to fourth or ninth grade, students were required to score at or above the 26th national percentile in both reading and mathematics on the TerraNova test. Students who scored somewhere between the 20th and 25th national percentiles could be promoted if they maintained strong academic records and 90 percent attendance and no major disciplinary problems.

At the same time, systems of mayoral control implement a wide range of initiatives to build school capacity and expand learning opportunities for students. Both Chicago and Philadelphia, for example, created an office of accountability, which conducts ongoing, on-site school-quality assessment and initiates school-specific intervention in low-performing schools. Philadelphia also focused on high school and middle school improvement based on strategic planning that involved stakeholders throughout the community. Among the strategies were a ninth-grade academy, a doubling of the number of counselors, a "credit recovery" program to address high school dropouts, and consolidation of middle schools and high schools. Students who did not make the grade were offered summer programs and a second-chance summer test for promotion.

Strategic Management of Resources

Mayor-led integrated governance as a reform policy is distinguished by its efforts to improve management efficiency throughout the system. Mayors are in a position not only to support teaching and learning in schools but also to improve the financial and management conditions in which teaching and learning occur. In addition to improving fiscal stability, integrated governance allows the central decisionmaking authorities more flexibility in terms of resource allocation. In particular, mayors may be able to reduce school district central office inefficiencies, thereby allowing for greater investments in teaching, learning, and provision of student services. At the same time, they are operating in an environment that is often hostile to change. Whether mayors can make good on their promise to improve fiscal efficiency remains an open question; to address the issue, we conducted extensive additional rounds of statistical analysis.

To consider the relationship between mayor-appointed school boards and measures of effective management and improvements in human capital, we once again employed a panel data approach. We obtained financial and staffing data for all of our 104 sample districts and for the entirety of our eleven-year period of observation, 1993–2003. The financial outcome data come from the Annual Survey of Government Finances conducted by the United States Bureau of the Census. The survey gathers data on revenues, expenditures, and debt from more than 15,000 school districts. In addition to these financial data, we use the Common Core of Data from the National Center for Education Statistics as a source for our demographic control variables, as well as data on district staffing patterns. Both sources provide data that are comparable across time and across districts.[8] Using our time series (1993–2003) and cross-sectional (104 districts) data, we employ a fixed-effects regression model similar to the achievement model to examine the effects of mayoral control.[9]

Does mayoral control lead to greater revenues per pupil? Our results suggest that it does not.[10] The power to appoint a majority of school board members is significantly and negatively related to per pupil revenues. Returning to the general question of whether a mayor can overcome institutional inertia and broader economic trends, the negative relationship between mayoral control and per pupil revenues suggests that factors beyond the mayor's control may determine revenue levels. Faced with limited options for raising new funds themselves, and dealing with urban districts that already rely heavily on state and federal compensatory funding, mayors may have to reframe their financial aims. Rather than depending on an infusion of new money to the school district, they may be forced to work more efficiently with the same or even fewer resources.

Our analysis finds that at baseline, mayoral control is inversely associated with the level of per pupil spending on instruction and support, but given five years, the percentage spent on instruction and support increases. The distinction between percentage allocation and overall expenditure levels is an important one. Mayor-led districts are not spending more, but they are spending differently. Mayor-led districts are reallocating resources to instruction and instructional support.

Although mayors may be able to institute changes in school district financial management, it appears that district employees may be insulated from sweeping changes brought in by mayoral control regimes. The effects of mayoral control measures on increases in the percentage of district staff who are teachers, administration, or student support are not statistically significant.

Synthesizing the findings of our analysis of mayors and school finances, we believe that most education mayors are becoming more strategic in prioritizing their resource allocation and management. Central to this strategy is the notion of fiscal discipline in constraining labor costs. We see this in the inverse relationship between mayoral control and expenditures. Education mayors, while continuing to partner with labor unions, seem able to leverage cooperation (or concessions) from the school employees' unions. Our case analyses suggest that the education mayors are able to negotiate multiyear contracts with teachers unions and administrators unions. Mayoral success in managing unions has been aided by the enabling legislation that grants mayoral control. For example, the 1995 Illinois reform act precluded a teachers strike during the first eighteen months of mayoral control.

Another aspect of mayors' strategic priorities seems to be improving bureaucratic efficiency by reducing expenditures on general administrative purposes. Mayoral control lowered the level of spending on general administration and also reduced the percentage of expenditures spent on general administration. By reducing general administrative costs, mayors free up more money for instructional purposes and may improve public confidence that wasteful spending is not occurring in the district. The trend in which mayors spend more on instructional purposes is also seen in their decision to prioritize this type of spending over noninstructional services such as support services, transportation, and some operations costs.

A third aspect of mayoral control emerging from our analysis is the need for leadership to do more with less, presumably by improving district efficiency. Although we do not have a direct measure of efficiency, we find some circumstantial evidence to suggest new spending priorities under mayoral control systems. Given five years to implement their strategies, mayor-led systems allocate more salaries and wages to instruction, thus prioritizing the resources that most directly affect teaching quality.

From a broader institutional perspective, city hall is likely to apply fiscal discipline and accountability to the school system in both formal and informal ways. During the late 1970s and the 1980s as well as the early years of the present decade, when cities faced severe fiscal stress, mayors began to adopt a new governing culture, which may be characterized as the new fiscal culture.[11] Mayors oriented toward the new fiscal culture tend to focus on management efficiency and emphasize quality-of-life issues. Growingly responsive to concerns of the taxpayers, these mayors move away from policies defined by traditional party labels and organized interest groups. In local governance that adopts this new culture, the traditional party labels become less relevant as the relation between social and fiscal issues weakens. Fiscal responsibility and social conservatism are no longer strongly linked.[12] In reforming management of agencies, mayors who adopt the new fiscal culture accelerate contracting out, hold down taxes, focus on management efficiency, and introduce outcome measures for periodic evaluation. These changes tend to overlap with the policy vision of civic-spirited business leaders and the taxpaying electorate. Quality-of-life issues are often defined in terms of the city's physical environment, parks and recreation, and public education.

In mayor-led school systems, consistent with the new fiscal culture, improvement in financial management tends to occur during the first couple of years. Analysis of documentary sources in mayor-appointed boards suggests improvement in financial and administrative management. These districts seem able to show financial solvency, often turning a deficit into a balanced budget. Mayoral control systems seem to be associated with improved bond ratings, labor peace, better client satisfaction, and greater efficiency at the central office. For example, in response to labor peace and balanced budgets, Standard & Poor's raised the Chicago district's bond rating from BBB– to BBB in March 1996 and then to A– in 1997. The favorable bond rating enabled the appointed board to raise billions of dollars to finance the first citywide capital improvement project in decades.

The appointed school board in Chicago was able to draw on a broad pool of expertise in operation, finance, and management. An analysis of 111 top administrative appointments made in the central office between July 1995 and February 1998 showed diversity of expertise. More than 40 percent of these appointees came from outside the school system—from the private sector, nonprofit organizations, and city agencies. In areas that were not directly related to education practices, such as finance and purchasing, more than 60 percent of the appointees came from outside the school system. In Philadelphia, the school board, jointly appointed by the mayor and the governor, moved rapidly to apply district-wide standards to all schools, including those that were contracted with educational maintenance organizations. The board and the chief executive officer launched a $1.5 billion capital plan to build new schools, modernize facilities, and reduce overcrowding.

The education mayor also institutes a broader climate of fiscal accountability across local governmental agencies, including school districts. By sharing financial, management, and auditing expertise with the school system, city hall can improve capital projects, balance the budget, and even support negotiations between unions and management. A key effort is to contain the escalating labor cost, which is in part driven by medical costs as well as collective bargaining agreements. Mayors have cautiously taken steps to leverage incremental concessions from the school employees unions. Many cities are contracting services to competitive bidders who in turn must show results. The lessons municipal agencies have learned by outsourcing various services are transferable to many services that school districts provide in-house, such as transportation, food service, information technologies, human resource management, and safety services, among others.

Taking into consideration both academic and management performance, our analyses generally support the claim of integrated governance that mayor-appointed school boards can have a significant, positive effect on district performance. Mayoral control has realized the promise that integrated governance is a viable policy reform in urban education. The success of mayoral control is beginning to attract the attention of many mayors who are dissatisfied with their cities' independent school systems.

Exploring Implications for Governance Redesign

Because the No Child Left Behind Act identifies takeover as an option in restructuring low-performing districts, it is likely that mayors in a growing number of cities will seek control over the school boards. Even in cities that may not allow the mayor to exercise direct control, mayors seem to become more active in school board governance. For example, in San Francisco, Mayor Gavin Newsome successfully backed his education adviser to run for a seat on the school board. In Los Angeles, Mayor Antonio Villaraigosa, having failed to gain control of the district, has gained substantial control as his close allies form the majority bloc in the elected school board.

As this chapter suggests, mayoral control has led to measurable progress in urban districts. First, city-appointed school boards have been effective in raising student achievement, particularly when the mayoral control system has been in place for more than two years. Second, mayoral control improves financial and administrative management because these districts are able to broaden the pool of management expertise, institute fiscal discipline, and deploy innovative strategies. Third, mayoral control is more likely to institutionalize pressure and support, implementing oversight and direct intervention to improve school accountability.

Although districts vary in their reform effectiveness, the education mayor generally assumes a stronger institutional mandate than does an elected school board. As an institution, the office of the mayor can play an instrumental role in improving district performance. The institutional form of charisma does not depend on a charismatic person for its foundation. Instead, "corporate bodies—secular, economic, governmental, military, and political—come to possess charismatic qualities simply by virtue of the tremendous power concentrated in them."[13] Because the office of the mayor carries stature and respect independent of the particular person who occupies the position, mayoral involvement can add substantial value to the school reform process.

From the perspective of institutional charisma, the office of the mayor holds a broader mandate than the city's elected school board. For example, a typical mayoral election receives a 45–55 percent voter turnout, which is several times more than a typical nonpartisan school board election. In New York City, just before passage of the state legislation that granted Mayor Michael Bloomberg control over the school district, fewer than 5 percent of eligible voters turned out to cast ballots in the local community school board elections. Similarly, in Chicago there was a continuous decline in turnout for the election of local school council members: between the first election in 1989 and the last in 1993, before the mayoral takeover of the district, there was a 68 percent drop in parent turnout.

By contrast, when a mayor is granted the power to appoint the school board, he or she can focus on mobilizing electoral support for school reform. In Boston, for instance, when Mayor Thomas Menino named seven members to the first mayor-appointed school board in 1992, he proclaimed himself an education mayor. Voters validated his strong platform on education in 1996, when 54 percent of the electorate opposed the referendum that called for a shift back to an elected school board. That 1996 election saw an unusually high turnout of 68 percent. Mayor Menino and his appointed superintendent, Thomas Payzant, established an unusually long and stable working relationship until the latter retired in 2006.

The office of the mayor is uniquely positioned in leveraging commitments and resources from nonpartisan institutions, such as universities and museums, to improve public schools. Although they vary in scope and visibility, collaborations between city hall and universities often result in additional political benefits to the mayor's office. For instance, in Providence, Mayor David N. Cicilline, who appoints his city's school board members, asked the president of Brown University to lead the search for a new school superintendent in 2005, thereby broadening the legitimacy of the search process and outcome. Mayor Cicilline also negotiated successfully with Brown University and other higher education institutions to make additional voluntary contributions to local property taxes. In Chicago, the mayor's office, city council members, and the University of Chicago collaborated in an effort to restructure a set of low-performing schools on the city's South Side. Many mayors also have encouraged universities and nonprofit organizations to establish charter schools in low-income neighborhoods. Mayors and their appointees often invite academic researchers to conduct evaluation studies on a wide range of educational problems.

Successful mayoral control tends to be associated with several factors, all of which are within the mayor's power: clear and attainable strategic goals, community and parental engagement, willingness on the part of the city to put financial and political resources to use in leveling up failing schools, the capacity for the mayor to work with the existing district administration for a smooth transition, managers who bring diverse expertise, implementation of innovative strategies and diversification of service providers, and accountability for results on the part of the administrative heads as well as the principals, teachers, and students. When these factors are in place, mayor-appointed boards are ready to raise education performance. In light of these findings and the enormous policy challenge in large urban systems, mayoral control offers a viable strategy that is likely to benefit students, parents, taxpayers, and the district as a whole.

Notes

1. Reported in Lowell C. Rose and Alec M. Gallup, "The 39th Annual Phi Delta Kappa–Gallup Poll of the Public's Attitudes toward the Public Schools," 2007 (Bloomington, Ind.: Phi Delta Kappa International, September 2007), p. 38.

2. Diane Ravitch and Joseph Viteritti, eds., *New Schools for a New Century: The Redesign of Urban Education* (Yale University Press, 1997).

3. Kenneth Wong and others, *The Education Mayor: Improving America's Schools* (Georgetown University Press, 2007). In particular, Francis Shen has provided valuable technical assistance to the project.

4. Mayor Richard M. Daley, keynote address at the Delivering Sustainable Communities Summit, Communities and Local Government, Manchester, U.K., February 1, 2005; emphasis added.

5. Paul E. Peterson, *City Limits* (University of Chicago Press, 1981), p. 43.

6. Ibid.

7. Larry Cuban and Michael Usdan, eds., *Powerful Reforms with Shallow Roots: Improving America's Urban Schools* (Teachers College Press, 2003).

8. In analyzing the financial data, we construct two general types of variables from the raw Annual Survey of Government Finances data. The first type is a measure of allocation, examining financial subcategories as a percentage of the whole. The second type is a measure of magnitude, exploring the amount (dollars per student) being spent in various subcategories. All of our allocation measures are reported as percentages, and all of our magnitude measures take enrollment into account and are therefore reported as dollars per student. For each of the revenue and expenditure measures, we consider both allocation and magnitude.

9. In addition to this baseline model, we consider models with five-year lagged governance. We cluster on the school district to provide for robust standard errors. For details, see Wong and others, *The Education Mayor*.

10. For more details, please see our online data supplement (brown.edu/Departments/Education/Education_Mayor/7-22-07_EducationMayor_Chapter7-Supplement.pdf).

11. Terry N. Clark and Vincent Hoffman-Martinot, *The New Political Culture* (Boulder, Colo.: Westview Press, 1998).

12. Kenneth Wong, Pushpam Jain, and Terry Clark, "Mayoral Leadership in the 1990s: Fiscally Responsible and Outcome Oriented," paper presented at the 1997 annual conference of the Association for Public Policy Analysis and Management, Washington, D.C., November 6–8, 1997.

13. Edward Shils, "Charisma, Order, and Status," *American Sociological Review* 30 (April 1965): 199–213, quotation on p. 207.

City Case Studies

PART

II

JOHN PORTZ AND ROBERT SCHWARTZ

5

Governing the Boston Public Schools: Lessons in Mayoral Control

In recent years a number of cities in the United States have turned to mayors to help improve public education systems. Through appointment of school board members and superintendents, mayors have assumed a central role in school reform efforts. As policymakers and citizens assess the impact and effectiveness of this turn to mayoral control, it is instructive to consider the experiences of cities that have ventured down this path.

Boston provides such an example. Since January 1992, the mayor of Boston has appointed the seven-member Boston School Committee, the formal name of the city's school board. The mayor's acceptance of this appointing authority was a major break from the days of an elected school committee, when mayors avoided and often battled the school system. Under mayoral appointment the Boston public school system has enjoyed a level of stability and cooperation in its governance that is near unique among urban school systems. Between 1995 and 2006, the same two individuals—Mayor Thomas M. Menino and his superintendent, Thomas W. Payzant—constituted the core political and educational arms of the governance team and worked closely with the school committee and the Boston Teachers Union. This continuity in leadership among key education actors stands in sharp contrast to the typical turnover, and frequent turmoil, in urban school districts. The story of how Boston arrived at this governance arrangement and what it has meant for the school system are this chapter's central concerns.

Governance and Public Schools: The Context for Mayoral Control

School governance is about the structure of authority by which major decisions are made and resources allocated within a school system. As defined in a report by the Education Commission of the States, "Governance arrangements establish the rules of the game, that is, . . . who is responsible and accountable for what within the system."[1] As noted by a longtime observer of school politics, "Governance is about control—who drives the educational bus."[2] A recent study of school boards describes governing as "steering" the school district. Governing involves the establishment of educational goals and policies that follow a vision and a set of core beliefs about how academic achievement can be realized.[3]

Several key actors are involved in school governance. Historically, school boards have played a central role. Typically elected, school board members represent the community as they oversee and guide the school district. In recent years, they have come under criticism for a host of reasons, including their frequent involvement in managerial aspects of school operations, such as hiring principals, teachers, and other staff, as well as their ineffectiveness in improving overall educational outcomes.[4] Superintendents also are key governance actors. As managers for the school system, superintendents play a key role in implementing school policies, and they advise school boards on policy development. School boards and superintendents do not act alone or unfettered. In particular, they operate within a growing set of rules and regulations established by state governments and federal authorities.

In recent years mayors have become more involved in school governance, particularly in larger cities.[5] Mayoral involvement can take different forms, but the most common involve appointment powers and fiscal controls. With respect to appointments, mayors are given authority to appoint school board members and, in some instances, the superintendent as well. With respect to fiscal controls, mayors are granted authority over the total funding support received by the school system. These appointment and budget powers move the mayor to center stage in the debates over school reform. In contrast to Progressive Era efforts to depoliticize school systems, mayoral control makes city hall a key actor in determining the allocation of resources in the school system. Reaching this level of mayoral involvement, however, is not simple or without controversy, as is evident in the Boston experience.

Fragmentation and Limited Accountability: 1970–1992

The debate over school governance in Boston is long-standing. Since at least the early 1970s, concerns have been raised over the fragmented nature of the school system and the lack of accountability both within the system and between the school department and other units of local government, particularly the mayor's office. In addition, the 1960s and 1970s saw a growing crisis over school segregation in which the school department faced mounting challenges over its allocation of resources and other decisions that were perpetuating a system of segregated schools.

During this period—from 1970 through the 1980s—the schools were often political battlegrounds. In addition to desegregation issues, the separation of the school department from general government set the stage for political battles between the school committee and superintendent on one side and the mayor and city council on the other. With no meaningful control over the school department, mayors typically kept their distance from school politics. From the perspective of the business community, infighting among these various political actors and the controversies around desegregation made working with the school system problematic. Educational leadership and policy coherence were sporadic, at best, and generally lacking during this period.

There were, however, periodic efforts to improve the school system. In the early 1970s, for example, under the leadership of Mayor Kevin H. White (1967–83), a group of reformers came together to develop and advance a restructuring plan for the school system.[6] Included in the restructuring plan were several key changes: decentralization of the school department into thirty-six districts with school councils that would facilitate greater citizen participation and accountability at the school level; appointment of the superintendent by the mayor; and replacement of the elected school committee with a citywide advisory committee.

Although at least part of this reform agenda received the support of many in the community, it ultimately failed to receive voter support. The plan to eliminate the school committee was particularly controversial and generated opposition from various quarters. Furthermore, several other restructuring proposals competed for attention. The reformers' proposal emerged from debates within the city council and was placed on the November ballot in 1974. Before the election, however, Judge W. Arthur Garrity, of the U.S. District Court, issued the first of many orders to desegregate the public schools. This order changed the political dynamic in Boston and turned the focus to busing and public reactions to this desegregation strategy. Amid this controversy, the proposal to restructure the schools failed at the ballot box.

The business community also explored several connections with the school system, albeit with mixed success. In the early 1970s a number of business corporations created partnerships with high schools under the auspices of a new organization, the Tri-Lateral Council for Quality Education. In a more comprehensive approach, in 1982, the Boston Compact was created as a partnership of the business community, the school system, and city govern-ment. Under this agreement, businesses pledged to provide a job opportunity for every public school graduate entering the labor market, in return for meas-urable improvements in performance in the school district's high schools.

Although these business initiatives and forays into school governance were important, the city's struggle with school desegregation dominated much of this period. Between 1974 and the late 1980s, Judge Garrity issued more than four hundred court orders involving school closings, student assignment, per-sonnel hires, textbook adoption, community partnerships, and a host of other school matters. For much of this period the federal district court governed the Boston school system.

The mayor's role in the schools was limited. Boston's strong-mayor form of government granted the mayor extensive authority over general govern-ment services but a limited role in school policy. Administrative control of the schools resided with the superintendent and school committee. Fiscal author-ity was blurred. Under Boston's governance structure, the mayor and city council set the total appropriation for the school department, but the school committee controlled the allocation of resources within the school budget. In this fiscally dependent arrangement, the elected school committee often decried city hall for providing financial resources inadequate to operate the school system, while city hall complained of having no control over the allo-cation of school monies. The school committee typically refused to make expenditure adjustments equal to those requested by city hall and would end the year in a deficit, requiring a last-minute appropriation from the mayor and city council. This divided responsibility inevitably led to acrimonious finger-pointing, with the public not sure whom to hold accountable for budgetary decisions.

In this environment, Boston's mayors typically kept at arm's length from the public schools administration. Mayor White, like most other urban may-ors, was keenly aware of the political price John Lindsay had paid for his attempts to intervene in the governance arrangements in New York in the mid-1960s. In his first term, White concentrated on improving city services in the departments over which he had control, paying only passing attention to the problems of the schools. By 1971, however, it was clear to the mayor that the school committee's continued defiance of the Commonwealth's Racial Imbalance Act would most likely lead to court-ordered desegregation, at which point the problems of the schools would land directly in his lap. This realization led him to hire a full-time education adviser at the beginning of his second term and to invest political capital in the unsuccessful proposal, described above, to abolish the school committee and gain direct control over the school department.

By the late 1980s federal court involvement in the schools had diminished, but governance and accountability concerns remained prominent.[7] The school committee, which in 1983 was expanded from five members (elected citywide) to thirteen members (four elected citywide, nine by the district) was at the center of the debate. Criticisms from the early 1970s continued: the school committee was widely criticized for political opportunism, policy fragmentation, and fiscal irresponsibility.[8] Battles over school closures were commonplace, and racial divisions were prominent. The difficulty of working with this school committee led Robert R. Spillane, the most competent and nationally respected Boston superintendent in memory, to resign after one term to accept a superintendency in Virginia.

Calls for a change in governance became increasingly widespread in the media and among many in the city.[9] The Boston Municipal Research Bureau, a business-supported government watchdog organization, had long advocated for greater clarity in governance roles by having the school committee focus on policymaking, and the superintendent manage the school system.[10] During the late 1970s and mid-1980s, several legislative changes were made to clarify the relationships among the superintendent, school committee, and city hall, but problems persisted, with the school committee receiving most of the attention. A *Boston Globe* editorial described the school committee as "a disaster, . . . [with] infighting, grandstanding, aspirations for higher political office, and incompetence. . . . The system is floundering."[11] A mayoral commission declared that "frustration with school performance had reached an historic high" and that changes in governance were critical to the future of the system.[12] After reviewing the governance system for the schools, the study concludes, "Boston is unique. The buck does not appear to stop anywhere."[13]

Mayor Raymond Flynn (1984–93), who early in his tenure had been hesitant to get involved in school politics, became more vocal in his criticisms and began to propose changes in governance. Among the reform proposals floated for consideration were elimination of the school committee and direct appointment of the superintendent by the mayor; a less drastic alternative proposed a school committee composed of a mix of mayoral appointees and elected members.

The most popular governance proposal, particularly among state officials, was to replace the elected committee with one appointed by the mayor. In November 1989 a citywide advisory referendum on the issue yielded mixed results: 37 percent in favor of an appointed committee, 36 percent opposed, and 26 percent not voting. The movement to an appointed committee was temporarily shelved, but in late 1990 efforts resumed, resulting in an April 1991 vote by the city council to forward a petition to the state to create a seven-member committee appointed by the mayor. The two black members of the city council voted against the change. From their perspective, an appointed school committee reduced voting opportunities for all residents of the city, and it eliminated an elected body that could provide a gateway into politics for Bostonians, particularly those in the minority community.[14] Debate continued, but the new committee structure received state approval, and Mayor Flynn appointed seven individuals from a list provided by a nominating committee to begin terms in January 1992.

The Stars Align: 1992–2007

The shift to mayoral appointment marked a sharp break in school governance. Yet to be resolved, however, was how leadership within the school system would mesh with the new political control exercised by the mayor. More specifically, Lois Harrison-Jones, Boston's second black superintendent, hired in mid-1991 by the elected committee, now found herself working for the newly appointed committee and, indirectly, for the mayor. The honeymoon was brief. Disagreements between the mayor and superintendent became increasingly public. The controversy subsided, at least temporarily, when Mayor Flynn resigned in mid-1993 to join the Clinton administration as ambassador to the Vatican. City council president Thomas Menino became acting mayor, then won the special election in November 1993.

With a new mayor in city hall, the relationship between the superintendent, the school committee, and the mayor was less volatile, but tensions continued. The superintendent pointed to the intervention of Boston politics into public education, while the mayor and others became increasingly critical of the superintendent's performance. In early 1995 Harrison-Jones was informed that her contract, due to expire in July, would not be renewed. The school committee initiated a broad public search process. In July and August three finalists were interviewed and an offer was extended to Thomas Payzant, assistant secretary in the U.S. Department of Education and a former superintendent in four communities, including San Diego and Oklahoma City. Payzant accepted and became superintendent in September 1995.

The key ingredients for the governance of school reform were now in place. As one school principal commented, successful school reform requires that the mayor, superintendent, school committee, and school administrators be in accord, or as he put it, "All the planets have to be lined up."[15] Between 1995 and 2006, the continuity in school governance was striking. Payzant remained as superintendent for almost eleven years, retiring on July 1, 2006. He was the longest-serving superintendent in the Boston schools since 1960. Thomas Menino, elected in 1993, continues as mayor, having won elections in 1997, 2001, and 2005. In 1997 he ran unopposed and won easily in the subsequent two elections. This continuity of the mayor and superintendent has provided a degree of stability in Boston that is rare among urban school systems.

Continuity is also the theme on the mayor-appointed Boston School Committee as well as the Boston Teachers Union. The current chair of the school committee, Elizabeth Reilinger, has served in that capacity for ten years (since January 1998) and has been a committee member since January 1994. In fourteen years on the school committee, she has worked closely with both Payzant and Menino. Edward Doherty served as president of the Boston Teachers Union for twenty years, leaving the post in 2003. His replacement, Richard Stutman, is a longtime union member and teacher in the Boston school system.

This alignment of individuals has played an important role in fostering communication and cooperation around school improvement. As Payzant notes, "The strong and sustained alliance among the mayor, school committee, and superintendent has set a tone for the district to move from fragmentation to coherence."[16] To be sure, tensions sometimes develop, but for the most part these leaders have developed relationships that recognize the interests and leadership styles of each. The mayor and superintendent, for example, have a working relationship that accommodates the political interests of the mayor while acknowledging the educational expertise of the superintendent.

Payzant's retirement in 2006 posed one of the first major challenges to this governance arrangement. After almost eleven years of the Payzant-Menino partnership, mayoral control would be tested by a new superintendent. A national search process resulted in the hiring of Manuel Rivera from New York, only to see him withdraw before coming to Boston. An interim superintendent continued as the search was renewed. In the summer of 2007, Carol Johnson, the superintendent in Memphis, was chosen to succeed Payzant. As an African American woman with teaching and administrative experience in Tennessee and Minnesota, Johnson brings a different set of skills and perspectives to the governance partnership. Thus far, her transition has proceeded smoothly, and she appears to have established a good working relationship with the mayor.

This governance arrangement has received general support from Boston voters over the years. The clearest test of public approval came in November

1996, when a ballot question was put to the voters. Required by the state legislation that authorized the appointed committee, this ballot issue gave voters the choice of returning to a thirteen-member elected committee (a yes
vote) or keeping the seven-member appointed committee (a no vote). The
appointed committee won the day, receiving 53 percent of the votes compared with 23 percent for returning to an elected committee; 23 percent of the
ballots were left blank on this issue. As Menino proclaimed, "The message was
clear throughout Boston that we should continue the progress we've made in
the schools."[17]

Although the appointed committee won by a margin of two to one among
votes cast, it received less support within the minority community.[18] In two of
Boston's twenty-two voting wards—minority areas in Roxbury and Dor-
chester—the appointed committee option lost in the balloting. In general, in
predominately black precincts, the average vote in favor of returning to an
elected committee was 55 percent; in predominately white precincts the comparable vote was 28 percent. The African American community was consid-
erably more inclined to support a return to an elected committee. As noted
earlier, to many in the minority community an elected committee represented
an important expansion of voting opportunities as well as fertile ground for
involvement in city politics. Overall support in the city, however, remained
strong for the appointed committee.

What has this new governance system meant for school politics and public education? In several areas, the change is quite significant. Mayor Menino
raised the agenda status of education while increasing financial support for
the schools. The change in governance also led to a shift in the general nature
of public discourse around education. Finally, continuity in leadership and
governance facilitated focused and sustained reform efforts from the school
department. Each of these changes warrants exploration.

Mayoral Support for Education

One of the most significant changes prompted by the new governance
arrangement is strong mayoral support for public education in Boston. As
noted earlier, under the elected committee structure, mayors had kept their
distance from a school system over which they had little control. With the
power to appoint committee members, however, this changed. Particularly in
the middle and late 1990s, there was a clear focus by the mayor on public
education. This shift is evident in at least two ways: first, attention to the
schools in the policy process and second, financial support for the schools.

Setting the policy agenda is one of the most important sources of mayoral power. Particularly in strong-mayor cities, mayors have numerous opportunities to direct the course of public policy. Inaugural addresses, State of the City speeches, budget messages, executive appointments, and public forums provide mayors with opportunities to shape the policy process.

The mayor's new authority over school affairs has been accompanied by a significant elevation of public education on the policy agenda. Exemplifying this shift in attention are two excerpts from different annual State of the City speeches. In early 1991, when the city's schools were still administered by an elected committee, Mayor Flynn emphasized the traditional goals for Boston: "The priorities in Boston are clear. Government has a job to do. We're going to keep providing the basic city services that you need and deserve, like maintaining the parks, picking up the trash, and having dedicated fire fighters and EMTs there when you need them. . . . Our number one priority is safe neighborhoods."[19] Five years later, with an appointed committee in place and Payzant as superintendent, Mayor Menino outlined a distinctly different list of priorities in a State of the City speech delivered at the Jeremiah Burke High School, which had just lost accreditation: "Economic security. Good jobs. Safe streets. Quality of life. Public health. Those are the spokes of the wheel—but do you know what the HUB of that wheel is? Public education! . . . GOOD PUBLIC SCHOOLS ARE AT THE CENTER OF IT ALL!" In fact, Menino started that address with the statement, "I want to be judged as your mayor by what happens now in the Boston public schools. . . . If I fail to bring about these specific reforms by the year 2001, THEN JUDGE ME HARSHLY."[20]

This dramatic shift in attention is captured by a content analysis of State of the City speeches. In the last seven years of an elected committee, from 1985 through 1991, Mayor Flynn's State of the City speeches devoted an average of only 3.7 percent of each speech to education (see figure 5-1). In contrast, a review of the first seven years under mayoral control (1992–99) shows mayors Flynn and then Menino devoting an average of 28.4 percent of each speech to education. Mayor Menino's quote cited above is from his 1996 address, of which 68 percent was devoted to education issues.

Nineteen ninety-six proved to be the peak year for attention to school issues. As figure 5-1 demonstrates, subsequent years showed an up-and-down pattern. Mayoral attention to education in these annual addresses dipped from 2002 to 2004, but on average, it remained well above the pattern that existed before the change to mayoral control. State of the City messages have become important venues for the mayor to identify key education goals,

Figure 5-1. *Focus on Education in State of the City Speeches, Boston, 1985–2007*[a]

Percent

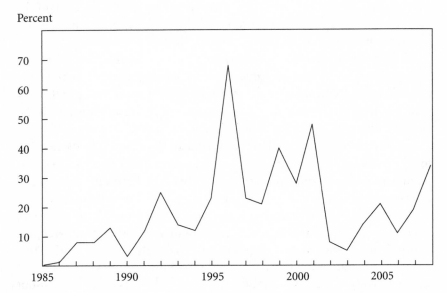

Source: Review by authors of annual State of the City speeches published by the city of Boston in the *City Record*.

a. Percentage of speech focused on education is calculated by the number of lines in the printed speech devoted to education divided by the total number of lines in the speech.

which include such proposals as more extended-day programs, more computers in the classroom, more and better school buildings, more literacy programs, better teacher recruitment, and improvements in test scores. As one longtime observer of school politics notes, Mayor Menino is the school system's "biggest cheerleader."[21]

The budget provides a second measure that demonstrates mayoral support for the schools. From the state and the city, Boston's public schools have received a growing piece of the city's fiscal pie, particularly in the middle and late 1990s. The agenda status accorded to the schools has translated into financial support. Although the economic and fiscal downturn in the early part of this decade has hit the schools as well as most other departments, the overall level of financial support remains significant.

One measure of financial support for the schools is the percentage of general fund expenditures made by the school department. Based upon this measure, the school department's portion increased from the years of an elected committee to those of an appointed committee. During the last seven years of an elected committee, the school department accounted for an average of 31.3 percent of the city's general fund expenditures. During the first seven years of an appointed committee, this average increased to 35.2 percent.[22]

This pattern of support has continued. From 1997 to the present, the Boston school system has continued to account for approximately 35 percent of general fund expenditures. However, it should be noted that an increase in state school aid to Boston, particularly in the mid- and late 1990s, is a major source of general fund support for the school department. The school department is not immune from cuts during difficult fiscal times, as took place earlier in this decade, but the mayor has often provided the schools a fiscal buffer from the ups and downs of urban finances. Most recently, for example, the mayor allocated an extra $10 million to the school department for the fiscal year 2009 budget to provide the new school superintendent with more time to achieve cost efficiencies and make program changes in light of lower enrollments.

Changing Public Discourse

Mayoral appointment and the new governance system have contributed to a change in the public discourse around school issues. As one business leader commented, "We have a mayor, a superintendent and a school committee singing from the same sheet of music."[23] Since 1992 this accord, along with a state and national focus on school accountability and student achievement, has resulted in a shift in public discourse from conflict and sharp debate to a more consensual environment focused upon education issues.

This change in discourse is evident in the way the school committee operates and relates to the public. Under an elected school committee, discussions concerning public education were often contentious and lengthy. Committee meetings were noted for their duration, averaging three hours in 1989 and 1990, and a divided committee was typical. In 1989 and 1990 there was at least one dissenting member in 88 percent of committee votes.[24] On occasion, a member would leave the meeting in disgust. Racial divisions were sometimes prominent in these debates. In 1990, for example, the four black members walked out in protest before the remaining members of the committee voted seven to one to fire Laval Wilson, the district's first black superintendent.

Under an elected committee, interaction with the public was frequent and service oriented. Public access to committee members was heralded by many as an important feature of the system. In 1989 and 1990 the committee held ten public hearings on a range of topics. Outside of hearings, committee members frequently responded to complaints from parents. Each committee member received a $52,000 office allotment that was typically used to hire a staff person to receive phone calls from parents and other residents with complaints about school services. This constituent orientation provided a readily accessible avenue for citizen concerns and also prompted committee involvement in school operations.

Public interaction and discourse have changed significantly under an appointed committee. A more consensual, elite dialogue has replaced contentious debate, racial divisions, and constituent services. In contrast to the long meetings and divided votes, the typical meeting of the appointed committee is shorter and less contentious. In 1994 and 1995, for example, committee meetings averaged one hour and thirty-five minutes, half as long as those under the elected committee, and the board voted unanimously on 98 percent of the votes during those two years.[25] A recent tabulation of committee votes finds a similar pattern: all but 1 out of 121 nonprocedural votes in 2004 and 2005 were unanimous.[26]

In this consensual decisionmaking environment, public participation is less constituent based and has generally declined. Appointed committee members lack the electoral incentives to seek parental input. For outreach, the appointed committee occasionally holds meetings in school buildings around the city and sponsors periodic public forums, but citizen participation is generally less than it was under the elected committee. In 1994 and 1995, for example, the committee held five public hearings, compared with twice that number in 1989 and 1990 under the elected committee.

The style of the appointed school committee reflects the generally professional background of its members. Most appointed members have professional or administrative experience that includes higher education, business, and community organizations. Although the elected committee also included some individuals with such backgrounds, by their nature, elected members were more attuned to the campaign trail of community meetings and voter forums.

The professional orientation and consensual nature of school politics has raised the stature of business and institutional partners, such as the Boston Plan for Excellence and the Boston Private Industry Council. The Boston Plan for Excellence, for example, shifted its focus in 1995 from supporting individual student scholarships and small grants to teachers to a much more involved role as a partner with the school system in designing and implementing school reform. The Boston Plan supported whole-school improvement throughout the district, and it focused considerable effort on developing and implementing a teacher coaching model known as Collaborative Coaching and Learning.[27] In the past few years, the Boston Plan for Excellence also has been working with the Boston Private Industry Council and Jobs for the Future to support the school department's initiative to create smaller learning communities at the district high schools. To support these and other activities, the Boston Plan played a key role in raising more than $65 million between 1995 and 2004. This included two grants from the Annenberg Foundation as well as grants from the Carnegie Foundation, Gates Foundation, and other donors.

The Boston Private Industry Council hosts the Boston Compact, an agreement among city government, the public schools, business, labor, higher education, and community groups to support the Boston public schools. As noted earlier, the compact was first signed in 1982, then reauthorized in 1989, 1994, and most recently in 2000. As Mayor Menino said at the last signing ceremony, "The only way we are going to meet the goals we share for our students . . . is if we all work together. Everyone here today recognizes that he or she is a stakeholder in education reform because our students are the future of this city."[28] Although the agreement is less visible today, the Boston Private Industry Council continues to play a key role in supporting school- and employment-related initiatives.

This change in public discourse has both critics and proponents. A common criticism is a decline in opportunities for discussion and debate of key policy decisions. As one longtime observer of the schools notes, there is limited "space for discussion" of positions that conflict with those of the mayor, superintendent, and other key actors. A consensual dialogue among education leaders and institutional partners is viewed as less receptive to criticism and challenges from community-based organizations and advocacy groups.[29]

With respect to school committee meetings, a common critique is that few issues are truly debated by the appointed committee and that many decisions are made before any public meeting, resulting in few dissenting votes. One community activist described the committee as a "rubber stamp," while a longtime educator questioned the committee for not "challenging" more of the proposals from the superintendent and mayor.[30]

Increasingly, community activists and others are turning to the Boston City Council as a venue to raise concerns and grievances. The council's committee on education holds public hearings on the school department's annual budget request as well as other issues facing the school system. A recent hearing, for example, focused on the school district's efforts to increase the number of teachers of color, to support participation by students of color in the exam schools and advanced courses, and to increase foreign language offerings in the district high schools. Although the committee and city council have no legal authority in these areas, they have become an important setting for discussion of school issues.

General public critiques of the school system still exist, but they are more episodic in nature. Critical Friends of the Boston Public Schools, for example, was a citizen and community-activist watchdog group formed at the time of Payzant's appointment. The group produced several reports critical of reform efforts, encouraging school leaders to make a "shift from rhetoric to radical action" to produce "significant, long-term and systemic" change.[31] By the late 1990s, Critical Friends had faded as an organization, although some of the key actors continued to observe and comment on the school system. With Payzant's departure imminent, several were joined by others in the community to produce a report entitled *Transforming the Boston Public Schools: A Roadmap for the New Superintendent*. While recognizing some accomplishments over the past eleven years, the report focused on numerous shortfalls in the schools, concluding that the school system "urgently needed transformative change" if all students were to succeed.[32]

Proponents, however, point to the successes and accomplishments of the school system as well as the recognition received by superintendent Payzant, the school committee, and Mayor Menino. The school department has sustained a sharp focus on teaching and learning, and overall test scores have risen during this period. The school committee, although less connected to the electorate, is seen by many as a more efficient and effective forum for discussions of education policy. Even among many in the minority community, there is recognition that the appointed school committee has been relatively successful in focusing on education matters. The committee, for example, approved successive district-wide improvement plans, citywide learning standards, and other reform initiatives.

The key education players in the governance system have received national recognition. Mayor Menino is widely identified among urban mayors as a leader in building and sustaining political support for public education. Superintendent Payzant received much recognition, including the 2004 Richard B. Green Award in Urban Excellence from the Council of Great City Schools and a 2005 Public Official of the Year award from *Governing* magazine. The Green Award for urban school leadership was also given to school committee chairwoman Elizabeth Reilinger in 2007. In 2004 the Boston School Committee received the first Award for Urban School Board Excellence from the National School Boards Association and the Council of Urban Boards of Education. Finally, in 2006 the Boston public schools won the prestigious Broad Prize for Urban Education. A finalist in each of the previous four years, the city's school system has been consistently recognized by a panel of educators and civic officials as a leader among urban school districts in the effort to improve student achievement.

A Focus on Teaching and Learning

A common criticism of school systems, particularly urban school systems, is the frequent turnover of leaders and change in reform policies, resulting in little, if any, improvement in the system. Rick Hess refers to "policy churn" and the constant "spinning of wheels" as the norm in urban education.[33] Boston is not immune to this tendency, but in general, with the support of its governance structure, it has sustained a focus on reform that is unusual among urban school systems. As two observers of the Boston experience note, "Without question, the legacy of Tom Payzant's superintendency in Boston will be the laser-like focus on improved instruction."[34]

Superintendent Payzant launched a number of major reforms within the school system. In 1996 the superintendent proposed, and the school committee adopted, a five-year reform plan for the schools called Focus on Children. Whole-school change is the guiding educational philosophy of this plan. With an emphasis on instructional improvement, the plan highlights six areas essential for whole-school improvement: literacy and mathematics instruction, applying student work and data, professional development, replicating best practices, aligning resources with an instructional focus, and community engagement. Support for this reform effort came from the business community and a grant from the Annenberg Foundation. In 2001 the school committee adopted Focus on Children II as the next five-year plan to continue whole-school improvement within the system. Supporting two successive and complementary five-year plans as a framework for reform is quite unusual in urban school systems.

A number of other reform initiatives have been put in place, some of which have been prompted by the Massachusetts Education Reform Act of 1993. The school department, for example, adopted citywide learning standards that are aligned with state standards. With these standards and the extension of whole-school change, there is now a major focus on improving literacy and mathematical skills. A rigorous promotion policy was adopted, and at the high school level, a number of schools are being restructured into smaller learning communities to support closer teacher-student interaction and better learning opportunities. The act also greatly strengthened the superintendent's control over personnel appointments, especially principals, who for the first time were removed from collective bargaining.

School reforms have been instituted in a number of other areas as well. Since 1998, for example, all five-year-olds are guaranteed full-day public kindergarten. The school committee negotiated a plan with the teachers union to reduce class size, and a technology initiative dramatically increased the number of computers in the classroom. To expand school options, the school committee and Boston Teachers Union agreed to the establishment of pilot schools within the district, which are allowed to operate with greater flexibility from school department regulations and union work rules. To increase accountability, the school department put in place an extensive review system that includes an in-depth analysis with site visits at all schools. In addition, beyond reforms within school buildings, the superintendent now sits as a member of the mayor's cabinet and works with other city departments to provide services that benefit school-age children.

Certainly, implementation of these many reform strategies has been challenging. Altering instructional practices in the classroom, for example, has met with mixed success. It has been difficult to build a sustained effort, supported by school-level leadership, to implement literacy and math instructional reforms across the district.[35] Upon reflection, Payzant has recognized that he "should have accelerated the literacy work [and] narrowed the program choices" as a way to push for more effective and broader instructional improvement.[36]

The result of all this work has been important improvements in student academic achievement, although the record is mixed. On the positive side, the school department can point to significant gains in student test scores. As noted in table 5-1, based upon the state-mandated Massachusetts Comprehensive Assessment System tests, the city's public schools have demonstrated across grades an increase in the percentage of students achieving proficiency and advanced scores, while the percentage of students scoring in the warning or failing category has decreased. On the fourth-grade math test, for example, between 2000 and 2007 the percentage of students scoring in the top two categories, advanced and proficient, rose from 14 percent to 27 percent, while the percentage of students scoring in the warning or failing category decreased from 46 percent to 27 percent. Table 5-1 shows a similar relationship in grades 8 and 10 for both math and English language arts. Comparable improvements are important, although it should be noted that these test scores statewide also have improved.

The National Assessment of Educational Progress offers another perspective on academic achievement, allowing comparison of Boston with other school systems. In general, Boston fares well among city school systems,

Table 5-1. *Massachusetts Comprehensive Assessment System Test Results in the Boston Public Schools, by Achievement Level, 2000 and 2007*[a]
Percent

Achievement level	Grade 4		Grade 8		Grade 10	
	2000	*2007*	*2000*	*2007*	*2000*	*2007*
Math						
Advanced or proficient	14	27	15	27	22	55
Needs improvement	40	46	19	31	12	27
Warning-failing	46	27	66	42	66	18
English language arts						
Advanced or proficient	6	31	36	55	22	50
Needs improvement	60	43	37	31	22	37
Warning-failing	34	26	27	14	56	13

Source: Massachusetts Department of Elementary and Secondary Education, Massachusetts Comprehensive Assessment System test results (www.doe.mass.edu/mcas/results.html).

a. The Massachusetts Comprehensive Assessment System includes a series of criterion-referenced tests based on the learning standards adopted by the state. Scoring for the test includes four levels of performance: advanced, proficient, needs improvement, and warning-failing.

although it lags behind national averages. On the 2007 tests for cities in the Trial Urban District Assessment, which is made up of ten cities and the District of Columbia, Boston tied for third place in the percentage of eighth- and fourth-grade students scoring at or above the basic level on the math test. On the reading test at the fourth- and eighth-grade levels, Boston ranked fifth among the eleven jurisdictions in the percentage of students scoring at or above the basic level.[37]

These test scores show progress, but significant challenges remain. For example, to meet the federal standard of proficiency for all students by 2013–14, many more students will need to score in the top categories (advanced or proficient). Among tenth-grade students, 45 percent scored below proficiency in math, and 50 percent on the English language arts test. The achievement gap also is a major concern. On the math portion of the 2007 state assessment test, for example, 89 percent of Asian and 74 percent of white students in grade 10 scored proficient or higher, while only 45 percent of African American and 48 percent of Hispanic students scored at that level. This general pattern exists at other grade levels as well. Finally, the high school dropout rate is a major concern. A recent report notes that approximately 40 percent of high school students in the Boston public schools do not graduate within four years.[38]

Summing Up: A New Dynamic in School Politics

Changes in governance are rarely neutral. Introducing mayoral appointment of the Boston School Committee reshaped political and policy processes, shifting advantages and disadvantages among different individuals and groups. Boston's move to a new governance structure for public education has altered the city's political and policy world. The city is now fifteen years into this experiment. The public appears to accept the system, although an occasional note of dissent persists. This governance system is praised for the continuity in leadership, attention, and resources it has brought to public education, but it also has raised concerns over the changing nature of school politics, policy debate, and citizen participation.

Placing the mayor at the center of school politics has raised the visibility of public education, and it has linked city hall and the school department in a cooperative manner not seen under the elected committee structure. Mayor Menino's frequent references to education in his State of the City speeches are indicative of this trend. The substantial financial resources provided to the schools also highlight significant city support. Along with this support and visibility has come a consensual style of decisionmaking in which the mayor plays an important governance role. As the mayor stated in a speech before the Education Writers Association, "In a nutshell, when it comes to school change, the mayor must be like the hub in a wheel—you have got to be in the center to keep things rolling."[39]

Boston has benefited from stable leadership that is rare among big-city school systems. Menino and Payzant were partners in education for eleven years, and the Boston Teachers Union and Boston School Committee have had stable leadership. It is possible that this continuity and stability in leadership could be achieved under an elected committee structure, but it is less likely, given the dynamics of the electoral process and Boston's history, especially during the desegregation years, when Boston had six superintendents in ten years. This period of stable leadership has been described by Richard Wallace, a highly acclaimed superintendent in Pittsburgh in the 1980s, as the necessary period to bring about significant change in an urban school system.[40] Receipt of the Broad award and other recognition is indicative of the accomplishments in Boston, although major challenges remain.

Mayoral Control of Urban Schools: Lessons to Be Learned

The Boston experience offers some interesting lessons for cities involved in school governance reform. Such lessons come with a word of caution: changes in policy and politics are heavily influenced by the particular circumstances of a specific city. Every city has a political history and a set of institutional arrangements that will shape its own experiences. Such uniqueness does not negate comparative study, but it does encourage us to view the experiences of other cities as instructive rather than determinative.

Mayoral Control as Enabling Reform

Perhaps the most important lesson from Boston is the role mayoral involvement has played in enabling school reform. The change in governance that put Mayor Menino on center stage and Thomas Payzant in the role of superintendent has created a platform for coherent, consistent, and focused reform efforts for more than a decade. This is a major accomplishment in any policy system and particularly in an urban educational arena. Given the history and experience in Boston before 1991, it is quite unlikely that such a platform for focused reform efforts would have developed without the change in governance that brought the mayor into the education process.

It is important to recognize, however, that enabling school reform through changes in governance does not guarantee that such reforms will actually take place or that student learning will improve. Indeed, the causal connection between governance and improved academic achievement is complicated and indirect. Governance is important in determining the allocation of resources and assignment of responsibilities, but it is one or more steps removed from the immediate and critical ingredients for student learning, such as effective instruction in the classroom, targeted professional development, and analyses of student assessment data. As Hess notes in a recent study of mayoral leadership, "Governance reform is not a strategy to directly improve schooling; instead, it seeks to provide effective leadership for improvement efforts."[41]

Thus governance changes are not a silver bullet. They provide an important context for reform and setting for leadership, but raising academic achievement requires hard work at every level within a school district to improve teaching and learning. Improved student performance also requires partnerships with parents and community organizations that can address the many economic and social challenges that confront students in U.S. cities. Boston's success in improving academic achievement, though significant challenges remain, is a testament to the difficult task any urban school district faces in formulating and implementing successful school reform strategies.

Leadership and a Focus on Teaching and Learning

The enabling effect of governance changes in Boston fostered a period of unprecedented continuity in leadership of the school system. Menino and Payzant worked as partners for eleven years, and they were joined by stable leadership on the school committee and in the teachers union. This alignment of leaders is indeed powerful. As Payzant argues, "A critical element of the Boston story that cannot be overstated is the sustained, stable leadership provided by the mayor and the appointed Boston School Committee. . . . Without this governance structure, I believe that the Boston schools could not have made the progress that they have made over the past decade."[42]

In Boston, this alignment and continuity in leadership allowed the district to apply a greater focus on reform efforts and to attract the financial resources needed to support those efforts. Boston's adoption of two successive five-year plans that focused on teaching and learning in the classroom provided important continuity in school reform strategies. Without doubt, implementation sometimes lagged, and the generally incremental pace of reform came under criticism; but the Boston schools benefited from a reform approach that was consistent and cumulative. Furthermore, to support reform efforts the school department received a higher level of financial support from the mayor and city government than had been true in the past. With school accountability clearly pointed toward the mayor's office and city hall, Mayor Menino was more supportive of school budget requests and took a proactive role in helping to shape broad school policy.

Another substantial benefit of this aligned governance structure is the inclusion of the superintendent on the mayor's cabinet. Under the old structure, there was little incentive for other department heads to work collaboratively with the school department, and when tensions arose over responsibility for school safety, for example, there was no single point of resolution. Having the police chief and the school superintendent at the same table and part of the same mayoral leadership team greatly increases the likelihood that such turf disputes will be resolved quickly. More affirmatively, having the superintendent at the cabinet table makes it much easier for the city administration to create a coordinated strategy linking the schools to other critical services for children or develop a unified approach to workforce development by bringing together secondary school and community college leaders, job training centers, and employer associations.

Alignment and continuity in leadership are critical, but a word of caution is in order. A tightly aligned governance structure can sometimes sacrifice policy debate and critique for an interest in moving forward in a chosen direction. Particularly with an elected mayor at the center of this governance system, criticisms can become politically charged instead of seen as critiques of education policies. Information is often controlled in this setting. It is not a system of checks and balances in which alternatives receive systematic attention. As the authors of one study of Boston note, "Maybe there is too much stability, and perhaps the stars are *too* aligned," a situation that thereby reduces the pressure for reassessment and alternative reform strategies.[43] As the experience in Boston attests, striking a balance between moving forward with focused reform efforts and at the same time providing opportunities for debate and critique can be challenging.

The Dynamics of Leadership

A related lesson from the Boston experience is the critical importance of the relationship between the two key leaders in this system: the mayor and the superintendent. If a mayor is going to exercise control over a school system, he or she must come to an agreement with education leaders, particularly the superintendent, about how they will work together. Mayors, by their very nature, are political actors, with expectations and needs that revolve around elections and the broad range of issues that constitute city politics. Superintendents are certainly attuned to the political world, but they also have the responsibility to administer a school system. Creating a marriage between these two around the assignment and responsibility for the politics, policy, and practice of education is no small task.

This marriage for leadership depends as much on compatible personalities as on formal governance arrangements. With Mayor Menino and the city's schools superintendent Payzant, Boston has been quite successful in forging this partnership. The chemistry between these two very different individuals has worked well for the system. As a politician and elected figure, Mayor Menino expects to be on center stage in public events, including those involving education. He plays a general role in education policymaking, particularly when it affects other areas of the city, such as after-school programs, but he defers to the superintendent and other education experts to shape overall policy for student learning. He uses the bully pulpit of the mayor's office to put a spotlight on education.

Superintendent Payzant, for his part, was quite comfortable with the mayor's taking the lead in political settings. He saw his primary role as formulating and implementing a successful education policy. A common scenario for a public event had Mayor Menino proclaiming the importance of public education to the future of the city, then introducing Payzant as the person who would make that a reality. Payzant has noted in an interview that this partnership came at a time in his career, after many years as a superintendent, in which he had already achieved recognition for his accomplishments, and ambitions around future job possibilities were not a factor. As

Paul Reville notes in a recent analysis of the Boston schools, "Most observers agree that the Payzant-Menino partnership was vital to the success of the school system."[44]

This compatibility of personalities and interests—over eleven years—is quite impressive in a political setting. While achievable elsewhere, it is highly dependent upon the individuals involved. Describing the current structure, one longtime observer of school politics in Boston suggests that "it all depends on who the mayor is." Mayor Menino has been a strong supporter of public education, but a future mayor may be less inclined. There is also the danger that a mayor could turn the schools into a political commodity for patronage and other political purposes.[45] Mayor Menino has not pursued this path, although it could happen under a different mayor. A superintendent must find a fit in this partnership. Deference to an elected mayor is important, as is the ability to shape and implement an education agenda to improve student learning.

The Changing Nature of School Politics

A fourth lesson from the Boston experience revolves around the changing dynamic of school politics. Under an elected committee structure, school politics in Boston was noted for its divisiveness. Disagreements along racial lines were common, and disputes between city hall and the school committee were frequent. School committee members often saw their role as constituent oriented, and micromanagement within the system was standard practice.

Mayoral appointment of the school committee, along with governance changes required under the Massachusetts Education Reform Act of 1993, significantly changed this dynamic. Education went from being a broadly contested political arena to one in which debate and critique are more structured around key players in the system. This is not to say that politics is gone but rather that the nature of the political dynamic has changed.

School politics under mayoral control is focused around institutional partners that support the school system. This focus is not surprising given the prominence of strong leadership exercised by the mayor and superintendent. The shift of authority and power from the school committee to the mayor and superintendent, and the separation of the school committee from a direct connection with the electorate, has served to highlight the role of institutional partners working with the leadership team and play down the role of community and parent groups that worked through the school committee. As a result of these changes, the Boston Plan for Excellence and other school partners have played a prominent role in school reform.

This shift in the nature of school politics has both proponents and critics. To some, this alignment among key institutional actors has brought more resources to the district, particularly through outside grants, and it has played an important role in maintaining the stability and coherency of school reform efforts. To others, however, the school district has lost some of its connection to the community and has become more distant from the interests and concerns of parents and community-based organizations. Lacking the electoral connection to the school committee, some parents and voters in the city have turned to the Boston City Council and its education committee as a venue for discussion and debate of school issues.

The challenge for Boston, New York, and other cities with mayoral control in urban education is to strike a balance that ensures multiple opportunities and venues for participation in school issues while moving the district forward with coherent and focused reform strategies. Parent and community participation are important, as is the involvement and support of institutional partners. It is the responsibility of mayors and other school and community leaders to forge a system that will serve this broad purpose.

In our review of lessons from Boston, it is important not to lose sight of the big picture. The Boston experience with mayoral control is instructive, but the real issue is building and sustaining effective leadership. This is the fundamental challenge of governance. In Boston, given its history and institutions, the case is quite persuasive that mayoral control has had a major positive impact on the Boston public schools. This governance structure has fostered effective leadership that has put Boston on a path to reform. It has created opportunities for innovation and change in a relatively stable political environment. It is not perfect, but the building blocks are present to carry the district forward. The new superintendent, Carol Johnson, began her tenure in September 2007 by reviewing the accomplishments of the past decade as the first step in extending Boston's reform efforts.

As a governance strategy, mayoral control reverses the Progressive Era reforms put in place early in the last century. One important goal of those reforms was to separate and insulate schools from the political machines and electoral nature of city politics. With mayoral control, the pendulum has swung back. In Boston and other cities that have followed this path, schools are back in the arena of city politics. There are trade-offs with such a strategy, but in an era of generally tight fiscal constraints, as exist in most large cities, winning a share of resources requires competing in the political process. In this regard, casting one's lot with the mayor may be the most viable governance strategy for improving urban education.

Notes

The interviews cited in this chapter were conducted with a promise of confidentiality; for that reason, names have been withheld.

1. Education Commission of the States, *Governing America's Schools: Changing the Rules* (Denver, November 1999), p. xiii.

2. Joseph Murphy, "Governing America's Schools: The Shifting Playing Field," paper prepared for the annual meetings of the American Educational Research Association, Montreal, April 1999, p. 2.

3. Donald R. McAdams, *What School Boards Can Do: Reform Governance for Urban Schools* (Teachers College Press, 2006), p. 9.

4. See Jacqueline P. Danzberger, Michael W. Kirst, and Michael Usdan, *Governing Public Schools: New Times, New Requirements* (Washington: Institute for Educational Leadership, 1992), and William G. Howell, ed., *Besieged: School Boards and the Future of Education Politics* (Brookings, 2005).

5. Larry Cuban and Michael Usdan, eds., *Powerful Reforms with Shallow Roots: Improving America's Urban Schools* (Teachers College Press, 2003); Jeffrey R. Henig and Wilbur C. Rich, eds., *Mayors in the Middle: Politics, Race, and the Mayoral Control of Urban Schools* (Princeton University Press, 2004); Stefanie Chambers, *Mayors and Schools: Minority Voices and Democratic Tensions in Urban Education* (Temple University Press, 2006); Kenneth K. Wong and others, *The Education Mayor: Improving America's Schools* (Georgetown University Press, 2007); Frederick M. Hess, "Looking for Leadership: Assessing the Case for Mayoral Control of Urban School Systems," *Policy Study* 7 (St. Louis: Show-Me Institute, February 6, 2007) (http://showmeinstitute. org/publication/id.44/pub_detail.asp).

6. David Seeley and Robert Schwartz, "Debureaucratizing Public Education: The Experience of New York and Boston," in *Communities and Their Schools,* edited by Don Davies (McGraw-Hill, 1981), pp. 60–82.

7. John Portz, Lana Stein, and Robin Jones, *City Schools and City Politics: Institutions and Leadership in Pittsburgh, Boston, and St. Louis* (University Press of Kansas, 1999).

8. Mayor's Advisory Committee, "The Rebirth of America's Oldest Public School System: Redefining Responsibility" (Office of the Mayor, Boston, 1989).

9. John Portz, "Problem Definitions and Policy Agendas: Shaping the Education Agenda in Boston," *Policy Studies Journal* 24 (Autumn 1996): 371–86.

10. Boston Municipal Research Bureau, "Special Report: Bureau Supports Appointed School Committee," Research Report 89-4, prepared for members and for general distribution (Boston, July 26, 1989).

11. *Boston Globe,* "Shortchanging the School Children," editorial, August 30, 1992, p. 26.

12. Mayor's Advisory Committee, "The Rebirth of America's Oldest Public School System," p. 1.

13. Ibid., p. 27.

14. Michael Rezendes, "Council Votes to Back Appointed School Panel, Abolish Current Board," *Boston Globe,* April 11, 1991, p. 40.

15. Elementary school principal, in-person interview with author, September 23, 1993.

16. Thomas W. Payzant, with Christopher M. Horan, "The Boston Story: Successes and Challenges in Systemic Education Reform," in *A Decade of Urban School Reform: Persistence and Progress in the Boston Public Schools,* edited by S. Paul Reville (Harvard Education Press, 2007), pp. 243–70, quotation at p. 247.

17. Quoted in Richard Chacon, "Menino: School Panel to Be More 'Accessible,'" *Boston Globe,* November 7, 1996, p. B13.

18. John Portz, "Boston: Agenda Setting and School Reform in a Mayor-Centric System," in *Mayors in the Middle,* edited by Henig and Rich, pp. 96–119.

19. Mayor Kevin Flynn, "State of the City, January 9, 1991," *City Record* 83, City of Boston (January 21, 1991), p. 29.

20. Mayor Thomas M. Menino, "State of the City Address," *City Record* 88, City of Boston (January 29, 1996), pp. 70–71.

21. Mayoral staff, interview with author.

22. These figures are calculated from data on City of Boston expenditures received from the Boston Municipal Research Bureau and exclude spending on health and hospitals and the Boston Public Health Commission.

23. *Boston Globe,* "Massachusetts Business Roundtable: Six Views from the Top," editorial, December 1, 1996, p. F1.

24. Karen Avenso and Patricia Wen, "Elected, Appointed Panels Show Differences in Style," *Boston Globe,* October 28, 1996, p. A1.

25. Ibid.

26. Tracy Jan, "Where NAY Is Rarely Heard: Is the Boston School Committee Working for You?" *Boston Globe,* October 9, 2005, p. B1.

27. Barbara Neufeld and Ellen Guiney, "Transforming Events: A Local Education Fund's Efforts to Promote Large-Scale Urban School Reform," in *Research Perspectives on School Reform: Lessons from the Annenberg Challenge* (Providence, R.I.: Annenberg Institute, 2003), pp. 51–68 (www.annenberginstitute.org/Challenge/pubs/research report/chapterthree.pdf).

28. Boston Public Schools, "City's Business, Higher Ed, Non-Profit Leaders Back Boston Schools on MCAS, Ed Reform," April 14, 2000 (www.bostonpublicschools. org/node/1332).

29. See Steven Taylor, "Appointing or Electing the Boston School Committee: The Preferences of the African American Community," *Urban Education* 36 (January 2001): 4–26.

30. Quoted in Anand Vaishnav, "Are They Acting as Advocates or Appointed Rubber Stamps?" *Boston Globe,* January 28, 2001, p. F1.

31. Critical Friends of the Boston Public Schools, *Status Report on Boston's Public Schools after Two Years of Reform* (Boston, 1997), p. 3.

32. Citizen Commission on Academic Success for Boston Children, *Transforming the Boston Public Schools: A Roadmap for the New Superintendent* (Boston, 2006), p. 7.

33. Frederick M. Hess, *Spinning Wheels: The Politics of Urban School Reform* (Brookings, 1999), p. 5.

34. Karen Mapp and Jennifer Suesse, "Leadership Development at the Boston Public Schools: 1995–2006," in *A Decade of Urban School Reform,* edited by Reville, pp. 79–110, quotation on p. 85.

35. Barbara Neufeld, "Instructional Improvement in the Boston Public Schools: The Limits of Focus and Stability," in *A Decade of Urban School Reform,* edited by Reville, pp. 133–52.

36. Payzant and Horan, "The Boston Story," p. 251.

37. U.S. Department of Education, National Center for Education Statistics, *The Nation's Report Card: 2007 Trial Urban District Assessment in Mathematics* (www.nces. ed.gov/pubsearch/pubsinfo.asp?pubid=2008452); U.S. Department of Education, National Center for Education Statistics, *The Nation's Report Card: 2007 Trial Urban District Assessment in Reading* (www.nces.ed.gov/pubsearch/pubsinfo.asp?pubid= 2008455).

38. Parthenon Group, "Strategic Planning to Serve Off-Track Youth: Data Review and Strategic Implications" (Boston, September 2007) (http://bostonpublicschools. org/files/Parthenon%20Report.pdf).

39. Thomas Menino, "Mayors' Roles in School Change," remarks to Education Writers Association, April 16, 1999.

40. Richard Wallace, *From Vision to Practice: The Art of Educational Leadership* (Thousand Oaks, Calif.: Corwin Press, 1996).

41. Hess, "Looking for Leadership," p. 17.

42. Payzant and Horan, "The Boston Story," pp. 246–47.

43. Cuban and Usdan, *Powerful Reforms,* p. 49.

44. Paul Reville, "Setting the Stage," in *A Decade of Urban School Reform,* edited by Reville, pp. 1–14, quotation on p. 6.

45. Richard Hunter, "The Mayor versus the School Superintendent: Political Incursions into Metropolitan School Politics," *Education and Urban Society* 29 (February 1997): 217–32.

DOROTHY SHIPPS

6

Updating Tradition: The Institutional Underpinnings of Modern Mayoral Control in Chicago's Public Schools

The promises of mayoral control are significant and well known. Managerial logic suggests, and Chicago's recent experience corroborates, that mayors may be especially adroit at stabilizing system leadership, focusing civic elites on education, mobilizing resources, and straightening the lines of organizational accountability.[1] Some argue that these organizational benefits lead to improved student performance.[2]

Chicago's experience with mayoral control also points to negative consequences that require policy attention. Mayors who have staked their reputations on progress in the schools have no incentive to reveal bad news and often spin negative data to appear neutral. Families, especially low-income families without the social resources to command special accommodation, feel left out of key decisions when school boards cease to be forums for community debate. Mayors may bring additional resources, but they also add new programs, which can balloon budgets. The ethos of city hall affects the schools: systemic corruption, chronic budget problems, or a willingness to accept performance gaps may all be reasons to question the wisdom of mayoral empowerment.

To address these crosscutting observations, I draw upon seventeen years of research. I have written about the precursors of Chicago's mayoral control, the crucial role of corporate actors in initiating the changes, the racial implications of these changes, consequences for school media coverage, and the city as a case of urban regime change.[3] This chapter differs from what I have written before. The passage of time and the longevity of Chicago's modern mayoral control experiment have raised an important policy question as yet unaddressed: How has the system's governing capacity been improved? Put another way, How has mayoral control at the turn of the twentieth century avoided the problems that led to its denunciation at the turn of the nineteenth?

The Chicago Model

Chicago has been promoted for more than a decade as a national model of mayoral control. When he was president of the U.S. Conference of Mayors in 1997, Richard M. Daley told the National Press Club, "If the Chicago Public Schools can be managed, any school system can. . . . The lesson for all school systems is that no problem is unmanageable."[4] Daley then linked his control of the schools to Chicago's ability to attract and retain middle-class families and maintain corporate employers, goals many urban mayors find both practical and pressing.[5] President Clinton found Daley's arguments compelling and commended his efforts as a "model for the nation," singling him out in both the 1998 and 1999 State of the Union addresses.[6]

Daley was also quick to use his new authority. In his first year as education mayor he began a series of accountability experiments that included basing student promotion on test scores and curtailing the autonomy of schools whose aggregate test scores fell below a benchmark. Similar ideas were subsequently adopted by many districts in response to the No Child Left Behind Act. Chicago's experience has been widely studied, arguably amassing more evidence than any other mayoral control city.[7] Moreover, Chicago's results are uncompromised by the complicating factors of mayoral turnover, since the long-serving mayor Daley is not subject to term limits and has no prospect of being defeated by a rival.

A Chicago Political Tradition, Updated

Chicago is one of a handful of U.S. cities that has never had an elected central school board. Every Chicago mayor since the middle of the nineteenth century has had the statutory authority to appoint the school board, subject to the city council's pro forma approval.[8] Until 1979, mayors were also expected to influence school system budgets because key school accounts were housed in city hall. These powers have led to a range of high-profile abuses, for which mayors have been repeatedly censured. In one infamous case, Mayor William Hale Thompson (1915–23, 1927–31) admitted to following "the dictation of a political boss" in appointing new board members and dismissing the seated ones. Challenged by a well-respected superintendent, Thompson responded by stripping him of his powers. The next two and a half years of chaos saw two warring school boards and multiple court challenges.[9]

Such political opportunism is not limited to the distant past. For example, when struggling to maintain her electoral credibility with the white ethnic coalition that had kept her predecessor in office for decades, Mayor Jane Byrne (1979–83) summarily dismissed two African American businessmen she had appointed just three months earlier. She replaced them with two white women, one of whom was known for participation in anti-integration demonstrations. This time the outrage was largely confined to the African American community, which by then represented 38 percent of the central office staff, 30 percent of principals, 43 percent of teachers, and 60 percent of students.[10]

Outraged Chicagoans did occasionally convince a mayor, Richard J. Daley (1954–76) among them, to consider the advice of a citizen nominating commission, but its advice was most often ignored. Before he was given complete control of the schools in 1995, Richard "Rich" M. Daley (1989–) became the first mayor to be legally constrained by such a commission. His response was to indignantly and routinely turn back whole slates, leaving half the seats vacant during the few years that the commission functioned.[11]

Chicago's city hall has long had a troubled relationship with the schools budget. The most notorious example came just as the Great Depression hit the city; a group of the city's corporate leaders and bankers approached the profligate Mayor Thompson with demands for school cutbacks. Neither they nor most small-property owners were able to pay their taxes. When Thompson refused, the businessmen took matters into their own hands and eventually got their way with his successors. Notwithstanding protests by dozens of community organizations and the teachers unions, Democratic machine mayors Anton Cermak (1931–33) and Edward J. Kelly (1933–49) both supported the resulting Committee on Public Expenditures, whose corporate and banking members cut educational services, closed programs, and fired teachers in order to balance the school budget, although city hall's school patronage hires were not touched.[12] The ensuing havoc temporarily lost Chicago's high schools their accreditation.[13] Disbanded in 1939, the committee left an abiding legacy: today Chicago has almost no junior high schools because the businessmen considered them expendable.

The elder Daley took the opposite approach to the schools budget. After granting the Chicago Teachers Union collective-bargaining rights, he acquired the habit of personally settling nearly biennial strikes with promises of money the system did not have. He prevailed upon state legislators to alter state aid formulas and loosen legal constraints on school borrowing. But he also used questionable accounting maneuvers to keep the district's bond ratings artificially high. Most egregious was the pro rata line in the district's budget in which a deficit was "balanced" by a transmittal letter from the board to itself saying how much it expected to fall short. Three years after the mayor's death, in 1976, these practices were publicly revealed by a legislative investigation triggered when Chicago's bankers slashed the district's bond ratings to below investment grade.[14]

Daley's shady bookkeeping cost the school system its fiscal independence for the next fifteen years. In exchange for buying the system's near-worthless bonds, Chicago's bankers, backed by the city's corporate leaders, insisted upon a School Finance Authority, which they would control. The authority cut personnel and services, abrogated union contracts, and kept the schools closed when the budget was unbalanced.[15]

Another product of outsized mayoral influence has been patronage employment. In the 1940s the school system was condemned by the National Education Association for rampant corruption, patronage, and a general lack of professional accountability in the hiring of teachers, principals, and faculty for the Chicago Teachers College.[16] School custodial positions, as well as half of the jobs emanating from city hall, remained patronage hires through the 1970s, until the Shakman decrees of 1979 and 1983 formally outlawed the practice in a posthumous rebuke to the elder Daley.[17] Even so, Harold Washington's mayoralty was punctuated by repeated claims that African American Chicagoans were simply using the district's central office to bootstrap into the middle class, a form of affirmative action patronage.[18]

Under federal investigation since 2004, Rich Daley's city hall has had an estimated five thousand patronage employees, several hundred of whom owed their jobs to falsified civil service test scores and sham interviews. Chicagoans are also currently paying for legal judgments to qualified, but excluded, contractors who refused to pay bribes to the city.[19] Although the schools have generally avoided corruption scandals, Daley has been unwilling to reveal the rationale behind capital spending in the school district, which has produced manifestly unequal benefits across schools, prompting one respected journalist to comment that "good old City Hall patronage is alive and well at Chicago Public Schools."[20]

Thus the 1995 law, far from being an unprecedented empowerment of Chicago's mayor, is actually an extension of the powers, both formal and informal, that all Chicago mayors have had, for better and worse. So why was the law written, and what actually changed in the summer of 1995?

The short answer is that Chicago's business community had tired of overseeing the schools through the School Finance Authority. They especially disliked the public scrutiny their decisions attracted. African Americans protested their cutbacks as racially motivated. A rapidly growing Latino community (20 percent of the population by 1990, 26 percent by 2000) thought the authority ignored their priorities, too. Nor could it balance the school budget. After a decade of relative peace, deficits and strike threats resurfaced, and the board's bond ratings were, once again, downgraded. Corporate leaders reasoned that because the mayor and the governor jointly selected the members of the School Finance Authority, the "bottom line . . . should be accountability with the mayor and the governor . . . [since] that's where the ultimate control is."[21] Using this logic, they thought it reasonable to hold a trusted politician publicly accountable and simultaneously back away from the limelight themselves.

A Gingrich-inspired Republican legislative takeover gave them the opportunity. At the request of Illinois senator James "Pate" Phillips and the newly empowered Republican House Speaker, Lee Daniels, the business executives crafted a school law giving Rich Daley greater authority over the schools than any of his predecessors had enjoyed. Corporate leaders believed Daley to be a mayor they could trust. They had backed his losing candidacy in 1983, ensured his election in 1989, and knew they had guaranteed access to him. "Our goals" said one to the legislature, "are to make him as accountable as possible."[22] The executives subsequently promoted mayoral control as a way Chicago's voters could hold a politician accountable for the system's performance. After 1996, however, all citywide electoral contests were made "nonpartisan," under a law passed at Daley's request. This eliminated primaries and access to the party apparatus that could finance and promote rivals. Consequently, the possibility of his losing an election became exceedingly remote.

Mayoral control also returned Chicago schools to the historical status quo following a much more radical governing experiment. A short-lived reform law, passed in December 1988, had created the nation's most decentralized school system. From the corporate leaders' perspective, reaffirming mayoral control of the schools was made all the more urgent by decentralization's shortcomings, which they summarized as misplaced micromanagement and insufficient accountability.[23]

The 1988 law mandated the creation of a local school council at each school: elected bodies made up of six parents, two community representatives (adults who lived in the school's catchment zone but had no children attending the school), and two teacher representatives.[24] Akin to an elected board of education, the local school council's main responsibility was to hire and fire the school's principal. Principals' tenure was eliminated, turning the position into a four-year renewable performance contract subject to the council's approval. Each local school council was also authorized to establish a reform strategy for the school and to approve its discretionary budget, expanded by the redirection of state and federal antipoverty funds.

The 1988 law also created two of three governing bodies that would be eliminated in 1995. Eleven district boards were established in 1988 as support organizations for local school councils, which selected their members. District board members, in turn, hired district superintendents. Council representatives also picked a school board nominating commission, which identified slates of candidates from among whom Rich Daley was formally obliged to select his central school board appointments. The district boards and the nominating commission were both eliminated in 1995, as was fiscal oversight by the School Finance Authority. To community activists who championed decentralization, the six years from 1989 to 1994 constituted a brief interregnum between two different versions of mayoral control.

What Changed and What Remained the Same?

The 1995 law strengthened the mayor's authority in a number of subtle ways. It mandated a corporate management structure, with enhanced fiscal and managerial flexibility. The law also limited union influence over school policy and sharply diminished the importance of the board of education by reducing its size and transferring to the mayor and his chief executive officer (CEO) a broad range of new, largely unspecified powers to sanction schools, students, teachers, and principals.

Corporate Management Structure

The legislation was drafted by a committee of corporate business executives who specified that the system be managed by a chief financial officer, a chief operating officer, a chief purchasing officer, and a chief education officer, all answerable to a chief executive officer not required to have any education credentials. Nevertheless, the CEO retained all the powers previously delegated to the general superintendent, including authority to establish the curriculum. Late in the negotiating process, Rich Daley asked for and received the unprecedented authority to handpick the chief executive of the system.

Neither of the two men Daley has selected as schools CEO since 1995 have been educators. Paul Vallas (1995–2001) had been the mayor's budget director for one year, a promotion from his job as city revenue collector, before becoming schools CEO. His chief credentials at the time were his budgetary abilities—Daley demanded a balanced budget within a few weeks of Vallas's appointment—and his loyalty to the mayor, who made no secret of not trusting educators. An aide explained that Daley thought that it "isn't realistic" to ask an educator to "run a $3 billion operation."[25]

Vallas was replaced six years into his tenure when test scores began to plateau, some of the many new programs began to unravel, and relationships with the teachers union grew strained. Arne Duncan (2001–), thirty-six when first appointed CEO, had briefly been Vallas's chief of staff after heading a small foundation and playing professional basketball in the European League. His tenure has been marked by an open-door policy toward grassroots reformers, whom Vallas had derided. His stated goal is to improve schools through instructional support, choice, and specialization, but he has a lower profile than Vallas, publicly deferring to the mayor.[26]

Fiscal Flexibility

Although Rich Daley had also asked the legislature for more school funds in 1995, he did not receive them. Instead, he was given unprecedented fiscal and managerial flexibility. The 1995 law lifted the requirement of a balanced budget, collapsed sixteen separate tax levies into one fungible source of support, and replaced twenty-five state categorical programs (for example, bilingual education, driver's education) with two block grants to the district. The consolidation initially "freed up close to $130 million," according to Vallas.[27] The law also removed all restrictions on outsourcing and contracting. Daley had long promoted "privatization," in his words, to "recast government as more of an overseer than a producer" and thereby reduce public cynicism.[28] The school system has taken full advantage of its new fiscal flexibility, although Vallas wondered "if we've saved money on privatization," since the budget grew by $1.5 billion over his tenure. Nevertheless, bankers showed their approval by repeatedly raising the district's bond ratings.[29]

This combination of new accounting rules and privatization initially calmed immediate budgetary fears but could not be sustained. Daley has frequently used anticipated revenue from the city's tax increment financing to underwrite borrowing for school construction. He also raised property taxes five times in Vallas's six-year tenure.[30] His close relationship with the Clinton White House facilitated federal grants, while his corporate partners helped pry additional dollars from the legislature. When the booming 1990s gave way to the belt-tightening twenty-first century, the specter of deficits began to reappear, and programs were cut back, largely because huge requests to Illinois for more funding were only partially met. Since 2003, Illinois budget shortfalls and partisan arguments about how to pay for education have derailed efforts to reform the state's school financing, requiring the mayor to beg for one-shot fiscal boosts each year and cut back capital spending and even some educational programs. In 2007 the mayor finally raised property taxes to the legal limit.[31]

A Hamstrung Teachers Union

The third major change in the school law was a set of restrictions on the Chicago Teachers Union's ability to achieve nonpecuniary gains through collective bargaining. Thirteen previously bargained school and workplace conditions (for example, class size, teacher assignments) were stricken from the school code. Teacher strikes were prohibited for eighteen months. Daley knew that this part of the law would jeopardize his relationship with unions, key members of his electoral coalition. He called them together in the spring of 1995, asking that they refrain from fighting the law, whose passage was virtually assured. In return, he promised to rescind most of its anti-union restrictions after he gained control. "Every right they took away, Daley gave them back in bargaining, every one," rejoiced a union leader.[32]

Finally, the mayor and his CEO were granted the special authority to sanction any Chicago school with remediation, probation, reconstitution, or intervention, although none of these punishments was spelled out in the law. After six years of decentralized accountability, in which local school councils made judgments about school effectiveness, this change promised to restandardize the determination of educational performance. Yet the law did not clarify what those standards would be, nor did it specify how they should be implemented. Instead, this was left to the mayor and his CEO.

Informal Influence

With such latitude, the law could not anticipate some of the most important developments. Those came from Rich Daley's style of governing. Daley, who cultivates the image of the "chief executive of a nearly $5 billion corporation," moved quickly to jettison the symbols of the "old" school bureaucracy.[33] The school system's central administration was relocated from the Pershing Road barracks in Chicago's black South Side to a newly renovated building in the Loop, near city hall. The move signaled the importance of the schools to the economy and the close relationship between Vallas and Daley.

Another consequence of Daley's style has been a shift to a corporate-style school board. Like the city council—which votes unanimously with the mayor on one thousand to two thousand pieces of legislation each year, and on the twenty-nine divided votes from 2003 to 2005 sided with the mayor 85 percent of the time—the board now serves a pro forma function.[34] In twelve years, Rich Daley's school board (initially five members, increased to seven in 1999) has only split its votes three times. Citizens are permitted the opportunity to address the board for two minutes but not to hear its deliberations, since the board does not publicly debate issues.[35] This is a big difference from both the pre-1995 board and the school boards selected by mayors before 1988. Nearly all were legislative bodies, casting public votes, debating issues, and developing factions that could derail the mayor's plans.

Daley also saw the schools as a magnet to attract the middle class, linked to his role in providing the infrastructure to revitalize economic growth. Both meant focusing on downtown development—94 percent of new development in the 1990s took place in seven of the seventy neighborhoods that surround Chicago's Loop, and 91 percent of the improvements leveraged by tax increment financing were in the downtown business district.[36] After 1995, Daley demolished three crime-ridden low-income housing projects to make way for gentrification and began a school building and remodeling program in West Town and the Near North Side.[37] It mushroomed to a $2.6 billion initiative for twenty-eight elementary schools and seven college preparatory academies by the end of Vallas's tenure.[38]

Daley has maintained close ties to a shrinking unionized labor force through abundant building contracts and higher-than-typical union wages. Consequently, he has moved gradually when threatening outsourcing, preferring to delay job losses through attrition or simply requiring contractors to hire union labor.[39] Even so, Chicago has shifted from industrial production to a service economy in which only about 13 percent of the workers are unionized.[40] The Chicago Teachers Union is one of the few large public sector employee groups with which he negotiates, and he has been nearly as generous as his father. Since 1995, Daley has offered the teachers a series of four- to five-year contracts, each with 3–4 percent yearly raises. In return, he has asked the union to accept his initiatives and steer clear of reform.

The bargain was kept until 2001, when a "reform" slate, led by a former employee of the national American Federation of Teachers under Al Shanker, won leadership of the Chicago Teachers Union. Deborah Lynch demanded that the union have a role in school governance. Since Vallas resigned two weeks after her election, it was CEO Duncan, Mayor Daley, and President Lynch who signed the agreement allowing the union to comanage ten failing schools. They also convinced the legislature to restore the union's legislative rights to bargain. But three years later, Lynch lost the union leadership in a bitter runoff election. Her African American challenger was reelected in 2007 by an overwhelming majority on a platform that kept to bread-and-butter bargaining and, once again, left reform to the mayor.[41]

The most controversial change has been Daley's insistence on changing the process of promoting children from grade to grade. In spring 1996, eighth-grade elementary school students were told that their scores on the reading portion of the nationally normed Iowa Tests of Basic Skills (ITBS) would determine their promotion to high school, a policy Daley championed as the end of "social promotion."[42] Those whose scores fell below a benchmark level set by CEO Vallas were required to attend remedial test-taking instruction in summer school, after which a retest would determine promotion or retention. A year later the same policy was extended to third and sixth graders, and the math test was added. Each year the cut score was raised. When multiple retentions encouraged students to drop out before reaching high school, alternative schools were created for fifteen-year-olds still in elementary school.

Educators' accountability came in the way that Daley interpreted probation and the other school sanctions he was authorized to impose. Turning again to ITBS test scores, he determined that schools would be put on probation if not more than 15 percent of the school's students scored at or above national norms. This performance standard was incrementally raised until 2006, then substantially complicated with additional criteria. The local school councils of probationary schools lost their authority, and principals were subject to dismissal by the CEO. Initially, probationary schools were assigned external assistance providers including a probation manager to guide planning and evaluate the principal. Probation schools were further required to contract with an external partner for professional development and other services, which necessitated redirecting the school's discretionary budget. Failure to get off probation with these measures could lead to more severe sanctions.

In June 1997, seven of thirty-eight probation high schools were reconstituted because they were deemed the system's worst performers. Their local school councils were disbanded and all principals and staff were required to reapply for their jobs. Increased shame, less autonomy, some new faculty, and mandated district-created scripted lesson plans in four subjects—9,360 plans in all—were expected to turn around these and the troubled schools on probation. "This is not rocket science," Vallas explained. "If you're a new teacher, or a weak teacher, or a teacher that doesn't have skills, or if you have a teacher that's burned out . . . if you stick to that curriculum you'll be able to deliver quality instruction."[43]

In 2000 the mayor initiated parent report cards, aiming to increase the accountability of parents of children in the prekindergarten to third grades. Twenty-three evaluation marks, including items like "spends quality time" with a child, were sent home every five weeks, because "the school system has got to identify the things that parents are clearly not doing."[44] But "insulted" parents and local school councils resisted, and only half the schools agreed to use the accountability device.[45]

After six years, Daley replaced Vallas just as news reports were revealing less performance gain than city hall had promoted. Mayor Daley and his new CEO Arne Duncan backed away from scripted lessons to emphasize reading instruction. Duncan, who counts faculty from Northwestern University, the University of Illinois, and the University of Chicago among his advisers, took a different path to student and school incentives. Among his changes was the tacit acknowledgment, under threat of a U.S. Justice Department probe, that holding children back in grade based on a single test score could be found discriminatory. He expanded the retention criteria, permitting grades and attendance to count. It had already been revealed by then that retention was not administered equally: about one-third of all retained students were unaccountably waived through, and the odds of receiving such a waiver were higher for whites than for African Americans.[46]

In 2004 Daley adopted another corporate-initiated plan for the schools, dubbed Renaissance 2010, which aimed to close one hundred low-performing schools and reopen them as charters, small schools, or "performance" contract schools. Corporate leaders justified their new strategy as providing much-needed competition for the "virtual monopoly" of public schools they still judged "radically dysfunctional."[47] Daley agreed on condition that a business entity would raise one-third of the seed money for Renaissance 2010, a goal largely met.[48] Meanwhile, shifting criteria for school probation increased the pool of schools eligible to be closed to 206 in 2007. By 2008, seventy-five new charter, contract, or performance schools had opened.[49] Most of them do not have local school councils.

With all the other governance changes, it surprises some observers that local school councils were not eliminated in 1995. They still underpin Chicago's mayoral control today, serving primarily as the representative voice of Chicago school parents, albeit with constrained school improvement and budgetary powers. Principals in most schools are still selected by the councils.

Although the mayor has several times tried to end parents' power to fire principals, Illinois legislators favor giving parents a check on city hall and have so far rejected Daley's requests. Consequently, Chicago parents still have a clear option if they do not believe a child's school is performing well: run in the biennial local school council elections, and if conditions continue to worsen, change the principal.[50]

Does It Work?

Mayoral control can be judged by several standards. One is aggregated student test scores. Mayor Daley promoted test scores as the key measure of accountability for students and schools more than six years before No Child Left Behind became law. During those years, scores on the ITBS rose significantly, while the proportion of low-achieving students fell.[51] However, attribution of all the gains to the reinstatement of mayoral powers has been contested. The proportion of students whose scores were counted fell from 82 percent to 74 percent, even though student enrollment had increased, which may have inflated the improvements.[52] Some analyses suggest that the rise in test scores began before mayoral control was initiated and the scores flatlined in 2000.[53] Moreover, ITBS improvements did not transfer to other tests. Chicago students' initial performance was much poorer on the Illinois State Achievement Test. In 2000 only 20 percent of eighth-graders met its standards in math, for example, as compared with 45 percent on the ITBS.[54] Nor do Chicago students fare well on National Assessment of Educational Progress exams relative to other big-city systems, as the second chapter in this volume demonstrates. Reasons given include differences in the tested content across tests and strategic choices by teachers who focused on ITBS tested skills.[55]

Since 2002, test score trends have been harder to untangle. One reason is that the district changed the national norming sample it was using for the ITBS, automatically boosting scores and severely complicating comparisons with trends before 2002. Only a few years later, in 2005, the Illinois State Achievement Test replaced the ITBS as the testing standard. The following year saw significant changes in the state test scale that sent scores soaring again. One comparison study of the two tests between 1999 and 2002, when both were given, showed no clear trend overall, small increases in third grade, declines in fifth grade, and mixed results (for example, trend lines that ran in opposite directions on the two tests) in the eighth grade.[56] Even so, beginning in 2005 test scores on the state achievement test began to rise, 2 to 7 percent more students met Illinois standards on the test in 2006 than in the previous year, and 2007 saw somewhat smaller gains.[57] Since the first two cohorts of eighth-graders were hit by the retention policy, subsequent graduation rates have also steadily improved, although Chicago researchers believe them to be lower (54 percent in 2002) than the rates reported by the state (64.8 percent).[58]

Another way to examine success is by tracking test score performance gaps between Chicago's white and Asian American students, who represent about 12 percent of the school population, and its large majority of African American and Latino students. Asian Americans and whites were both scoring at national norms before 1995, and their scores rose significantly above those norms in the latter half of the decade. Latinos, 34 percent of the students, saw smaller gains in their scores. But African American students (53 percent of the student body) saw test score gains for only a few years, after which the scores stalled and in some grades declined. By 2001 the test score gap between African Americans and all other groups had widened.[59] The gap between graduation rates of African American students and others has widened as well, the rates for African American boys being substantially lower than all others, with only about 39 percent graduating by the age of nineteen.[60] Researchers explain the disparity by differences in student performance (that is, grade point average, attendance, and number of Fs) during their first year of high school.[61]

In 2006 a lack of comparable data across years encouraged researchers to weigh African American and Latino students in Chicago against their counterparts in the rest of Illinois, with some surprising results. These two groups of students in Chicago began with performance levels much lower on average but approach parity with their Illinois counterparts by the eighth grade, though they still remained far below those of white and Asian American students (for example, the median reading score for third-grade African Americans was 31 points below the median white score, but the gap on the eighth-grade reading test that year was a smaller 21 points).[62]

Retention and Promotion as Measures of Success

For the dozen years Daley has been in control of the schools, poor test scores have had two consequences: students were held back in grade (that is, retention, no "social promotion") and schools lost autonomy (for example, through probation sanctions). Both create their own measures of success. How, one can ask, has retention affected the students held back? And have sanctioned schools turned around?

Although the numbers fluctuated from year to year, from 1996 until 2001 about seven thousand to 10,000 Chicago elementary students have been retained in grade annually, almost 20 percent of the third graders and about 10 percent of both sixth and eighth graders. Retained third graders saw no improvement, and retained sixth graders showed 6 percent lower achievement growth, compared with their peers who had the same or similar scores but were not retained. On average, retained third and sixth graders were three times more likely to be placed in special education, where their scores did not count toward subsequent promotion decisions, than similarly achieving students who were not retained. Those unfortunate enough to be retained more than once or designated special education students experienced a considerable drop in their performance. Dropout rates also increased by 8–13 percent among the students retained, and 78 percent of those retained twice had dropped out by the age of nineteen. Nor did mandatory test-prep summer school alter the average student's long-term performance.[63]

Ninety-seven percent of those retained (in all three grades) between 1997 and 2002 for low test scores have been African American or Latino. Latino students in bilingual-education classes were exempted from retention for three (later extended to four) years.[64] Reasons given for this disparity include the research observation that predominately African American schools received by far the slowest instructional pacing, meaning these students have not had the opportunity to learn the tested material.[65]

Test-based school sanctions rapidly produced a schools hierarchy. At the top have been college preparatory schools, many of them new, with test admission criteria and accelerated programs. Some of their principals have been recently rewarded with additional autonomy to make fiscal and instructional decisions without central office oversight.[66] At the bottom, about one-fifth of the schools have been placed on probation. One hundred and nine schools were put on probation in 1996. Between then and 2001 about 150 got off probation, but some were reassigned a second time, while others languished. Throughout, the relative size of the three layers stayed much the same. In 2004 stiffer criteria resulted in a record high of 212 schools (one-third of the district) on probation, and these schools were required to spend their discretionary funds on district-specified interventions, such as reading specialists.[67] Thereafter, the criteria for probation were loosened, then tightened again. In June 2008, new probation criteria gave elementary schools points for attendance and test score achievement rates, trends, and gains over the district average on four separate Illinois State Achievement Tests. High schools earned points for attendance, drop-out rates, freshman grades and course completion rates, and four separate tests.

Low-performing elementary schools that had not been put on probation saw larger gains in student test scores (a 23.6 percent average gain in proportion of students meeting national norms on the English portion of the ITBS, 27 percent on the math test) than probation schools, which as a group remained far below national averages by 2003. Twenty-six percent of the low-performing elementary schools not on probation fell below the higher probation standard by 2005. Yet this was far better than the schools first placed on probation in 1996, of which 87 percent failed to meet the new standard.[68] Reconstitution, the sanction applied to a handful of the worst high schools, proved even less effective: test scores in those schools plunged, as did teacher morale. Reconstitution was eliminated in 2002.

Attracting the Middle Class

Another means for evaluating the system was provided by Mayor Daley, who sought to attract a tax-paying middle class. By this measure mayoral control has done somewhat better. The primary contribution the school system has made to attracting and retaining the middle class has been to construct new schools in gentrifying areas and to target college-bound students. Charter schools and Renaissance 2010 schools that open in buildings that once housed traditional schools consequently receive more resources than schools that are not included in the plans for this transformation process. Sixty-two percent of the new schools (attended by 3 percent of the system's 414,000 students) have had their capital needs fully funded compared with 45 percent of traditional schools. According to district officials, these schools are being prioritized in order to get them ready for their new students.[69]

Building Capacity for Reform

Given the uncertainty involved in sifting through the many possible measures of performance and the complexity of the reform strategy—nothing about Chicago's experience suggests that any current gains can be attributed simply to a reform law—it is useful to ask: What has built Chicago's capacity to bounce back from mistakes, continue to make incremental progress, and keep faith in city hall? Chicago's history teaches us that mayoral control of the schools is a governing strategy insufficient to guarantee reform. Yet the city has seen clear improvements, if also many missteps, in its school performance over the last dozen years. Instead of freighting mayoral control with all the credit or blame, and then drawing narrow distinctions between earlier and current versions, it is more useful to understand the capacity-building institutions that underpin governance change.

Independent of the mayor's authority, Chicagoans have created three institutions that give their system enormous capacity to ground improvements in research, evaluate mayoral initiatives, make school performance transparent, and enable parents and community members to act if the results are not what they want or need. One such capacity-building institution provides independent and credible research about what is working and for whom. Another is dedicated to interpreting this research for the general public, debating interventions, and investigating policy consequences. Both of these are dependent on a third: the institutionalized forums for grassroots debate and activism that are empowered to alter conditions in individual schools when needed. All three institutions had been functioning for half a decade before 1995. None depends upon tax dollars for its operation.

Independent Research

Mayors are not education professionals, and neither of Mayor Daley's school CEOs has been a professional educator. This is one of the arguments for giving them control. As generalists, mayors are less likely than professional superintendents to micromanage the schools.[70] But it is also a weakness. Nonspecialists are likely to make decisions based on intuition or to assume that a policy instrument producing gains in another domain—policing or economic development, for example—will also succeed in education. In Chicago, vague slogans like "no social promotion" and "accountability" have driven policy even when the processes for implementing these ideas were not understood.

Sloganeering makes it difficult to alter course when evidence suggests that unintended harm has undermined good intentions. For example, although criticized for "sacrificing everything for test scores" and censured by the National Research Council in 1998, Chicago's student retention policy was not altered until Vallas left his post.[71] The National Research Council had pointed out that the ITBS "had not been validated [for] identifying low-performing schools and students" and recommended multiple measures for these high-stakes decisions. But neither the mayor nor his CEO would budge, claiming that any change to a more suitable test or broader measures might cause the system a loss of credibility.[72]

Sometimes, for fear of losing momentum, mistakes were deliberately buried. High school reconstitution, for example, was revealed to be a failure; but because Vallas had commissioned the research, its lead author was not allowed to reveal findings to anyone except the CEO. When the results were finally made available, it was already well beyond the time the policy should have been stopped for the sake of the youngsters involved.[73]

Consequently, it has been crucial that Chicago have an independent research body with routine access to public school data, qualified to conduct technically high-quality research and prepared to follow the results wherever they lead. The Consortium on Chicago School Research has filled that analytical function since 1990. Founded by researchers Anthony Bryk and Penny Sebring, both at the University of Chicago, it is a collaborative effort involving the University of Illinois, Northwestern University, and Roosevelt University researchers among its directors and principal investigators. It engages, as well, a wide array of community stakeholders on its steering committee.[74] Policy analysis at the consortium is motivated by the practical problems of implementing reform in Chicago and so is called "place-based research."

Bryk initially argued that social science methods applied to school assessment could help local school council members in low-income districts to make good decisions about principal hiring and school improvement planning. "Pluralistic policy research" was intended to compensate for the social capital they lacked.[75] Parents and community members, as nonspecialists, would need ongoing longitudinal research based on Chicago's schools so that they could see the consequences of their decisions and learn from the successes of others under the same systemic constraints. To this end, the consortium created an individual school report that provides schools with the results of their own student performance (as well as teacher, principal, and student surveys) as compared with that of a peer group and the system as a whole. These reports are not used to evaluate schools, however, but to help them improve.

Since mayoral control was reasserted, the consortium's system-wide research reports have become more crucial. Major policy decisions intended for district-wide implementation almost invariably suit some schools but not others. And some decisions, like the mayor's first efforts at high school restructuring, have proved bad ideas altogether. Where the consortium has been given access to the school data, its reports have been a crucial source of credible analysis. The Consortium on Chicago School Research receives individual student achievement test scores, administrative data, and high school course transcripts every year from the school system and conducts biennial surveys of teachers, principals, and students, all under an agreement with the district that predates Mayor Daley's new powers. Its studies of retained students, for example, would have been impossible without these data and the ability to link student records by individual student codes. Consortium scholars provide Chicago's (and the nation's) most sophisticated analysis of retention ("no social promotion") policies to date, revealing nuanced implementation concerns, such as the differential effects on third graders and older children. Virtually none of the performance results reported above would have been possible, or fully credible, without the consortium's independent analyses.

Although initially skeptical and sometimes overtly hostile to the consortium, even CEO Vallas came to appreciate its research after he had taken over Philadelphia's schools, largely because the consortium had offered suggestions about how to improve programs and understand roadblocks and always took seriously his efforts to raise achievement. Arne Duncan has been more receptive all along.

The consortium has collected nearly twenty years of longitudinal data that enables the creation and ongoing monitoring of outcome indicators and the testing of alternative hypotheses and evaluation analysis. It also provides technical assistance to other researchers who perform their own independent analyses (under appropriate human-subject and professional competency constraints). These independent researchers test the consortium's conclusions, develop different metrics of success, and offer new ideas for improvement but rely on the consortium for their core data. In this way the consortium's longitudinal database and education mission perform a crucial public function: increasing the capacity of all Chicago researchers to develop education expertise among generalist policymakers and to help local school practitioners make improvements.

The consortium's governance structure enables this impact. The consortium operates under the direction of an executive director and several codirectors, researchers who lead major studies. These individuals are ultimately responsible for crafting the research agenda, maintaining the quality of the research, and guiding its dissemination and use in schools as well as sustaining the organization. The codirectors are greatly aided by a steering committee of about twenty members made up of stakeholders from across the city. Institutional members of the steering committee include the school district, the state board of education, the principals association, and the teachers union. Individual members, selected for their "expertise, diversity of opinions, and their involvement in school reform," outnumber these institutional actors.[76]

Steering committee meetings have several purposes: to review research designs and help researchers interpret their findings, to provide reactions to preliminary reports, and, periodically, to help create the research agenda. By the time a report is published, stakeholders have debated its methods, findings, and meaning, each bringing different concerns to the dialogue. All have a strong sense of how the research affects their education work, whether it is aimed at improving policy or adjusting implementation. Neither the mayor nor the CEO establishes the research agenda or has a veto over the consortium's work.

Transparency

Mayors have no incentive to reveal bad news. Even Mayor Daley must periodically run for office. His reputation is his reelection platform. Consequently, like all politicians, he cherry-picks data to enhance his standing and buries, or "spins," information that is negative. But when the topic is the public schools, where the life chances of the city's children hang in the balance, the results of this normal political process can be dire. Transparency is most needed just when all the incentives work to undermine it.

This does not mean that journalistic coverage of the schools falls off under mayoral control; on the contrary, its status is boosted on the local policy agenda.[77] An editor of one of Chicago's dailies put it this way: "One of the major changes that's occurred since the mayor took over the school system is that the mayor's office is holding press conferences now about schools. The biggest news events concerning change in the Chicago Public Schools are now announced at city hall . . . which means that all the city hall reporters are covering education issues."[78] But when their sources of information are employed by city hall, journalists covering the city hall beat stand to lose access if they annoy the mayor. Those inclined to challenge him are often unprepared to probe; they rarely understand how the school system works or how to interpret education data.[79] Add to the mix an activist CEO, savvy about media relations, and the public may learn little of importance about the schools, even from dedicated journalists determined to hold officials' feet to the fire.

Thus when initial impressions of success in Chicago were fostered by a city hall publicity campaign, "the mere perception of success [was] feeding itself."[80] According to an active foundation executive, one result was "more political support for the school system . . . than ever."[81] Paul Vallas was lionized in *Forbes* magazine as "Chain Saw Paul" for his "tough tactics" and "plenty of publicity" and because he came from "outside the education establishment."[82] With publicity came credibility; in 1997 civic elites overwhelmingly identified Vallas and his senior staff as their sources of information about the system. Vallas, admitted one journalist, "was a master at using the media. . . . He had everything that we want. He was accessible, he gave us his home phone number, he was plain spoken, and he didn't speak in educationese." The CEO also personalized contacts with the media by announcing reform initiatives at the last minute through phone calls designed to leave little time in which journalists could seek alternative perspectives. "Before long," commented one education editor, the relationship between district and press "was a love fest." Mayoral control and Vallas's extraordinary media skills also resulted in "very little, if any, skeptical reporting."[83] Even a corporate supporter claimed he was "not sure that [the media] are sufficiently critical."[84]

But Chicago had a means to counter the public relations barrage. In 1990 the city's foundations joined with the Community Renewal Society to create *Catalyst,* a newsmagazine solely dedicated to covering the city's schools. The year before, Linda Lenz, a local reporter frustrated by editors' preoccupation with advertising revenues, launched a plan to develop a new form of journalism that would support school reform rather than search out gotcha stories. She reasoned that reformers could only be effective if they had a source of independent information about how the education system worked and a cross-sector forum for debate that was "mindful of the complexities" when describing studies of program effectiveness.[85] To the extent that it meets these goals, *Catalyst* may have been more important since 1995 than it was when initially conceived.

One study has revealed that Daley's reassertion of authority had a significant chilling effect on the number of diverse opinions reported in *Catalyst.* But the magazine's editors explained that they were compensating for a deliberate lack of transparency on the part of the new central administration. After 1995, *Catalyst* provided the missing information, including detailed descriptions of policy changes no longer readily available to the public and assessments of their impact, drawn largely from the Consortium on Chicago School Research.

Nor were *Catalyst*'s editors content to explain the mayor's and Vallas's policies to a passive populace. They remained committed to providing a forum for all of Chicago's school stakeholders, from Latino parents to long-established city hall operatives, from education researchers to black activist organizations. Commissioned studies of *Catalyst*'s effectiveness around 2005 led the editors to revamp the newsmagazine's format and renew their attention to investigative journalism. One explicit focus has been the resource and implementation disparities between middle-class and low-income communities in the highly segregated city.

Citizen Representation and Involvement

Even an active media outlet dedicated to the schools, capable of interpreting research results and conducting its own investigations, requires a committed audience. Chicago has filled that need, too. As a Cleveland newspaper editor put it, "Chicago has a much, much, much more engaged community, both in terms of the academic concentration on schools as well as on the local neighborhood groups of either ethnic, or academic or human services."[86] Chicago public engagement processes began with a citywide summit called by former mayor Harold Washington. Even after his untimely death the summit continued, engaging the city for many months. A wide array of residents, representing all of the city's neighborhoods, influenced the decisions that led to the decentralizing law of 1988. This participatory democracy was subsequently institutionalized in the form of local school councils.[87]

After their euphoric first year of existence, local school councils fell short of their most idealistic supporters' hopes. Community activists had been pleased that the Illinois Supreme Court gave the councils legal status equivalent to the central school board. But corporate leaders sided with the one dissenting justice, who said their function was to "simply implement in the particular school the district-wide policies set by the board."[88] Such differences of opinion over the meaning of local school governance reflected different perspectives on who had the legitimacy to make substantive decisions about public schooling. Corporate leaders worried about the potential for corruption and poor decisionmaking. In the words of one, "A lot of these people never had *any* kind of experience like that before."[89] The costs of biennial electioneering and local school council training were recurring district expenses, for which there was no enthusiasm among those concerned with balanced budgets. One survey conducted in the early 1990s reported that 10–25 percent of the local school council respondents characterized their councils as being rancorously divided or lacking in transparency, and the press has reported examples of a few councils' signing contracts with organizations that did not provide the contracted services.

The greater concern has been electoral apathy. Steep declines in the numbers of candidates who ran for local school council slots began almost immediately. Fewer than half as many candidates came forward in 1991 as had in 1989. Turnout declined from 192,771 in 1989 to 175,845 in 1996, demonstrating that the councils draw voters in no greater numbers than elected school boards. Today, council elections are considered a success if at least one candidate runs for each open seat; only sixty-two schools had fully contested elections in 2006. There is little evidence that the teachers union is engaged in local school council slate making, a common criticism of decentralization. This is probably because teachers are allotted only two seats on each local school council and cannot vote for parents. But in some schools, community organizations have created electoral slates to ensure that a principal who represents them is seated.

Yet the concern about electoral legitimacy misses the greater contribution that local school councils make to Chicago's version of mayoral control. The councils assemble a body of engaged parents and community members in each school who have the means to turn conversation into action should they feel the school is being served poorly. Independent of their capacity to make sound education decisions—a question on which Mayor Daley and Illinois legislators so far disagree—they provide Chicago's only public forums for debate of school policies.

Absent local school councils, the system's governance is highly centralized and in the hands of a politically unaccountable mayor. He effectively holds his position for life, and city hall remains largely inaccessible to ordinary citizens. The school board serves as an advisory group to the mayor, not as a citizen forum. Chicago's central office is as bureaucratic as any big-city school system's. The Consortium on Chicago School Research's steering committee is an education forum for researchers and community elites, but local school councils provide the only political outlet for individual parents and community members, whose concerns and criticism would otherwise be ineffectual. And although council elections do not draw large numbers of voters or candidates, they remain a means to alter the implementation of the mayor's plans one school at a time. Notwithstanding interschool competition for capital improvements and extra resources that tilt the scales toward middle-class parents, this is the one place where even low-income parents and community members can affect the education their children receive. Perhaps this is why Chicago's local school councils are so strongly defended.

Councils are educative institutions in their own right. In theory, as many as 44,000 Chicagoans have learned about their schools firsthand while serving as local school council representatives. The councils also sustain both *Catalyst* and the Consortium on Chicago School Research. Absent the local councils, these two institutions would be addressing a small, elite audience of political leaders, education insiders, and a few civic activists. *Catalyst* speaks to local school council members as concerned residents with a need to know about the schools in their neighborhoods. Members of the councils also afford *Catalyst*'s journalists a legitimate grassroots alternative to information from official district and city hall sources. Councils create the structural conditions that permit democratic decisionmaking to survive, if only one school at a time, even in the context of centralized mayoral control at the top of the system. *Catalyst*'s award-winning journalists and the highly respected researchers of the Consortium on Chicago School Research bolster those conditions by providing local school councils with reliable information and school-based research. Evaluating a principal's performance is done more credibly as a result; so too is evaluating the mayor's latest initiative.

No other mayoral-control experiment in the nation has this bottom-up decisionmaking process. Ironically, without these three capacity-building institutions, many of Mayor Daley's initiatives would quite likely have had much greater local opposition. It may be the primary reason why Chicagoans have not revolted en masse when problems have surfaced.

Unsolved Capacity Problems

Notwithstanding its institutional resources and civic capacity, there are also problems Chicago has not solved. Despite fifteen years of oversight by the School Finance Authority, unprecedented flexibility to move funding from one need to another, a hamstrung teachers union, and the goodwill of businesses and foundations, Chicago's budgetary woes remain. Mayor Daley has used heroic measures each year since 1996 to balance the budget, and Chicagoans have seen large tax hikes, but the system remains fundamentally out of balance.

Part of the problem is that the school budget has ballooned. To be successful in improving school performance, mayors must initiate new programs. Finding ways to raise new funds for summer school, after-school programs, all-day kindergarten, wiring the schools, redressing long-deferred maintenance, and a host of other priorities has required every ounce of ingenuity the mayor possesses. When the strategy for improvement involves a large share of outsourcing, there are additional start-up, construction, and contract maintenance costs. In addition, Chicago has incurred substantial financing costs through tax increment financing loans and bonds, all of which eventually have to be paid.

Illinois contributes a relatively low share of baseline funding to the public schools compared with other states. This has had the consequence of making local funding disparities larger than they would otherwise be. Illinois legislators have repeatedly been asked to reexamine school funding on equity grounds. Yet to date, no plans have received sufficient legislative support. Until something is done to remedy this situation, Chicago's version of mayoral control will continue to strain the resources of the city. Without a more rational and reliable state funding stream, the finance costs of public education under this mayor's control are likely to outstrip the city's taxing capacity.

Qualified teachers and principals, bilingual staff in schools to serve Latino communities, informed parents to serve on local school councils, expert school-support teams, reliable partners for new schools, and knowledgeable advisers for those still troubled are resources as important to schools as stable finances. Beyond funding, each of these resource streams requires community support and an organizational base upon which to draw. Chicago is fortunate in having many institutions of higher education, all of which have agreed to alter their preparation of principals and teachers, serve as partners to help turn around schools on probation, perform evaluation studies, and provide advice. The city is also blessed with a wide range of activist community-based organizations.

These resources have been consolidated and sustained in one of two ways. Some have been acquired through costly district contracts. To the extent that Rich Daley has chosen the first option, it provides him with loyal contractors while allowing him to support Chicago's large organizational base with focused material incentives, at the expense of adding new costs to the schools budget.

Alternatively, extraschool organizations have been motivated to participate as part of a larger reform coalition willing to raise its own private, philanthropic funding. To the extent that Chicagoans have demonstrated an autonomous interest in reforming their schools, they are independent of city hall, free to criticize and audit its educational performance. They can also add ideas and voices, providing political protection for politicians worried about seeming indecisive if their policies do not work out as planned. Crucially, this mobilization strategy relies on philanthropic persistence among funders who often want only to seed organizations and then turn to other priorities. Chicago is lucky to have a philanthropic community with remarkable tenacity that has so far maintained the Consortium on Chicago School Research, *Catalyst,* and several other capacity-building institutions. Added recently are mission-driven foundations that aim to seed new types of schools. But when the private philanthropy dries up, the need for these human resources remains. Chicago has not yet solved this sustainability problem.

Breaking with Tradition

By some accounts, mayoral control in Chicago represents a new and unprecedented governance structure. This narrative argues that Richard M. Daley is a new-style mayor, one who takes his school leadership and management responsibilities seriously. If so, this means success for Chicago's schools is dependent on one man remaining in charge of the city. It raises two questions: How are the traits that make Daley a school leader transferred to the next mayor? And what should the electorate look for in replacing him, when the time comes? Even if there were technical answers to these questions, they might not be useful. Politicians are seldom elected to fulfill a predecessor's mandate, and most political executives prefer to put their own governing stamp on the offices they hold.

This narrative about an education mayor ignores the capacity-building institutions that Chicagoans created, independently of mayoral control, to assist school improvement. These institutions are Chicago's bulwark against another less-than-ideal mayor, lowering the risks of this governing strategy for everyone concerned. They are arguably more important institutional changes than any mayoral power shifts. Whatever governing strategy is adopted in the future, Chicagoans have, in the Consortium on Chicago School Research, dedicated and independent research on which to base program evaluation and improve activities; in *Catalyst*, a means to receive credible information about the schools; and should it be needed, the ability to redress problems at one school at a time in elected local school councils. Each of these institutions contributes crucial external resources that Chicago's mayors can rely on but that also can correct glib claims, reveal the underlying processes of success, and keep the media spotlight on the schools and students still struggling. Although some cities have one of these institutions, among U.S. cities only Chicago has them all.[90]

Notes

Interviews referenced in this chapter were conducted by the author unless otherwise noted. The names of the education editors and the names of their papers have been withheld at their request.

1. Kenneth J. Meier, "Structure, Politics, and Policy: The Logic of Mayoral Control," in *Mayors in the Middle: Politics, Race, and Mayoral Control of Urban Schools*, edited by Jeffrey Henig and Wilbur Rich (Princeton University Press, 2003).

2. Kenneth K. Wong and others, *The Education Mayor: Improving America's Schools* (Georgetown University Press, 2007).

3. See, for example, Dorothy Shipps, "Chicago: The National 'Model' Reexamined," in *Mayors in the Middle*, edited by Henig and Rich, pp. 59–95; Dorothy Shipps, "Pulling Together: Civic Capacity and Urban School Reform," *American Educational Research Journal* 40 (Winter 2003): 841–78; Dorothy Shipps, *School Reform, Corporate Style: Chicago, 1880–2000* (University Press of Kansas, 2006); Dorothy Shipps, "The Invisible Hand: Big Business and Chicago School Reform," *Teachers College Record* 99 (Fall 1997): 73–116; Dorothy Shipps, Elisabeth Fowlkes, and Alissa Peltzman, "Journalism and Urban School Reform: Versions of Democratic Decision Making in Two American Cities," *American Journal of Education* 112 (May 2006): 363–91.

4. Quoted in Frank James, "Daley Lectures on Schools: If Chicago Can Turn Around, Others Can, Mayor Says," *Chicago Tribune,* Metro Chicago, June 6, 1997, p. 3.

5. U.S. Conference of Mayors, *Best Practices in City Governments,* volume 3, *Focus on the Mayor's Role in Education* (Washington, 1997).

6. William J. Clinton, "State of the Union Address by the President" (White House Office of the Press Secretary, January 27, 1998); Federal News Service, "Full Text of President Clinton's State of the Union Address as Delivered on January 19, 1999," *Washington Post,* January 20, 1999, p. A12.

7. In addition to the above, see, for example, Elaine Allensworth, *Graduation and Dropout Trends in Chicago: A Look at Cohorts of Students from 1991 to 2004,* Research Report (Chicago: Consortium on Chicago School Research, 2005); William Ayers, "Chicago: A Restless Sea of Social Forces," in *A Union of Professionals: Labor Relations and Educational Reform,* edited by Charles T. Kerschner and Julia E. Koppich (Teachers College Press, 1993); Marilyn Bizar and Rebecca Barr, eds., *School Leadership in Times of Urban Reform* (Mahwah, N.J.: Lawrence Erlbaum, 2001); Anthony S. Bryk and others, *Charting Chicago School Reform: Democratic Localism as a Lever for Change* (Boulder, Colo.: Westview Press, 1998); Jim Carl, "Harold Washington and Chicago's Schools: Between Civil Rights and the Decline of the New Deal Consensus, 1955–1987," *History of Education Quarterly* 41 (Fall 2001): 311–43; Civic Committee of the Commercial Club, *Left Behind: A Report of the Education Committee,* Research Report (Commercial Club of Chicago, 2003); Paul T. Hill, Lawrence C. Pierce, and James W. Guthrie, *Reinventing Public Education* (University of Chicago Press, 1997); Michael M. Katz, Michele Fine, and Elaine Simon, "Poking Around: Outsiders View Chicago School Reform," *Teachers College Record* 99 (Fall 1997): 117–57; Pauline Lipman, *High Stakes Education: Inequality, Globalization, and Urban School Reform* (New York: Routledge Falmer, 2004); William S. McKersie, "Reforming Chicago's Public Schools: Philanthropic Persistence, 1987–1993," in *Advances in Educational Policy,* edited by Kenneth Wong (Greenwich, Conn.: JAI Press, 1996); Jeffrey Mirel, "School Reform, Chicago Style: Educational Innovation in a Changing Urban Context, 1976–1991," *Urban Education* 28 (July 1993): 116–49; Donald Moore, *Chicago's Grade Retention Program Fails to Help Retained Students,* Research Report (Chicago: Designs for Change, 2000); Jennifer O'Day, "Complexity, Accountability, and School Improvement," *Harvard Education Review* 72 (Fall 2002): 293–329; Melissa Roderick and Mimi Engel, "The Grasshopper and the Ant: Motivational Responses of Low-Achieving Students to High-Stakes Testing," *Educational Evaluation and Policy Analysis* 23 (January 2001): 197–227; Alexander Russo, ed., *School Reform in Chicago* (Harvard Education Press, 2004); Shipps, *School Reform, Corporate Style;* Deborah Lynch Walsh, *Labor of Love: One Chicago Teacher's Experience* (Lincoln, Neb.: Writers Club Press, 2000); Wong and others, *The Education Mayor.*

8. Dick Simpson and others, *Chicago City Council's Newly Found Independence: Chicago City Council Report, May 7, 2003–December 7, 2005* (University of Illinois at Chicago, Department of Political Science, 2006), p. 2.

9. Quoted in Julia Wrigley, *Class Politics and Public Schools: Chicago 1900–1950* (Rutgers University Press, 1982), p. 141.

10. Shipps, *School Reform, Corporate Style,* p. 95.

11. Mayor's Daley's chief of staff, interview with author, June 25, 1997.

12. The cuts are detailed in Mary Herrick, *The Chicago Schools: A Social and Political History* (Beverly Hills, Calif.: Sage Publications, 1971).

13. Citizens' Schools Committee, *Chicago Schools* 1 (July 1934); 1 (August 1934); 1 (September 1934).

14. Joint House and Senate Chicago Board of Education Investigation Committee, *Report to the 81st Illinois General Assembly: The Chicago Board of Education's 1979 Financial Crisis and Its Implications on Other Illinois School Districts, Final Report,* edited by the Illinois General Assembly (State of Illinois, January 13, 1981).

15. Citizens' Schools Committee, "Report III" (Chicago, January–February 1980); G. Alfred Hess Jr., *School Restructuring, Chicago Style* (Newbury Park, Calif.: Corwin Press, 1991).

16. National Commission for the Defense of Democracy through Education, *Certain Personnel Practices in the Chicago Public Schools,* report prepared for the Citizens' Schools Committee (Washington: National Education Association, 1945).

17. Stephen P. Erie, *Rainbow's End: Irish-Americans and the Dilemmas of Urban Machine Politics* (University of California Press, 1988). The Shakman decrees were court orders initiated by Michael Shakman, an independent candidate for the Illinois Constitutional Convention in 1970 when he filed suit against the Democratic organization of Cook County, which the elder Mayor Daley chaired. A 1979 ruling led to a court order in 1983 that prohibited taking any political factor into account in city hiring. The intent was to outlaw patronage employment in Chicago.

18. Douglas Gills, "Chicago Politics and Community Development: A Social Movement Perspective," in *Harold Washington and the Neighborhoods: Progressive City Government in Chicago, 1983–1987,* edited by Pierre Clavel and Wim Wiewel (Rutgers University Press, 1991), pp. 34–63.

19. Amanda Paulson, "Chicago Scandal Takes Its Toll," *Christian Science Monitor,* August 12, 2005 (www.csmonitor.com/2005/0812/p02s01-uspo.html); Fran Spielman, "City's Hiring Still Not Clean, Monitor Says; 'Subtle Types of Manipulation,'" *Chicago Sun-Times,* December 19, 2007, p. 12.

20. Veronica Anderson, "Equity and Transparency Elusive," *Catalyst Chicago,* May 2007, p. 2.

21. Henry Mendoza, cochair, Chicago United, interview with author, November 26, 1991.

22. Arnold Weber, President of the Civic Committee, to The Honorable Mary Lou Cowlishaw, in *Cowlishaw Papers* (New York, 1997) (in author's possession).

23. David Paulus, Chicago United Education Committee, interview with author, September 30, 1991; B. Kenneth West, chairman of the board, Leadership for Quality Education, interview with author, November 14, 1991.

24. High schools also had one student representative on the council.

25. Mary Sue Barrett, interview with author, June 25, 1997.

26. *Catalyst Chicago,* "Duncan Charts a New Path for Chicago Public Schools," September 2001, pp. 24–29.

27. Paul Vallas, telephone interview with author, September 3, 1997.

28. Richard M. Daley, "Chicago City Government: Smaller in Size, but Greater in Performance," *Business Forum,* January 1, 1994.

29. Vallas, interview.

30. Rosalind Rossi, "Board OKs $48 Million Tax Levy for Schools," *Chicago Sun-Times,* December 18, 1997, p. 20; Rosalind Rossi and Fran Spielman, "School Tax Hike on the Table," *Chicago Sun-Times,* May 23, 2001, p. 6.

31. Aaron Chambers, "CPS Budget Hanging in the Balance," *Catalyst Chicago,* December 2007 (www.catalyst-chicago.org/news/index.php?item=2331&cat=30); John Myers, "CPS Releases 'Keep Afloat' Budget," *Catalyst Chicago,* August 2007 (www.catalyst-chicago.org/news/index.php?item=2234&cat=23).

32. Margaret Blackshire, secretary-treasurer of the AFL-CIO, interview with author, October 27, 1997.

33. James L. Merriner Jr. and Mike Cramer, "The Stealth Boss," *Illinois Issues,* March 1998, pp. 14–17.

34. Simpson and others, *Chicago City Council Report.*

35. John Myers, "Rubber Stamp or Glue?" *Catalyst Chicago,* September 2007, p. 20.

36. Eli Lehrer, "The Town That Loves to TIF," *Governing Magazine,* September 1999, p. 44.

37. Alan Ehrenhalt, "Pleasure and Guilt on Michigan Avenue," Assessments, *Governing Magazine,* July 1999, p. 7.

38. Brett Schaeffer, "Watchdog Group: CPS Capital Plan a Project Wish List," *Catalyst Chicago,* April 2001, p. 23.

39. Steven Alexander, "Black and Latino Coalitions: Means to Greater Budget Resources for Their Communities?" in *The Collaborative City: Opportunities and Struggle for Blacks and Latinos in U.S. Cities,* edited by John L. Betancur and Douglas Gills (New York: Garland Press, 2000), pp. 197–213, 206.

40. Kim Phillips-Fein, "The Still Industrial City: Why Cities Shouldn't Just Let Manufacturing Go," *American Prospect,* September–October 1998, pp. 32–33.

41. John Myers, "Bread and Butter v. Reform Agenda," *Catalyst Chicago,* May 2004, pp. 19–20; John Myers, "Web Extra: Teachers Ratify 5-Year Contract," *Catalyst Chicago,* September 2007 (www.catalyst-chicago.org/news/index.php?item=2267&cat=30).

42. Rosalind Rossi and Fran Spielman, "Daley Backs Board: Mayor Opposes Sham Graduation for 8th Graders," *Chicago Sun-Times,* June 5, 1997, section D, p. 10.

43. Vallas, interview.

44. Vallas, quoted in Amanda Paulson, "In an Era of 'Accountability,' Parents Get Report Cards Too," *Christian Science Monitor,* July 18, 2000, p. 17.

45. Rosalind Rossi, "Parents to Get Grades: Chicago Schools Chief Paul Vallas Wants to Issue Report Cards to Tell Mom and Dad How They Are Performing Too," *Chicago Sun-Times,* May 18, 2000, p. 1.

46. Jenny Nagaoka and Melissa Roderick, *Ending Social Promotion: The Effects of Retention,* Research Report (Chicago: Consortium on Chicago School Research, 2004).

47. Civic Committee of the Commercial Club, "Left Behind," p. 51.

48. The Renaissance Schools Fund, *Free to Choose, Free to Succeed: The New Market of Public Education,* Renaissance Schools Fund Symposium, Chicago, May 6, 2008, p. 3.

49. See the Chicago Public Schools website "Renaissance 2010: 100 New Schools for Chicago" (www.ren2010.cps.k12.il.us).

50. Aaron Chambers, "Web Extra: No Traction on Plan to Strip LSC Powers," *Catalyst Chicago,* May 2007 (www.catalyst-chicago.org/news/index.php?item=2212&cat=30).

51. John Q. Easton, Todd Rosenkranz, and Anthony S. Bryk, *Annual CPS Test Trend Review, 2000,* Research Report (Chicago: Consortium on Chicago School Research, 2001); Melissa Roderick, Brian A. Jacob, and Anthony S. Bryk, "The Impact of High-Stakes Testing on Student Achievement in Promotional Gate Grades," *Educational Evaluation and Policy Analysis* 24 (January 2002): 333–58.

52. Todd Rosenkranz, *2001 CPS Test Trend Review: Iowa Test of Basic Skills,* Research Report (Chicago: Consortium on Chicago School Research, 2002).

53. Anthony S. Bryk and others, *Charting School Reform: Democratic Localism as a Lever for Change* (Boulder, Colo.: Westview Press, 1998).

54. Designs for Change, *The Big Picture: School-Initiated Reforms, Centrally Initiated Reforms, and Elementary School Achievement in Chicago (1995–2005),* Research Report (Chicago, 2005).

55. Brian A. Jacob, "Accountability, Incentives, and Behavior: The Impact of High-Stakes Testing in the Chicago Public Schools," *Journal of Public Economics* 89 (June 2005): 761–96.

56. John Easton and others, *How Do They Compare? ITBS and ISAT Reading and Mathematics in the Chicago Public Schools, 1999–2002,* Research Report (Chicago: Consortium on Chicago School Research, 2003).

57. Designs for Change, "The Big Picture."

58. Allensworth, "Graduation and Dropout Trends in Chicago."

59. Rosenkranz, *2001 CPS Test Trend Review.*

60. Allensworth, "Graduation and Dropout Trends in Chicago."

61. Elaine Allensworth and John Easton, *What Matters Most for Staying on Track and Graduating in Chicago Public High Schools,* Research Report (Chicago: Consortium on Chicago School Research, 2007).

62. John Q. Easton, Stuart Luppescu, and Todd Rosenkranz, *2006 ISAT Reading and Math Scores,* Research Report (Chicago: Consortium on Chicago School Research, 2007), pp. 4–7.

63. Elaine Allensworth, *Ending Social Promotion: Dropout Rates in Chicago after Implementation of the Eighth-Grade Promotional Gates,* Research Report (Chicago: Consortium on Chicago School Research, 2004); Nagaoka and Roderick, "Effects of Retention"; Moore, "Grade Retention Program Fails"; Melissa Roderick, Mimi Engel, and Jenny Nagaoka, *Ending Social Promotion: Results from Summer Bridge,* Research Report (Chicago: Consortium on Chicago School Research, 2004).

64. Nagaoka and Roderick, "Effects of Retention," p. 20.

65. Julia B. Smith, Valerie E. Lee, and Frank M. Newmann, *Instruction and Achievement in Chicago Elementary Schools,* report prepared for the Chicago Annenberg Challenge (Chicago: Consortium on Chicago School Research, 2001); Julia B. Smith, BetsAnn Smith, and Anthony S. Bryk, *Setting the Pace: Opportunities to Learn in Chicago's Elementary Schools,* report prepared for the Chicago Annenberg Challenge (Chicago: Consortium on Chicago School Research, 1998).

66. *Catalyst Chicago,* "School Report Card," special supplement, February 2007.

67. *Catalyst Chicago,* "Reform History: 2004 News Briefs," *Catalyst* online, 2004 (www.catalyst-chicago.org/guides/index.php?id=52).

68. Designs for Change, "The Big Picture."

69. John Myers, "Going to the Head of the Class," *Catalyst Chicago,* May–June 2007, pp. 6–10.

70. Meier, "Structure, Politics, and Policy."

71. Suzanne Kerbow, interview with Karin Sconzert, July 10, 1997.

72. National Research Council, quoted in Jay P. Heubert and Robert M. Hauser, *High Stakes: Testing for Tracking, Promotion, and Graduation* (Washington: National Academy Press, 1998), p. 31.

73. G. Alfred Hess Jr., personal communication with author, April 22, 2003; Dave Newbart and Rosalind Rossi, "Scores Drop at Schools under Tightest Rein: Vallas Says 'Intervention' Won't Be Used at More Sites," *Chicago Sun-Times,* June 6, 2001, p. 12.

74. Between 1996 and 1999, I was a director at the consortium.

75. Anthony S. Bryk and Kim L. Hermanson, "Educational Indicator Systems: Observations of Their Structure, Interpretation, and Use," paper prepared for the Conference on the Research Agenda for Assessing School Reform, Chicago, Consortium on Chicago School Research, March 8, 1991.

76. Melissa Roderick and John Q. Easton, *Developing New Roles for Research in New Policy Environments: The Consortium on Chicago School Research,* Research Report (New York: Social Science Research Council, July 16, 2007), p. 11 (http://nycresearch partnership.ssrc.org/Paper%202.pdf).

77. John Portz, "Boston: Agenda Setting and School Reform in a Mayor-Centric System," in *Mayors in the Middle,* edited by Henig and Rich, pp. 96–119.

78. Chicago education editor, interview with author, October 24, 2003.

79. Shipps, Fowlkes, and Peltzman, "Journalism and Urban School Reform."

80. Greg Hinz, "Executive of the Year: Schools CEO Vallas Goes to the Head of the Class," *Crain's Chicago Business,* June 8, 1998, p. 3.

81. Patricia Graham, interview with author, July 16, 1997.

82. Bruce Upbin, "Chain Saw Paul," *Forbes,* April 6, 1998, pp. 66–68.

83. Anonymous remarks quoted in Shipps, Fowlkes, and Peltzman, "Journalism and Urban School Reform," p. 383.

84. Ronald Gidwitz, interview with author, July 8, 1997.

85. Linda Lenz, interview with author, December 12, 2003.

86. Cleveland newspaper editor for education, interview with author, February 23, 2003.

87. Carl, "Harold Washington"; Mirel, "School Reform, Chicago Style."

88. *Arthur Fumarolo et al.* v. *The Chicago Board of Education et al.,* 142 Ill.2d 54; 566 N.E.2d 1283 (Ill. 1990), 838–39; 1990 Ill. LEXUS 136; 153 Ill.Dec. 177 (1990).

89. West, interview.

90. For example, Cleveland has its own *Catalyst* but nothing equivalent to local school councils or the Consortium on Chicago School Research. Philadelphia has a dedicated and independent research institution in Research for Action but nothing like *Catalyst* or the local school councils.

WILBUR C. RICH

7

Who's Afraid of a Mayoral Takeover of Detroit Public Schools?

Reforming public schools may be analogous to sewing buttons on Jell-O. It does not matter how hard one tries, the buttons will not stay put. So it is with school reform. No amount of grafting and repair seems to have lasting effects. In groping for a more enduring impact on the urban public school crisis it was inevitable that mayors would volunteer, or allow themselves to be drafted by state legislatures, to rescue the school system. Assuming control of the public schools represents an extraordinary opportunity to exemplify mayoral leadership. For generations public school districts have enjoyed structural, if not political, autonomy from city halls.[1] As statehouses turn to big-city mayors to solve the continuing school crises, the traditional wall between city politics and schools has disappeared. Although Americans have endeavored to keep elected municipal politicians out of school administrations, the public has apparently acquiesced to these mayoral takeovers out of widespread frustration with low student achievement scores, fiscal management, and violence in the public schools.

This change in governance and structure reflects a lack of confidence in elected boards and their superintendents. Critics of public schools in the 1990s were particularly harsh.[2] Many have attacked public school professionals as unwitting contributors to the current state of organizational malaise and pedagogic bankruptcy. Even defenders of the public school system have raised questions about the efficacy of school leadership, curriculum shortcomings, and low student achievement scores. Conversely, neither critics nor supporters would have recommended city hall control of public schools as the solution.[3]

Mayoral takeover of schools is not without its perils. In some cities it has worked well; in others the record is mixed. Mayoral takeover's short life in Detroit revealed some of the difficulties a mayor faces in trying to bring about change with a skeptical constituency. Although the takeover law (Michigan Public Law 10) empowered Detroit's mayor to appoint the school board and hold the chief executive officer (CEO) accountable, it did little to change attitudes in the city. Such a radical structural change was expected to shake up the current players in school policy and produce "real school reform." Instead, takeover raised new questions: Would mayor-appointed school boards be independent or just rubber stamps for city hall? If the mayor can fire the CEO, then what is the policy role of the school board? Could city hall control the school budget through the CEO?[4] Could the mayor assume a micromanaging role?

This chapter examines whether the process of the state-mandated mayoral takeover of Detroit schools shaped the legitimacy crisis it encountered. Although the new board appointment process was legal, state law does not confer absolute legitimacy. Replacing an elected school board with one appointed by the mayor represented a fundamental institutional change and as such it needed to be legitimated. If Detroit residents accepted the change as appropriate and just, then the change would have acquired legitimacy. Without this acquired legitimacy, residents would not feel obligated to respect the appointed board or follow its edicts. Moreover, the process of acquiring legitimacy can be contested by what I have called the "public school cartel."[5] To understand how this group reacted to state takeover, a brief description of the political context for the city's public schools is required.

Shrinking City, Dwindling School Enrollments

Detroit has been forced to bear the burden of changing demographics. For the past forty years the city has been shrinking. In 1970 the city had a population of 1,514,063, 43.6 percent of whom were black. By 2000 the population was 951,270, and the black proportion had grown to 81.6 percent. Meanwhile, the school population continues to shrink from its 1960 peak of nearly 300,000 to just over 100,000 in 2007. According to the 2000 census, 26 percent of the residents were living below the poverty line.

The image of the city of Detroit has reflected the course of the automobile industry through its inception, triumphs, and decline. As the quintessential Rust Belt city built on top of an actual salt mine, Detroit is one of the cities that has led the deindustrialization of America. By the 1980s, its heavy-metal economy had lost out to globalization and foreign automobile makers. Detroit can no longer sustain assembly-oriented manufacturing production. Academics have announced that the era of Fordism (assembly line–based work) is over.[6] The postindustrial world has arrived. Since the 1970s, Detroit's city politics, now dominated by African Americans, has shifted its emphasis from being a host community for autoworkers to one fighting to hold on to its population. Detroit has evolved into a has-been city, and a disproportionate percentage of its residents receive some form of welfare.[7]

The transformation of Detroit from a thriving lunch-box working-class city into one with street urchins operating an underground drug economy has taken forty years. On many streets there are abandoned houses and decaying infrastructure. City politicians have attempted to reverse this situation, but redevelopment has been slow and largely unsuccessful. One academic has suggested that trying to change the image of Detroit is like trying to put lipstick on a gorilla.[8]

Yet Detroit remains one of the largest urban school districts in the United States. Most of the students in Detroit's public schools come from low-income families, as exemplified by the high percentage of students eligible to receive free school lunches. Since 1990, the school district has turned over six superintendents. Although every type of school reform measure, from site-based management to charter schools, has been tried, no reform scheme has turned the system around. Like most American inner-city school systems, Detroit Public Schools continues to struggle with recurring fiscal problems and a daunting history of poor student achievement. When mayors in similar cities were given control of the schools, some state politicians thought mayoral takeover was worth trying in Detroit.

Mayors versus the Public School Cartel

In an earlier work, *Black Mayors and School Politics*, I suggested that a coalition of school activists, which I called the "public school cartel," worked as a veto player in the struggle for the school system. I use the term to describe a coalition of professional school administrators, longtime board members, union leaders, and school activists organized for what I see as the protection of the organizational culture and policies of the system.[9] Public school cartels are not cartels in the pure economic sense. However, in its behavior this group of school activists is similar to a cartel. In Detroit, they have maligned school reformers, fought competitors (in the form, for example, of charter schools and vouchers), dictated workplace conditions in union contracts, and harassed superintendents. In addition, they help elect the school policymakers (school boards). For various reasons, these activists come together to fight certain school reform measures. The public school cartel does not meet on a regular basis, nor does it have a single leader. Mobilization is triggered by threats of change, whether real or imagined.

Public school cartel leaders have convincingly made the claim that current school policies are not the source of the school predicament. They have been equally successful in labeling elected politicians as power grabbers and in charging that conservative politicians are trying to divide the black community. Leaders also identify, nurture, and recruit ordinary citizens to their cause. The public school cartel leadership has not been reluctant to remind members that public disagreements invite unwanted attention and interlopers. Unitary interest transcends the particularistic interests of individual members. Group socialization plays an important part in keeping members committed to the ideology of policy commitment.[10] Members are taught that patience has its rewards. The cartel wins most battles by simply waiting out the tenure of its political opponents.

Over the years the public school cartel has fashioned a working relationship with state legislators. Usually the state refrains from interfering with local control of schools. The tacit agreement is that the state will only intervene in cases of fiscal mismanagement, board malfeasance, or scandal.[11] City hall is not party to these agreements. As a result, cartel leaders have few, if any, political obligations to elected mayors, and the mayors feel no particular allegiance to the cartel. Accordingly, mayors in cities like Detroit have criticized the cartel leadership, particularly members of the board of education and sometimes union leaders. Mayoral criticism is expected, but the real threat for the public school cartel is a state-mandated structural change in governance. Since the mid-1990s, state legislatures have been inclined to impose a 1995 Chicago Model school governance system on big cities.[12]

Once a mayor is granted the power to appoint the board and CEO, that power allows him or her an opportunity to assert leadership in the education arena. Leadership style determines how deeply a mayor will go in the school system. James McGregor Burns divides leaders into two types: transformational and transactional.[13] Transformational leaders seek to destabilize existing social and political arrangements, create a new agenda, and change the political attitudes of their followers, whereas transactional leaders are less interested in making fundamental changes and more interested in negotiating and bargaining as a way to resolve disputes. For them, peace in the policy arena is the realization of their policy goals. Change does occur during the tenure of a transactional leader, but it is incremental change. Dennis Archer's and Kwame Kilpatrick's experiences with the Detroit takeover illustrate these two different leadership styles.

Dennis Archer and Detroit Schools

In 2000 the Detroit school system reported that it had 182,332 students enrolled. Today the number is close to 100,000. The overwhelming majority of students are black (91.3 percent), 4.3 percent are white, and 4.4 percent are listed as other. In a 1999 *Detroit News* study, the student-teacher ratio was reported to be twenty-one to one. The district had a 25 percent dropout rate, the average ACT score was 16.7, and the median SAT score 923. The Detroit School District current website reports the average ACT score as 15.4 (2007 data).[14]

Despite these statistics, few cities can match the flamboyance of Detroit school politics.[15] The Detroit Federation of Teachers is arguably one of the strongest and best-led teacher unions in the nation. As the vanguard of the public school cartel, it has won fights over issues such as millage increases and choice of both superintendents and school board members.

Given its record, it seems that Detroit's version of the public school cartel could have prevented the takeover. The 1999 Detroit mayoral takeover represented a breakdown of the tacit agreement that had existed between the school district, the cartel, and the state government. Simply put, the Detroit school takeover was the result of the failure of the public school cartel leaders to maintain their side of the agreement. It could not prevent mismanagement or improve student performance. These failures created an atmosphere that allowed a Republican state legislature to repudiate local control in Detroit's case and to turn over the system to city hall. For several years, elected members of the Detroit school board have engaged in embarrassing board meeting antics and disruptions that have eroded their image as competent trustees. In the past, Mayor Coleman Young, through his fund-raising and endorsements, protected board members from electoral challenges.[16] Mayor Young had enough political clout in Lansing (the state capital) and support in the city to limit state encroachment into the district's affairs. His successor, Dennis Archer, never achieved sufficient political clout to offset state encroachment. This perception was in part a function of his short tenure, rumors of his ambition for higher office, and his leadership style. The journalist Barry Franklin, however, has suggested that Archer's leadership was lacking.

> The takeover offered Archer's African-American rivals the perfect opportunity for expressing their antipathy toward him. Archer's ongoing

problems, particularly the recall attempt, his botched effort to deal with snow removal, and the criticism of his conciliatory approach to addressing city problems have rendered him vulnerable to attacks from his opponents. At the same time, the Mayor's African-American support for the takeover was weak.[17]

City politicians with ambition for higher office often try to avoid risky and embarrassing incidents that may compromise those ambitions. Accordingly, these politicians (for example, former Baltimore mayor Martin O'Malley, now governor of Maryland) take a hands-off approach to school politics. It is also possible that Mayor Archer felt powerless in his dealings with the public school cartel and welcomed state control of the schools in order to make what he believed were essential changes.

A more plausible explanation for the timing of the takeover is related to Republican governor John Engler's attempts to shake up the political situation in Democratic Party–dominated Detroit and unseat the discredited elected board members. In 1996 Engler had suggested a takeover with Mayor Archer, which Archer rejected.[18] Engler also promoted the idea of a takeover in his 1997 State of the State address. At the time, a *Detroit Free Press* poll found a split among Detroit residents on mayoral takeover, 42 percent in favor and 43 percent opposed. In anticipation of the 1999 State of the State address, board of education president Darryl Redmond asserted that the board should plan a series of "revolutionary and unprecedented" reforms for the system.[19] Schools superintendent Eddie Green also opposed the takeover. In his 1999 State of the City address, Mayor Archer expressed reservations about the takeover and asked for more time.

A *Detroit Free Press* poll taken a month later, in early February, found that 54 percent of Detroiters favored mayoral takeover and 32 percent opposed it.[20] Again the governor's State of the State address advocated a mayoral takeover of the schools. He also sent a bill to the state legislature to that effect. Within a week of the governor's speech, Archer changed his position and supported the bill. Barry Franklin believed that a deal negotiated by state senator Virgil Smith to get an additional $15 million for implementing the initiative persuaded Archer to change his position on takeover. Archer told the media that he would "take the bull by the horns."[21]

The Republican-dominated state legislature approved a Chicago-style takeover (Michigan Public Law 10) and gave the mayor the power to appoint the school board.[22] This action occurred after the Democratic legislators from Detroit tried to take the mayor out of the loop and force Governor Engler to directly control the schools. Detroit's thirteen school employee unions, which had supported the Engler plan, turned their allegiance instead to Archer, who had promised not to privatize janitorial, food, and transportation services.

The Detroit school takeover was a politics of deals. As the takeover became inevitable, concerned groups tried to cut separate deals. The dealing behind closed doors was a mix of partisanship, careerism, and personal attacks. Archer told the *Detroit News,* "It got very personal. It got very ugly and it didn't need to go that way."[23]

A Chief Executive Officer for Detroit Schools

Michigan Public Law 10 provided the chief executive officer of schools with the power to fire teachers and principals. The CEO could also waive provisions of union contracts and reconstitute failing schools. The new law also provided for a seven-member board, six of whom were appointed by the mayor and one by the governor. The board had power to appoint the CEO, but the mayor could fire him or her. The governor's representative on the new board was the state superintendent, Arthur Ellis. In effect, the Detroit school district was in partial receivership.

Mayor Archer appointed Freman Hendrix, his deputy mayor, as the chair of the new school board. Other members included New Detroit president Bill Beckman, a businessman; Marygrove College president Glenda Price; community activist Marvis Coffield; the CEO of Mexican Industries, Pam Aguirre; and DaimlerChrysler vice president Frank Fountain. Hendrix resigned in November 2000 and was replaced by Reginald Turner, a lawyer; Frank Fountain replaced Hendrix as chair. Otherwise the board membership remained relatively stable. For all intents and purposes, this was a blue-ribbon board.

The new law required that the board's decision in selecting the CEO be unanimous. Because this board could not agree on a candidate, it appointed an interim CEO, David Adamany, a former president of Wayne State University. Adamany promptly initiated a ten-week building repair program and attempted to install a new payroll management system. These management changes got good reviews, but the Detroit Federation of Teachers also wanted a pay raise. When it was not forthcoming, the members voted to strike. Under a threat of further state intervention, the district and the union settled on a contract that included a pay raise.[24] When the raise was stalled, the union sued the district. Union president John Elliot, who had remained relatively silent during the early part of Adamany's tenure, released a written statement saying, "Enough is enough. We have spent months battling both the ineptitude and intentional foot dragging by [district] administrators. The school system's behavior has been unconscionable."[25] This was the first in a series of attacks he leveled at Adamany.

Acting on a request from CEO Adamany, the state legislature passed a law prohibiting principals and assistant principals from joining unions. Most of the Detroit legislative delegation opposed the new law, calling it "union busting." The new law made principals middle managers.[26] The Detroit Federation of Teachers took its case to federal court and lost. Meanwhile, the new board continued to have trouble agreeing on a permanent CEO. Adamany took himself out of the search early in the process. This left him with some room to change things managerially, but it also shifted the discourse away from him.

The union leadership's general assessment of Adamany's tenure was that he had made minimal impact on the Detroit public school system. In a 2000 interview with this writer, John Elliot, then president of the Detroit Teachers Union, assessed Adamany's short tenure.

> You just don't turn a big old school system around overnight. The average superintendent tenure is about three to five years. Adamany had the same [central office] staff that he inherited. This staff had been there through four superintendents. You need subordinates you can trust and are in agreement with your philosophy. No one person can turn around the system. A general can issue orders but the sergeants must carry them out. [Adamany] did bring in four or five people from the private sector but they had to *be educated in the ways of the school system.* Methodology, strategy, and politics in the school system are different from the private sector.[27]

To succeed Adamany, the board appointed Kenneth Burnley, a Detroit native who had been superintendent of schools in Colorado Springs for thirteen years, as the new CEO. For his leadership and administrative skills, he won the 1993 National Superintendent of the Year Award. Burnley was greeted with great fanfare—a hometown man returning to save the system. He knew city leaders and brought the reputation of a good administrator. Burnley's reputation allowed Mayor Archer to lower his profile in the administration of the school system. In a *Catalyst* article comparing Cleveland, Boston, and Detroit's mayoral takeovers, Archer's role was described as "keeping his distance from school policy" after the new board appointed Burnley.[28] Archer's deputy press secretary, Michelle Zdrodowski, observed, "He has enough on his plate trying to run the 10th largest city in the country." State Treasurer Mark Murphy asserted, "We took all the normal powers of a school superintendent and a board and put them in the CEO position. It is a very strong position."[29] However, Archer's announcement that he would not seek reelection further compromised what leverage he had, real or imagined, in the struggle. Burnley became the face of the school system.

Burnley inherited a $1.5 billion bond construction project to build twenty-one new schools. He also inherited a shrinking school system in terms of enrollment and a budget that bled red ink. Jeffrey Mirel credits Burnley with the completion of a major system audit, contract renewal with Detroit's teachers union, introduction of money-saving practices, and reorganization of the payroll office. The deferred maintenance of Detroit school facilities had left buildings and equipment in disrepair. A new school technology center was established and an upgraded computerized payroll system enabled the teachers to get their checks on time and with correct salary figures. Burnley outsourced management of school maintenance, food service, and technology. The food service program improved so much that it won the Award for Food Quality presented annually by the Physicians Committee for Responsible Medicine.[30]

Burnley also moved the central administration staff from the old Maccabees Mutual Insurance Building to a new facility in the Fischer building, in the city's New Center. The Burnley administration also relocated Cass Tech and Renaissance High schools, the city's two premier public schools. However, it was Burnley's organizational and curriculum improvements that made the biggest impact. Burnley was able to create a strategic plan, spending $1.5 billion on new schools and technology.[31] Twenty-one new schools were built and four hundred new school buses were purchased. Student achievement saw fourth-grade reading scores reach the 70th percentile on the Michigan Educational Assessment Program test.

Burnley's first two years went well, and his performance was reflected in reports by the Detroit press. Yet the latter three Burnley years met with problems because of declining enrollments and state support. The district was sinking in a sea of red ink. For fiscal years 2004 and 2005 there was a $198 million budget shortfall. At the same time, the city's overall budget was facing a $389 million shortfall over three years. Mayor Kwame Kilpatrick, elected in 2001, had to lay off 686 employees and terminated overnight bus service. Burnley had to lay off 372 teachers. Michael Casserly of the Council of Great City Schools called the Detroit situation "the worst crisis of any large school district in the nation."[32]

The opponents of the mayoral takeover never relented in their attacks against it. The attacks became what Mayor Archer called "personal." They attacked both the law and the people associated with it. The text of Michigan Public Law 10 contained a sunset clause, according to which Detroit voters would decide in 2005 whether to continue the reform. With that deadline in mind, the new mayor of Detroit, Kwame Kilpatrick, began a campaign to allow the mayor to select the CEO and to support the idea of an elected board, albeit advisory.

Kwame Kilpatrick and School Reform

Kwame Kilpatrick, a former middle-school teacher at Detroit's Marcus Garvey Academy and state legislator, succeeded Archer. Elected in 2001 at the age of thirty-one, he became one of the nation's youngest mayors. For many political observers, Detroit seemed to be on the verge of a profound generational change as many of the old politicians were being passed over. Kilpatrick grew up in a famous Detroit political family. As the son of Congresswoman Carolyn Check Kilpatrick and Bernard Kilpatrick, a former high-ranking official in Wayne County government, he knew most of the political actors in the city.

As a state legislator, Kilpatrick had called the Republican-backed state takeover of the Detroit board "the injustice of 1999." While minority leader in the statehouse, Kilpatrick had opposed the idea of an appointed board.[33] Five years later, he supported a return to an elected board, albeit advisory, and proposed that city hall be given the power to hire and fire the school CEO. He told a writer for the *American School Board Journal*, "A return to the old board system runs the very high risk of undoing the progress that's been made, condemning ourselves to repeat the mistakes of the past, and forcing future generations to pay the price. That cannot happen."[34] Kilpatrick's proposal for an advisory board also included a provision prohibiting members from running for office while on the board and for one year after they left office.

After taking office, Kilpatrick appointed a new board; only one member of the Archer board was reappointed. Kilpatrick's board members were Geneva Williams, Bill Brooks, Belda Garza, Tom Watkin, and Michael Tenbursch. In an interview, Kilpatrick announced that he would keep current CEO Kenneth Burnley if his proposal were accepted.

In a separate short debate with this writer on Tavis Smiley's NPR radio show, Mayor Kilpatrick repeated his proposal for an elected advisory board.[35] I expressed doubt that such a scheme could work in Detroit. Why would anyone run for a board seat if the mayor had the power to hire and fire the CEO? What powers would such an advisory board have? Besides, the school board is one of the few starter venues for aspiring politicians who lack name recognition.[36]

In 2002 Kilpatrick appointed a blue-ribbon committee, called Redefining Reform, to explore what it would take to transform Detroit's schools. The committee was divided into five study groups. Irvin Reid, the president of Wayne State University, led the subcommittee on academic achievement. Shirley Stancato, the president of New Detroit, a coalition of business and civic leaders, headed up the group on community and corporate involvement. The group tasked with parental involvement was chaired by Larry Patrick, an attorney and former board member of the education coalition HOPE (who had run on a 1988 school reform slate), and Geneva Williams, a current board member. Bill Brooks, the president of the Detroit Board of Education, led the study group on school governance. Based on the school governance group's recommendations, Kilpatrick took a proposal to retain the mayor's power to appoint the CEO and the idea of an advisory elected board to the state. In a 2003 speech to the city, he asserted, "Detroit public schools have been a separate entity with no connection to the Mayor's office. But I have become involved in this because I have a passion for children, a passion for education, and a passion for this city."[37] He allowed that he had paid "surprise visits" to public schools across the city and claimed to have had confidential discussions with teachers and principals.

The state legislature rejected his proposal, and Kilpatrick decided to put it on the ballot (Proposal E) in the 2005 November election. The Detroit Chamber of Commerce, the New Marcus Garvey movement, the Detroit Urban League, and the Black Slate (the political arm of a church called Shrine of the Black Madonna) supported the proposal. Organizations opposed were the Detroit branch of the National Association for the Advancement of Colored People (NAACP), the American Federation of State, County, and Municipal Employees (AFSCME), Keep the Vote, and a group called the Coalition to Defend Affirmative Action, Integration, and Immigrant Rights and Fight for Equality by Any Means Necessary. Also opposed was one-time mayoral candidate and high-profile city council member Sharon McPhail.

Meanwhile Mayor Kilpatrick was in the midst of a miniscandal that threatened his reelection. The controversy involved his lifestyle and the lease of a sport utility vehicle for his family. Nicknamed the hip-hop mayor, his lifestyle was becoming a liability. As his approval ratings waned, Kilpatrick's attention shifted to his reelection campaign. Archer's former deputy mayor and school board chair Freman Hendrix decided to challenge Kilpatrick in the primary. It was a tough campaign, requiring Kilpatrick to admit his mistakes and get character endorsements from church leaders. Nonetheless, in some circles Kilpatrick's competence and ethics were permanently compromised. He spent a lot of political capital in the campaign and had little left to push Proposal E.

In the November 2005 elections, voters approved a measure to return the city to an elected school board. Proposition E was defeated by 65 percent of the vote. Before the election, the Skillman Foundation had conducted a survey and found 74 percent in favor of an elected board.[38] In a 1999 state senate committee hearing on takeover, Helen Moore, a longtime school activist, commented, "How dare you take away our rights as black people to vote. We can solve our own problems."[39] After the defeat of Proposal E, she asserted, "We stopped them [on] Nov. 2. We're going to stop them again. No to Kenneth Burnley, Mayor Kilpatrick and the Chamber of Commerce! Ask Compuware and Ford Field for the money!"[40] Superintendent Burnley did not see the vote as a referendum on his leadership. "For the whole time I was there," he later recalled, "I was considered the governor's [Engler's] appointee. Overriding this [campaign to return to the elected board] was the fact that some Detroiters wanted their vote back. A majority person had taken their vote away, and they wanted it back."[41]

When the new board was elected, it had to hire a new CEO because Kenneth Burnley's contract had run out. During his five-year tenure Burnley had tried to save the system from a fiscal meltdown. Under his leadership, twenty-one schools were built, and many others were renovated. Yet the system's fiscal problems continued. Burnley had to make budget cuts and lay off teachers. When he resigned in July 2005, Burnley alleged, the system had a $62 million fund balance.[42]

A Return to an Elected Board

In 2005 Governor Jennifer Granholm, a Democrat, signed a law that rescinded the 1999 takeover of the Detroit public schools. Governor Granholm appointed a 120-member Detroit Public Schools Transition Team to make recommendations for the new elected board. The transition team recommended, among other things, abolishing charter schools.

The newly elected board then selected William F. Coleman, a former deputy superintendent in Dallas, to be CEO. On August 28, 2006, during Coleman's watch, the teachers voted to strike. The strike got national attention and lasted for two weeks. The district had a $105 million deficit, and the board wanted the union to accept a 5.5 percent pay cut over two years to help close the gap in the district's \$1.36 billion budget. However, the union had gone two years without a raise. Teachers rejected the proposal and, negotiations having failed, went out on strike. After two weeks, the two sides signed a contract that included a one-year pay freeze with small raises in the two following years. Four months later Virginia Cantrell defeated Janna Garrison, the strike leader, for the presidency of the Detroit Federation of Teachers.

Another fallout of the 2006 strike was the firing of William Coleman, the district superintendent. A dispute arose regarding financial irregularities, and on March 8 the election board terminated his contract. They appointed Connie Calloway, the superintendent of schools at Normandy, Missouri, a small community outside St. Louis, to be the new CEO. Calloway took office on July 1, 2007, and faced her first school year the following September.

Takeover and Responses

Any new institutional arrangements must pass the test of legitimacy. Throughout the five years of mayoral takeover in Detroit, the mayor and his supporters were not able to convince Detroit residents that an appointed board, insulated from the electoral system, would yield better school governance and, more important, higher student achievement in the classrooms. As the political scientist James Gibson has suggested,

> In a new political system few resources are more coveted than political legitimacy. Legitimacy is an endorphin of the democratic body politic; it is the substance that oils the machinery of democracy, reducing the friction that inevitably arises when people are not able to get everything they want from politics. Legitimacy is loyalty; it is a reservoir of goodwill that allows the institutions of government to go against what people may want at the moment without suffering debilitating consequences.[43]

The vote to consummate the legitimacy of the appointed board was retrospective, not prospective. The state legislature had given the city five years to make the new board appointment process work and to win public support. The public school cartel and others told Detroit voters that this was their opportunity to recover their voting franchise, a one-time chance to get back what was rightfully theirs. A rational voter could decide that his or her vote was directed at the civil rights issue alone and was not an endorsement of the performance of the school system.

As a result, the outcome of the election was interpreted in a variety of ways. Some saw it as a restoration election, returning the board selection to the people. Others saw it as a referendum on the incumbent mayor's leadership. Still others saw it as sending a message to Lansing regarding home rule and local control. Few saw the vote as the final solution to the Detroit school problem.

It is also noteworthy that both Archer and Kilpatrick had appointed blue-ribbon citizens, not aspiring politicians, to the boards. None of these earlier members was elected to the new board. It is understandable that the winning candidates believed they had more legitimacy than their appointed predecessors.

The elected board had achieved electoral legitimacy but not necessarily command legitimacy, that is, the ability to make knowledgeable decisions based on expertise that would be accepted by the public. Ironically, the mere act of allowing people to vote to legitimate a selection procedure does not automatically confer a mandate on the winning candidate. In the board election, candidates ran as concerned citizens, not as education experts. None of the winners were experts in school governance or student achievement, so once they took office public attention regarding the schools situation shifted away from them. Research has shown that black representation on a school board contributes to a favorable evaluation of schools.[44] In this case, the symbolic ownership of the board may take school policy off the public agenda until there is another major crisis.

Summary

Former superintendent Burnley suggested that "takeover works best when the city is working well. New York City and Chicago were working well. Detroit was experiencing a huge outward migration, massive layoffs in the automobile industry, and school enrollment instability. The population went from 1.9 million in 1970 to 800,000 in 2000."[45] To borrow from an old ad campaign, "This is not your father's Detroit." City politics had transmogrified Detroit's image, and it became easy for journalists and academics to malign the city.[46] Residents may have internalized some self-doubt. As the automobile industry continued to decline in significance, steady and high-paying jobs also disappeared. Detroit was a shrinking city with little hope. As the economy weakened, the city did not have the resources to protect itself from outside political encroachment. Voters could not change the economic dynamics, but they felt that they could prevent the loss of the right to choose the members of the board of education. Fear of mayoral ambition played a minor role in the political discourse.

Archer and Kilpatrick were not the first mayors to covet the control of the school board. Coleman Young wanted control, but the state legislature was not interested in granting him that power. Lacking the popularity and political skill of Mayor Young, mayors Archer and Kilpatrick worked at a disadvantage in dealing with the education cartel. First, it was not clear that either mayor understood how the cartel works, which led to political mistakes and misjudgments. More important, they underestimated the resourcefulness of the public school cartel leadership. A mayor long on ambition but short on time and patience would not survive in the political maze of school politics. Second, CEOs from the outside do not have the time or the know-how to loosen the grip of the cartel over the schools. A reform CEO may need ten years to make lasting change in the system. No CEO had had that amount of time. Time seemed to be on the side of the public school cartel. It can wait out most politicians. Repudiating the work of a CEO is relatively easy, as Detroit's cartel demonstrated with Adamany, Burnley, and Coleman.

The interregnum between Detroit superintendents demonstrates how citizen demands for changes in student performance can be safely ignored. This constant rebuff may have resulted in Detroit's losing faith in its own capacity for school reform. Although it was obvious that some progress was being made under the mayoral takeover, voters were persuaded to return to the elected board. The cartel was able to make the argument that the vote was about the franchise rather than about school reform. When they mixed a racism charge into the election narrative, the voters wanted to send a signal to Lansing.

Moreover, the reaction of the public school cartel to mayoral encroachment varied with the tactics and personalities of the mayor. Both Detroit mayors had reelection issues. Dennis Archer's tenure was threatened with a recall effort and opposition from fellow Democrats. Barry Franklin characterized Archer as "more of a conciliator and more willing to try to work with Detroit's corporate leaders and white suburban communities."[47] Described as having a "frustrating leadership style," Archer was perceived as a transactional leader trying to keep the peace. The takeover of the school system was imposed, and he took a hands-off approach, allowing the state treasurer and superintendent Burnley to assume a public leadership role. As Archer had announced his intention not to run for reelection, the public school cartel regarded him as a lame duck. Besides, an open confrontation with the cartel would have tarnished his image as a political comer on the national scene.

The public school cartel may have perceived Kwame Kilpatrick as more of a threat. Apparently, Kilpatrick envisioned himself as a transformational leader. Having taught in the school system, he had some strong views about pedagogy and administration. He established a blue-ribbon committee, Redefining Reform, to study all aspects of the system. In the same 2003 speech he reminded the public that he had served in the state legislature and stood up against Engler's so-called reform efforts. Yet the voters rejected Kilpatrick's proposal to retain the power to appoint the CEO. Kilpatrick's tenure as mayor and his miniscandal did not engender trust from his constituency. The scandal allowed the media to question whether he should be reelected. It is not uncommon for local reporters to try to link extravagant lifestyle with incompetence.[48] Mayor Kilpatrick became entangled in a megascandal involving a romantic affair with his chief of staff and false statements he admits having made in court. In addition to receiving a vote of no confidence from the city council and being indicted for perjury, he was forced to resign. Kenneth Cockerel Jr. became acting mayor September 18, 2008.

Adamany, Burnley, Coleman, and Calloway were not members of the cartel. They were hired help and proved expendable in a crisis situation. Adamany's success as a university president did not carry over into public school politics. Burnley, a Detroit native, had some credibility when he first took the job, but when the fiscal crisis hit and he had to make layoffs, his political capital was eroded. Scapegoating superintendents for fiscal problems is a common tactic of the public school cartel.[49] The fate of the current CEO, Calloway, is yet to be decided, but the existing enrollment and fiscal condition of the district has not improved since the Burnley era.

This case study of Detroit demonstrates the folly of retrospective citizen participation. If citizen participation in school reform is going to be effective, it must be incorporated into the drafting of a new law. A public forum could have facilitated the legitimacy of the takeover and would have mobilized more support for the new institutional arrangements. Frederick Hess calls for transparency before another proposal for mayoral control is attempted.[50] Prospective citizen participation could be a vehicle for achieving an effective board structure and obtaining legitimacy for it. Even though the state legislators had consciously tried to involve the public through legislative hearings, they were not willing to put their plans prospectively before the voters.

By keeping Detroit voters out of the school reform drafting process, the governor, the state legislature, and the mayor were able to mount a campaign to save the reform. Moreover, Kilpatrick's attempt to salvage the concept of a mayor-appointed CEO played into the hands of the public school cartel. They were able to characterize Proposition E as a power grab. The election of a board seemed a trip back to the future. The background of the newly elected board members resembled the pre-takeover elected board. School politics had come full circle, and Kilpatrick found himself, ironically, as the lone city politician trying to make a case for "partial control" of the school system.[51]

The case study also demonstrates the adaptive strategy of the public school cartel to outside encroachment. The musical chairs played by the board and the superintendents gave the cartel time to regroup and rethink its strategies. Writers like Barry Franklin identify Republican governor Engler's motives in the takeover as pure partisanship. Since Engler did not need black votes, an alliance with Archer could allow his party to further divide state Democrats on the issue. Ironically, the 1999 takeover played into the hands of the Detroit cartel by helping to further politicize an already hyperpoliticized environment. The cartel was able to characterize the motives of state politicians as racist, partisan, and undemocratic. The narrative shifted away from student performance and the district's fiscal problems toward Detroit as a victim of state encroachment.

Franklin's essay, written nine months after the mayoral takeover but not published until 2003, could not have anticipated the collapse of the state initiative.[52] He may be correct about the narrow partisanship and personal ambitions of some of the actors. He was also prescient in pointing out the diminishing power of cities like Detroit in state politics and characterizing the takeover as "largely a black-black conflict."[53] However, Jeffrey Mirel disagreed with Franklin's assessment. He saw the conflict as "a multifaceted struggle marked by fluid alliances that defied traditional categories."[54] For him, there were no unified voices among Democrats and Republicans.

The 2005 gubernatorial election took place after the publication of Mirel's essay. The election of Democrat Jennifer Granholm changed the entire political context of the issue. She was willing to reverse Engler's reform initiative and to support the return of an elected board. In addition, her decision to appoint a large, inclusive transition team was a clever political move. The team, which included many long-standing members of the cartel community, produced a report that supported localism. Fortunately, Governor Granholm dissociated herself from an attempt by the transition team to ban charter schools.

Finally, mayoral credibility can be a legitimating mechanism. A mayor who enjoys widespread support and trust can make fundamental institutional changes that will be accepted by the public. Transformational mayors are more likely than transactional ones to engage in a legitimating endeavor.[55] Nonetheless, the public school cartel could safely return to its old norms within months. To prevent this possibility will take bold transformational leadership. This is unlikely, but I agree with Mirel that a third way is possible. Detroit must find a way to promote compromise among the various school actors. Otherwise, Kilpatrick's prediction that an elected board would be a return to pre-takeover board antics will come true. There also needs to be some type of alternative civic mobilization to push leaders toward real change in the Detroit schools.[56] Given the history and sociology of Detroit, such a radical change seems unlikely.

Notes

1. Michael D. Usdan, "Mayors and Public Education: The Case for Greater Involvement," *Harvard Education Review* 76 (Summer 2006): 147–52.

2. John Chubb and Terry Moe, *Politics, Markets, and American Schools* (Brookings, 1990); Myron Lieberman, *Public Education: An Autopsy* (Harvard University Press, 1993); Wilbur Rich, *Black Mayors and School Politics* (New York: Garland Press, 1996); Jonathan Kozol, *Savage Inequalities* (New York: Crown, 1991).

3. Charles Mahtesian, "Handing the Schools to City Hall," *Governing* 10 (October 1996): 36–40; Richelle Stanfield, "Bossing City Schools," *National Journal* 28 (February 1997): 272–74.

4. Paul T. Hill, "Getting Hold of District Finances: A Make-or-Break Issue for Mayoral Involvement in Education," *Harvard Education Review* 76 (Summer 2006): 158–77.

5. Rich, *Black Mayors and School Politics.*

6. See Ash Amin, *Post-Fordism: A Reader* (Cambridge, Mass.: Blackwell Publishing, 1994).

7. Thomas Sugrue, *The Origins of the Urban Crisis: Race and Inequality in Postwar Detroit* (Princeton University Press, 1996); Wilbur Rich, *Coleman Young and Detroit Politics* (Wayne State University Press, 1989).

8. William J. V. Neill, "Lipstick on the Gorilla: The Failure of Image-Led Planning in Coleman Young's Detroit," *International Journal of Urban and Regional Research* 19, no. 4 (1995): 639–53.

9. Jeffrey Henig and Wilbur Rich, eds., *Mayors in the Middle: Politics, Race, and Mayoral Control of Urban Schools* (Princeton University Press, 2004).

10. Norman D. Kerr, "The School Board as an Agency of Legitimation," *Sociology of Education* 38 (Fall 1964): 34–59.

11. Henig and Rich, *Mayors in the Middle,* p. 176.

12. See Dorothy Shipps, *School Reform, Corporate Style: Chicago, 1880–2000* (University Press of Kansas, 2006).

13. James MacGregor Burns, *Leadership* (New York: Harper and Row, 1978).

14. Data from Detroit School District (www.detroitk12.org.nyud.net/schools/reports/pdfs/district_profile.pdf).

15. Henig and Rich, *Mayors in the Middle.*

16. Rich, *Coleman Young and Detroit Politics.*

17. Barry M. Franklin, "Race, Restructuring, and Educational Reform: The Mayoral Takeover of the Detroit Public Schools," in *Reinterpreting Urban School Reform: Have Urban Schools Failed, or Has the Reform Movement Failed Urban Schools?* edited by Louis F. Mirón and Edward P. St. John, chapter 5 (Albany: State University of New York Press, 2003).

18. Jeffrey Mirel, "Detroit: There Is Still a Long Road to Travel, and Success Is Far from Assured," in *Mayors in the Middle,* edited by Henig and Rich, pp. 120–58, 129.

19. Franklin, "Race, Restructuring, and Educational Reform."

20. Cited in Associated Press State and Local Wire, "Poll: Most Detroiters Support Mayor Taking Over Schools," February 6, 1999.

21. Mirel, "Long Road to Travel," p. 132.

22. Michigan Public Act of 1999, MCLA 380.371.

23. Associated Press State and Local Wire, "Poll: Most Detroiters."

24. Mirel, "Long Road to Travel," p. 132.

25. Brian Harmon, "Detroit Teachers Sue District for Raises and Back Pay," *Detroit News,* November 23, 1999, p. D6.

26. Mark Hornbeck, "Principal Union Hits Detroit," *Detroit News,* December 9, 1999, p. A15.

27. John Elliot, telephone interview with author, April, 6, 2000; emphasis added.

28. Alexander Russo, "Detroit's Archer Keeps Distance from Schools," *Catalyst Cleveland,* May–June, 2001, p. 12.

29. Ibid.

30. Kenneth Burnley, telephone interview with author, September 13, 2007.

31. The additional funds were leftover monies from the 1980 bond issue.

32. Jodi Wilgoren, "Shrinking, Detroit Faces Fiscal Nightmare," *New York Times,* February 2, 2005, p. A12.

33. Mirel, "Long Road to Travel."

34. Glen Cook, "Mayor May Take the Reins in Detroit," *American School Board Journal* 191 (January 2004): 4.

35. This program was aired on January 28, 2004.

36. Rich, *Black Mayors and School Politics.*

37. Kwame Kilpatrick, "Education Reform," televised speech, November 18, 2003 (web.archive.org/web/20031206033741/www.ci.detroit.mi.us/mayor/speeches/Education+Reform+2003.htm).

38. Reported in Chastity Pratt, "Detroit: High Court Upholds Reform School Board," *Detroit Free Press,* February 25, 2003, p. A1.

39. Associated Press, "Michigan Governor's Plan to Reform Detroit School Divides City's Residents; Ditching Elected Board Looks Like Racist Power Grab, Some Are Charging," *St. Louis Post-Dispatch,* February 21, 1999, p. A3.

40. Diane Bukowski, "'We'll Stop Him Again' Say Activists," *Michigan Citizen,* November 27, 2004, p. 1.

41. Burnley, interview.

42. Ibid.

43. James Gibson, *Overcoming Apartheid: Can Truth Reconcile a Divided Nation?* (New York: Russell Sage Foundation, 2004), p. 289.

44. Melissa J. Marschall and Anirudh V. S. Ruhil, "Substantive Symbols: The Attitudinal Dimension of Black Political Incorporation in Local Government," *American Journal of Political Science* 51 (January 2007): 17–33.

45. Burnley, interview.

46. Ze'ev Chafets, *Devil's Night and Other True Tales of Detroit* (New York: Random House, 1990).

47. Franklin, "Race, Restructuring, and Educational Reform."

48. Wilbur Rich, *David Dinkins and New York City Politics: Race, Image, and the Media* (State University of New York Press, 2007).

49. Rich, *Black Mayors and School Politics.*

50. Frederick Hess, "Mayoral Control for Detroit Schools? If So, Do It Right," *Michigan Education Report,* Summer 2007, pp. 1–2.

51. Michael Krist and Fritz Edelstein, "The Maturing Mayoral Role in Education," *Harvard Education Review* 76 (Summer 2006): 158–64.

52. Franklin, "Race, Restructuring, and Educational Reform," p. 114.

53. Ibid., p. 119.

54. Mirel, "Long Road to Travel," p. 144.

55. See Kenneth K. Wong and others, *The Education Mayor: Improving America's Schools* (Georgetown University Press, 2007).

56. See Clarence Stone, "Civic Capacity and Urban Education," *Urban Affairs Review* 36 (May 2001): 595–619.

The New York Experience

PART
III

DIANE RAVITCH

8

A History of Public School Governance in New York City

Public debate should always be informed by a knowledge of history. To know where we are and where we are heading, it is important to know how we got to the present time. This is as true in education as it is in every other realm of public life.

The New York City public schools have an interesting and even fascinating history. Throughout the history of the nation's largest public school system, there has been a constant search by public officials for the right balance among different levels of political authority: the school, the local community, the central board, the borough presidents, the city council, and the mayor. Over the years, the state legislature and city officials have sought to find that balance to ensure both democratic participation by the public in its schools and efficient administration of the schools.

Those who do not know the history of school governance probably think that mayoral control is an aberration. This is not true. In fact, for most of the history of the school system, the mayor appointed every member of the central board of education. Mayoral control typically coexisted with some form of community authority, exercised through local boards that were appointed or elected.

For most of the history of New York City public schools, the typical form of governance consisted of an independent central board appointed by the mayor and local boards appointed by either the mayor, the central board, or other public officials. City officials who sought change in the schools' structure of governance always had to persuade the state legislature in Albany, since the city's public schools are organized by state law. Most legislative changes have been a response to the perception that power had become too centralized or too decentralized.

The Origins of Public Schooling

When did public education in New York City begin? One can choose different moments in time as the point of origin, depending on how one defines public education and whether one is looking at the experience of Manhattan (the original City of New York) or Brooklyn.

According to a cornerstone on a New York University building at the northeast corner of Waverley Place and Washington Square, the first public school teachers were Adam Roelantsen and six others who taught in the schools of the Dutch Reformed Church. Roelantsen arrived in 1633 as New Amsterdam's first schoolmaster and a salaried employee of the West India Company. One history says that he took in washing to supplement his meager salary. Certainly he and the other teachers who followed him had very specific religious duties; they taught catechism, led the students in prayer, and conducted other religious ceremonies in school. The church's schools were free, but because of their sectarian nature they were not the foundation of public education. Although interesting as New York's first free schools, the Dutch Reformed Church's schools did not grow into what we now know as the public education system.[1]

Another contender for the title might be the school opened in 1787 by the Manumission Society of New York for the children of slaves (renamed the African Free School in 1794). The leaders of the Manumission Society included two of the nation's founding fathers, John Jay and Alexander Hamilton. But the African Free School was a charity school open only to the children of slaves (who "have been or may be Liberated") and did not grow into a larger system of public education.[2] In the same category with the African Free School is the school established for poor girls by the Female Association, a group of philanthropic women who belonged to the Society of Friends (Quakers). This school, like the African Free School, was a corporate charity school that did not grow into a larger system of education.

The schools usually considered by historians to be the precursors of free public education on Manhattan Island were established by the Free School Society, beginning in 1805. The legislature granted the society a charter to open a free school to educate the children of the poor and allowed it to receive public funding, along with the city's religious schools. Currently, the city government recognizes the first school opened by the Free School Society as the first public school; a plaque in City Hall Park marking the site of the first school of the Free School Society identifies it as such. But like the plaque at New York University, the one at City Hall Park is misleading. The Free School Society was managed by a private corporation and dominated by Quaker men, many of whom served on the board for more than twenty years. When the society's first free school opened, it was intended for poor children whose parents did not belong to any church and could not afford to send them to a private school. Like the African Free School and the school of the Female Association, the schools of the Free School Society were privately managed charity schools for poor children, not public schools open to all children.

In 1825 the city's Common Council decided that sectarian schools would no longer receive public funding, and the Free School Society was left as the sole agency to provide tax-supported schooling. The following year, 1826, the Free School Society changed its name to the Public School Society and opened its doors to all children, not just children of the poor. After its name change, the society at first charged tuition but abandoned the fees when enrollment fell. In time, the fact that the Public School Society was managed by a private corporation, not by appointed or elected public officials, eventually undermined its legitimacy and led to the society's demise.

The Creation of the Board of Education

Public education in New York City truly began in 1842 with the establishment of the New York City Board of Education, created specifically to resolve a bitter conflict between the Public School Society and the Roman Catholic leadership of the city. The Catholics, led by Bishop John Hughes, considered the Public School Society to be a Protestant public school system and sought equivalent public funding for Catholic schools.

Governor William Seward led the effort to replace the highly esteemed and incorruptible Public School Society as the leading agency of free education in the city on the grounds that its powers were "not derived from the community whose children are educated." He urged the legislature to grant to the people of New York City "what I am sure the people of no other part of the state would, upon any consideration, relinquish—the education of their children."[3]

On April 11, 1842, the legislature established the Board of Education in the City of New York. The central board was composed of thirty-four people—two commissioners of common schools for each of seventeen wards, chosen at a special election; also to be elected in each ward were two inspectors and five trustees to oversee the public schools. Each ward was to be treated as a separate town under state law. Thomas Boese, the first historian of the New York City public school system, has written that the new organization seemed "incoherent, with as many independent boards as there were wards in the city—a complex machinery of trustees, inspectors, and commissioners from all classes of society. . . . With the central board of education virtually dependent upon the dictum of the local ones, with officers of every grade without experience, it would seem a wonder that the new system had not died at its very birth." Its peculiar advantage, wrote Boese, was that "it was based on a DIRECT and IMMEDIATE APPEAL TO THE PEOPLE."[4]

The legislature allowed the schools of the Public School Society to coexist with the new ward school system managed by the elected board of education and the ward trustees. However, by 1853 the Public School Society agreed to turn over its schools to the board of education, which henceforward was the sole agency responsible for overseeing free, tax-supported education for the city's children.

Thus starting in 1842 the public schools of New York City (Manhattan) were governed by an elected central board of education and by elected local trustees (ward boards, which today would be called local community boards). Because each ward was treated as a separate school district, the ward trustees controlled jobs and contracts for the schools in their districts at a time when there was neither a civil service system nor unions. Thus the trustees were free to hire anyone they wanted as teachers, and critics alleged that they tended to favor sisters, cousins, and aunts. The ward trustees had more power over the schools than the central board. By 1848, because of low participation in special elections, the school board elections were merged with the general elections.

Unlike Manhattan, the neighboring city of Brooklyn never had public schools run by a private corporation. Instead, it had a strong tradition of local control, known as the "local committee tradition." The town of Brooklyn was incorporated as a city in 1834. The following year, the legislature determined that the Common Council of Brooklyn should appoint three trustees to manage each public school, and each school was treated as a separate district. In 1843 the legislature created a board of education for the city of Brooklyn, composed of representatives from each school district. But the central board never had the power of the local committees, which controlled hiring and promotion of teachers, repairs, and other matters concerning each school. Again, with no civil service protections and no union, teachers served at the whim of local trustees.

Over the next half century, the size of the central board of education in Brooklyn fluctuated—from twenty-eight to thirty-three—and the power to appoint members of the central board shifted from the Common Council to the mayor (in 1882). What did not change was that each school continued to be run by a school committee of three persons. Defenders of the local committee system said that it kept the schools close to the people. Reformers, however, despised the local committee system, claiming that it was controlled by Democratic bosses and that jobs were bought and sold. Nonetheless, the local committees remained intact until 1902, when the whole city school system was reorganized.

Meanwhile, back in the City of New York, the elected board of education and elected local school boards continued to manage the public schools until the 1860s. In 1864 the legislature reduced the size of the board of education from forty-four members, elected by wards, to twenty-one, elected by districts (between 1842 and 1864, the number of wards had increased from seventeen to twenty-two). The trustees continued to be elected in each ward and retained the power to appoint teachers and janitors; for the first time, their choices for principals had to be submitted for the approval of the central board. The mayor gained power to nominate the inspectors of schools for each district, subject to confirmation by the board of education. This was the first time the mayor was permitted by law to select school officials, albeit subject to the central board's approval.

The Tweed Ring Gains Control of the Schools

That legislation, however, was trivial compared with the changes that lay ahead for the board of education in the next few years. Reformers and civic leaders kept up a steady din of criticism of the public schools and the men who ran them. Reformers complained about corruption, extravagance, and inefficiency, about the ties between ward trustees and Tammany politicians, and about the character and morals of the men who were elected as ward trustees and members of the board of education. Critics of the system derided the trustees as saloon keepers and illiterates.

School reformers launched a drive in 1867 to abolish the entire system of governance and to replace the elected boards with a paid commission appointed by the governor. Their hope was to turn control over to an independent, nonpartisan Metropolitan Board of Education. The *New York Evening Post,* affiliated with the Democratic Party, opposed the state takeover, saying that it "would remove even the modicum of interest now felt by the people in regard to the education of their children, by placing the control where the people have nothing at all to do with the schools." The *Post* proposed that the school system be turned into a department of the city government, run by a commissioner appointed by the mayor. Anti-Tammany forces, however, were unwilling to turn the school system over to the mayor to do with as he wished. Lacking any strong popular support or organizational backing, the bill proposing a state agency to run the schools failed. Tammany Hall was relieved; on the eve of its complete takeover of city politics, it did not want any municipal agencies turned over to the state.[5]

William Marcy Tweed was quite familiar with the school system. "Boss" Tweed was elected to the city's board of education in 1855. Over time he held many other elected positions, the most significant being a seat on the city's board of supervisors, which controlled the finances of various city departments. In 1863 he was selected as Grand Sachem of the Tammany Society, also known as Tammany Hall, which was the Democratic Party's political machine. The following year, he was chosen by the Seventh Ward school board to fill a vacancy as a ward trustee. In 1868 he was elected to the state senate, where he took charge of legislation that was important to Tammany Hall. In the same year, Tammany managed to elect the governor, the mayor, and the city comptroller.

With Tammany's power secured, the stage was set for the "reform" of the public school system. In March 1869 Tweed introduced legislation to dismiss the elected board of education and to replace it with an interim board of twelve, appointed by the mayor. The legislation promised that within the next eighteen months, an election would be held to choose a new board. Most of the daily newspapers opposed the plan. The *New York Times* warned that the scheme would allow the Tammany organization to dominate the schools, use them for patronage, and compel teachers and other employees to contribute to Tammany Hall's candidates. Nonetheless, the legislature passed the bill on April 30, 1869.[6]

Tammany's handpicked mayor, A. Oakey Hall, promptly announced his dozen appointees. The new board compliantly awarded contracts to firms connected to the Tweed Ring; it eliminated all textbooks published by Harper Brothers because of attacks on Tweed in *Harper's Weekly* by the caricaturist Thomas Nast. In the spring of 1871, to avoid the promised election of a new board of education, Tweed introduced a proposal in the legislature to abolish the board of education and convert it into a department of the city government. His proposal passed.

For the first time, complete control of the public schools was centralized in the mayor, who had the power to appoint all school officials, including ward trustees and inspectors. The popular election of ward trustees was eliminated. Under the new act, they were appointed by the mayor for a five-year term.

The trustees would not serve out those terms, however. The Tweed Ring's corruption—its use of its political power to loot the city treasury, award contracts for personal gain, inflate bills, and line the pockets of its friends—was exposed in the fall of 1871 and the empire built by Boss Tweed soon was disassembled.

The Restoration of the Board of Education

In 1873 the legislature passed a law reestablishing an independent board of education, along the lines of the district system of 1864. But the new school system had one major difference from the past: no school official would be chosen by election. Nor were school officials permitted to hold any other public office. The new board of education contained twenty-one members, appointed by the mayor. The board had the power to appoint five trustees in each ward, and the mayor appointed three inspectors in each of the city's seven districts. The local trustees had full power to appoint teachers and janitors; their choices for principal were subject to the approval of the central board. The local trustees were more powerful than the central board as they not only hired teachers but also selected sites for new buildings and awarded contracts for fuel, books, and other supplies. The job of the district inspectors was to oversee the work of the ward trustees; they countersigned all bills and payrolls, and their approval was necessary to remove a teacher. The single greatest power of the restored central board was to select local trustees.

In the board of education's annual report for 1878, the law of 1873 was described as follows:

> The controlling principle in this return to the former system was to remove the schools from political supervision. The erection of the Board of Education into a department of the City government brought it necessarily into so close a contact with the influences almost inseparable from the municipal administration, that it could not fail, sooner or later, to become an instrument of partisan aggrandizement and power. ... It became an exaggeration of conservatism to place the whole organization in the hands of a single individual.[7]

This system of governance, adopted in 1873, was essentially mayoral control, inasmuch as the mayor appointed the central board and the inspectors, and the central board appointed the local trustees. This balance survived for another quarter century, until a new reform movement arose in the mid-1890s.

The Reform Movement of the 1890s

The school reform movement of the 1890s sought to eliminate political influence from the public education system. It objected to the powers of the local trustees. Its leaders wanted a centralized school system in which most power was vested in experts in pedagogy. Reformers complained that the local trustees were too political and lacked the competence to run the schools in their ward; the defenders of the existing system included teachers as well as trustees and inspectors.

The reform movement was successful. In 1896 the state legislature passed a law eliminating the trustees and preserving the inspectors. It also created a powerful board of superintendents, which consisted of the city superintendent of schools and his deputies. This latter body was empowered to manage the schools and to select principals and teachers, subject to the approval of the board of education. The twelve-member board was authorized to divide the city into no fewer than fifteen inspection districts. The mayor would appoint five inspectors for each district, who were responsible for visiting the schools and reporting on their condition and on the efficiency of their teachers.

With the consolidation of Greater New York in 1898, the boards of education in New York (Manhattan) and Brooklyn ceased to exist. The former became the School Board for the Boroughs of Manhattan and the Bronx, and the latter the School Board for the Borough of Brooklyn. The members of these boards were allowed to serve out their terms; after they departed, the mayor appointed new members to replace them. In January 1898 Robert Van Wyck, the mayor of the newly consolidated metropolitan New York City, appointed school boards for Richmond and Queens, each with nine members. Each school board selected delegates to serve on a new central board, which consisted of eleven members from Manhattan and the Bronx, six from Brooklyn, and one each from the two remaining boroughs. The total on the central board was nineteen. A board of examiners was created to establish qualifications for teachers and other employees and to issue licenses to qualified applicants. The board of examiners was hailed as the cornerstone of the merit system because applicants for jobs as teachers or supervisors were required to pass tests to prove their competence (seventy years later, however, the tests came under legal challenge by civil rights groups because of disparate pass rates for different racial groups, and the board was eventually abolished).

The Brief Trial of Borough School Boards

For four years the city had four borough school boards, each responsible for its own schools. The New York City charter permitted Brooklyn to preserve its system of local committees, in which each school was managed by a committee of three. The central board was responsible for financial affairs, site selection and construction, examination of teachers, and purchasing and distribution of supplies. The city superintendent had the right to visit any school but not to interfere with its operation. There were frequent conflicts between the central board, which was Manhattan dominated, and the borough boards (especially Brooklyn). Critics complained that with each borough establishing its own course of study, there was a lack of uniformity in educational matters. There were complaints too about duplication of labor and the difficulty of fixing responsibility and accountability.

The first city superintendent was William Henry Maxwell, who had risen through the Brooklyn system to become the superintendent of Brooklyn schools. Because of his intimate knowledge of the deeply politicized Brooklyn system, he worked to remove all partisan influences from the public schools. He was chosen as superintendent for the entire city of New York in 1898 and served for twenty years. Because of his effectiveness in running the new school system, he won recognition as a national leader in education. Throughout his career as head of the New York City system, he staunchly opposed political interference in the running of the schools.

By 1901 the growing volume of criticism of the borough system convinced the legislature to abolish the borough boards and establish a single board of education for the entire city school system. This board consisted of forty-six members, all appointed by the mayor. Twenty-two were from Manhattan (two less than a majority, so that Manhattan could no longer control the entire city system), fourteen were from Brooklyn, four from the Bronx, four from Queens, and two from Staten Island. The board of education was directed to divide the city into forty-six local school districts, corresponding to the number of members on the board of education. The city charter provided that each local school district would have a local school board of seven members, five appointed by the borough president, one member of the central board chosen by the president of that board, and the district superintendent assigned to the district by the city superintendent.

The local school boards had no power to appoint teachers. Their primary responsibility was to inspect the schools in their district and report to the central board on their condition and progress. They also had the authority to report on the need for additional schools and to recommend sites for new schools.

The Maxwell Era

The city charter expanded the powers of the city superintendent, and Maxwell became the chief executive of the school system and the head of a powerful board of superintendents. All education decisions were placed in the hands of the board of superintendents. They set the rules for graduation and promotion; they established the qualifications for teachers; they recommended textbooks and courses of study; they determined the syllabuses for various subjects taught in school. Under the reorganization of 1902, professional educators took charge of education, the central board made policy decisions, and the local boards inspected the schools in their district.

Mayor Seth Low—a former mayor of Brooklyn and president of Columbia University—appointed the new board in January 1902. This board elected an executive committee of fifteen with power to award contracts and make decisions on behalf of the whole board. Under the brilliant educational leadership of city superintendent William Henry Maxwell, the New York City Board of Education embarked on a remarkable era of reform, innovation, and expansion. The most pressing need of the public schools, because of heavy immigration from Europe, was to increase the number of places for students. In the first three years after the establishment of the new system, new buildings and additions were constructed, adding one hundred thousand new seats. Several new high schools were opened, including Stuyvesant in Manhattan, Morris in the Bronx, Erasmus Hall in Brooklyn, Bryant in Queens, and Curtis in Staten Island. The number of kindergarten classes, school libraries, evening schools, summer schools, recreation centers, and playgrounds rapidly grew, as did lecture programs for adults (which reached more than a million adults each year).

Changes in Board Composition

In 1917, at the urging of Mayor John Purroy Mitchel, the legislature reduced the size of the board of education from forty-six to seven. Mayor Mitchel believed that the board was too large to be efficient, and he also had plans to reorganize the curriculum of the schools. His proposal to reduce the board size was defeated in the legislature in 1915 and 1916 but passed in 1917. That year, however, Mitchel faced Tammany candidate John Hylan in the general election. Hylan claimed that Mitchel planned to turn the public schools over to the Rockefeller Foundation, which represented the interests of an arrogant upper-class clique. Hylan won a smashing victory. In 1918 he selected the new seven-member board of education, abolished Mitchel's educational reforms, and launched a major building program to reduce overcrowding. Hylan's ambitious school construction initiative added nearly half a million seats during the 1920s.[8]

Nearly four decades passed without another significant change in governance. In 1961 state investigators uncovered a scandal in the bureaucracy involving payoffs and bribes to mid-level officials overseeing the school construction program. Governor Nelson Rockefeller called the legislature into special session; it removed the board of education and directed Mayor Robert Wagner to choose a new nine-member board drawn from nominations made by a screening panel of civic and educational leaders. The legislature also urged a strengthening of local school boards; henceforth, they would be appointed by the board of education, not the borough presidents. The new board consisted of nine prominent citizens and was usually divided equally among Catholics, Protestants, and Jews—by custom, not by law.

The Origins of Decentralization

This system of governance—a central board of education appointed by the mayor and local school boards appointed by the central board—lasted until 1969. Beginning in 1966, angry protesters in minority communities—dissatisfied with the quality of education in their schools—demanded racial integration or community control. The board of education authorized the creation of three small demonstration districts to test the concepts of decentralization and community control. Asserting control, the Ocean Hill–Brownsville district dismissed a group of teachers in the spring of 1968, triggering a series of lengthy teachers' strikes, which paralyzed the school system that fall.

Faced with an explosive social climate in the city and a variety of plans to decentralize the schools, the legislature reorganized the school system in 1969. The new law sharply reduced the power of the mayor in the selection of the board of education. It replaced the existing board with a paid, five-member interim board, one member appointed by each borough president. This board was supposed to be replaced a year later by an elected board (one member elected from each borough) along with two members appointed by the mayor. However, the election never took place because of a court ruling that the proposed board would give equal representation to boroughs of vastly different populations. So the board consisted of seven members—five appointed by the borough presidents and two appointed by the mayor.

The 1969 law empowered the interim board to divide the city into thirty to thirty-three school districts with roughly equal numbers of pupils. It provided for the election of community school boards by proportional representation. It granted substantial power to community boards to control the elementary and junior high schools in their districts; high schools remained under the control of the central administration. The community boards had the power to select their superintendents as well as to approve or veto the superintendent's choice of principals. (In 1996, after numerous complaints about the local boards, the legislature removed the local boards' power to appoint and remove community superintendents and gave it to the chancellor).

The 1969 law directed the board of education to appoint a chancellor with broad powers, including the power to suspend or remove a community school board for failing to comply with the law, rules, or regulations of the city board. It reduced the authority of the board of examiners, permitting the lowest 45 percent of schools to hire teachers who had passed an alternate examination; the role of the examiners was whittled away by court rulings, and the board was finally abolished by the legislature in 1990.

Debating Decentralization

Decentralization had its supporters and its critics. On one hand, it satisfied some of those who demanded greater involvement of parents and community members. Participation in school board elections was persistently low, never exceeding 10 percent of eligible voters, and critics charged that, because of the low turnout and lack of voter information, the boards were easily captured by organized groups.

Over the years of decentralization, criticism of that system of governance escalated. From time to time, a community school board became embroiled in political or financial scandal, with board members accused of various forms of corruption, such as selling jobs, taking kickbacks for contracts, and using their budgets for patronage to friends and relatives. Across the city, achievement varied widely, from relatively affluent and successful districts like District 26 in Queens and District 2 in Manhattan to districts at the other extreme, where poverty and low student achievement were typical. Graduation rates differed strikingly by race and ethnicity, and employers in the city regularly complained about the poor skills of high school graduates.

The board of education was frequently attacked by critics for its seeming lethargy and lack of focus. Its seven members were appointed by six different elected officials, and it appeared to be incapable of forging a clear agenda for improving the school system. Over the thirty-two years of decentralization, the city's mayors had a dualistic view of the board of education. On one hand, some complained about their inability to take control of the board; on the other, the problems caused by poverty and demography seemed so intractable that mayors may have been glad to be insulated from responsibility for them. It should be noted that the mayor was never powerless during decentralization; in addition to having two votes on the seven-member board and the ability to coax allies to vote with him on the choice of a new chancellor or some other important issue, the mayor controlled the board's purse strings through the city budget. At no time was the mayor a powerless bystander.

Nonetheless, the sense of frustration grew keenly during the mayoralty of Rudy Giuliani, who frequently excoriated the bureaucrats at the board of education and even recommended that its headquarters at 110 Livingston Street in Brooklyn be "blown up" or sold. He wanted to regain the power to appoint every board member, but the Democratic-controlled legislature was not about to cede power to this Republican mayor.[9]

The Return of Mayoral Control

The next mayor, elected in 2001, was Michael Bloomberg, who had promised in his campaign to gain control of the public schools and to be accountable for improving them. After his election, Mayor Bloomberg persuaded the legislature to reconstruct the governance of the city school system. Legislation passed in 2002 abolished the board of education, along with the elected local community school boards. The law turned the school system into an arm of city government. The legislature granted the mayor unfettered power to name the chancellor, who reported solely to him, and the chancellor appointed all other officials.

The statute created an education panel, consisting of eight members appointed by the mayor (including the chancellor), five appointed by the borough presidents, and two nonvoting students. This panel, however, is in no way equivalent to the old central board, as its members serve at the pleasure of the mayor and the borough presidents who appoint them. On the only occasion on which a majority of its members planned to vote in opposition to the mayor's wishes, three were removed from the panel on the day of the vote—two by the mayor and one by a borough president. (At issue was a controversial mayoral plan to end "social promotion," which passed easily after the three dissenting members were replaced.) Unlike the board of education, the Panel for Educational Policy is not an independent decisionmaking body. By statute, the panel is not permitted to exercise any executive powers or to perform any executive or administrative functions.

As part of his effort to remake public education, Mayor Bloomberg sold the board of education's headquarters in Brooklyn to a real estate developer and moved the headquarters of the new Department of Education to the building adjacent to City Hall in Manhattan. In one of those delightful ironies of history, the new department of education settled into the Tweed Courthouse, an elegant building erected by the all-powerful Tweed Ring at the height of its power. Whereas the previous board of education was popularly referred to as one-ten, with reference to its physical location (110 Livingston Street), the shorthand name for the new Department of Education is simply "Tweed." In another of history's ironies, the new department was relocated to a building constructed by an administration that had also turned the independent board of education into a municipal department.

The Lack of Checks and Balances

With the elimination of the central board of education as the governing agency, there is no longer any deliberative public body that holds open hearings about important decisions affecting education policy or budget and has the power to change executive decisions. The Panel for Educational Policy is widely perceived as a rubber stamp for decisions made by the chancellor and the mayor; it takes the power to change those decisions. In many instances, the chancellor has made major decisions and then told the Panel for Educational Policy what was decided.

The Department of Education has attempted in a number of ways to compensate for the absence of any meaningful parental or community involvement by appointing a chief family engagement officer; by convening meetings of community education councils; and by hiring parent coordinators for every school. None of these efforts, however, appears to have changed the perception of parent activists that they do not have a seat at the table when decisions are made; they are informed but not consulted about decisions that affect the well-being of their children.

The current system of governance must be judged in the light of history. Has it effectively met the historic challenge of ensuring both democratic participation by the public in school policy and efficient administration of the schools? Much has been written elsewhere about specific policies enacted since 2002, such as small schools, social promotion, and charter schools, and about student outcomes, such as test scores and graduation rates. These issues have been debated in the press. However, they are not the subject of this chapter.

What seems unquestionable is that the current system provides extremely limited opportunities for democratic participation in school governance, more so than at any time in the history of public schooling. The elimination of all public boards—both central and local—has left the public with no forum in which to question policies before they are adopted. It may be that democratic participation sometimes gets in the way of fast decisionmaking, but our constitutional form of government was designed to guarantee that the public and its representatives would be involved in the decisionmaking process, even at the cost of slowing it down. The absence of any meaningful checks and balances is a dubious proposition, whether applied to a public or a privately managed institution.

In addition, it would be inadvisable to ignore the clear lessons of history that schools must be insulated, to the greatest extent possible, from the partisan battles, patronage seeking, favoritism, and ambitions of parties and politicians. Even if such insulation is difficult, it is still a worthy ideal to strive for.

As one surveys the history of public education in New York City, it seems safe to say that the purpose of the public schools is not the same as that of the Sanitation Department or the Police Department or the Consumer Affairs Department. The public schools have a unique responsibility for children and thus an unusual responsibility to involve the parents of these children in reviewing and discussing of decisions that affect their children. This responsibility requires a greater degree of public engagement than is customary or necessary in other city agencies.

Issues for the Legislature

The education questions facing New York's state legislature in 2009, then, will be the same questions that have confronted the legislature since the early years of the nineteenth century. What is the right balance among the different levels of government? If the mayor controls the schools, what are the best ways to establish appropriate checks and balances on his or her exercise of that power? How can the public be assured that data about test scores and graduation rates are accurately reported? Which decisions should be made by the school, the local community, or the citywide agency? What is the best way to involve parents and local communities while still maintaining effective administration and equality of educational opportunity across the city schools? What governmental arrangements are likeliest to involve the citizenry in democratic discussion focused on the well-being and education of the rising generation?

Notes

1. A. Emerson Palmer, *The New York Public School* (New York: Macmillan, 1905), p. 3.

2. Ibid., p. 13.

3. William O. Bourne, *History of the Public School Society* (New York: William Wood, 1870), pp. 498–500.

4. Thomas Boese, *Public Education in the City of New York* (New York: Harper Brothers, 1869), p. 69; emphasis in original.

5. Diane Ravitch, *The Great School Wars: New York City, 1805–1973* (New York: Basic Books, 1974), p. 90.

6. Ibid., pp. 88–99, describes the period in which the Tweed Ring took control of the New York City public schools.

7. Palmer, *The New York Public School*, p. 164.

8. Ravitch, *The Great School Wars*, p. 223.

9. Quoted in Eric Lipton and Abby Goodnough, "Giuliani Leads New Effort to Take Control of the Schools," *New York Times*, December 7, 2000.

CLARA HEMPHILL

9

Parent Power and Mayoral Control: Parent and Community Involvement in New York City Schools

For more than one hundred years, New Yorkers have debated how best to educate the city's children. Is public education best left to paid professionals who, free from political pressure, work strictly in the interests of the children? Or should parents and community members have a role in deciding what children learn, how budgets are allocated, who is assigned to which school, and who is hired? The pendulum has swung between these two competing ideologies: community control of schools, which brings with it complaints of patronage and corruption, and centralized control, which shuts out parent and community voices even as it brings a level of professionalism to education.

In the nineteenth century, local wards controlled the schools. Reformers at the end of the century, reacting against the machinations of Tammany Hall, pressed for a highly centralized, professional school system, free of political influences. A central board of education controlled schools from the end of the nineteenth century to the middle of the twentieth century.[1] Then, at the beginning of the civil rights movement, the pendulum began to swing back toward community control, in response to the utter failure of the formally apolitical, centralized board of education to respond to community demands for desegregation and racial justice.

In the years following *Brown* v. *Board of Education,* the 1954 U.S. Supreme Court decision outlawing segregation, civil rights leaders, black and Puerto Rican parents, and white liberals in New York City pressed for measures that would stop the creation of segregated schools and encourage integration of existing schools. Despite the board of education's own policy pronouncements favoring desegregation, however, a massive, unresponsive centralized

187

bureaucracy resisted meaningful attempts at integration. As David Rogers argues in his 1968 book *110 Livingston Street,* the New York City public schools actually became more segregated between 1960 and 1965, partly because middle-class whites left the city for the suburbs but also because new schools were built in racially segregated areas rather than in "fringe" areas— on the boundaries between white and black neighborhoods. Attendance zones were drawn in a way that ensured that schools would remain segregated, even when housing patterns might have allowed integration. Even attempts at voluntary integration through open enrollment—a policy that allowed black and Puerto Rican children to transfer from their neighborhood schools to empty seats in white schools—were thwarted by the central board.[2]

Legislation in 1961 created local advisory boards, appointed by the central board of education, which were supposed to make the bureaucracy more responsive by providing an avenue for community members to air their concerns. But members of these boards complained that they were powerless and that the members of the central board of education ignored them.

"When you deal with them, you feel like their hearing aids are turned off," Rogers quotes a local school board member as saying of the central board. "It's such an enormous operation, like throwing spitballs at Gibraltar." The multilayered bureaucracy seldom responded to community pressures, and parents with legitimate complaints were left with nowhere to take them.[3]

By the end of the 1960s, black activists had largely abandoned attempts at integration. So many whites had left the city for the suburbs that large-scale integration had become nearly impossible. Furthermore, with the rise of the black power movement, many community activists believed that fighting for high-quality neighborhood schools, whatever their racial makeup, was more important than fighting for integration per se. These activists argued that schools controlled by local community members held the most promise not only for better education but also for the increased hiring of black and Puerto Rican principals, teachers, and school aides to teach black and Puerto Rican children.

Decentralization

Huge political battles—including a divisive teachers strike in 1968 that pitted a mostly white teachers union against black parents who wanted the power to hire people they felt shared their aspirations for their children—led to compromise legislation in 1969 that gave control of elementary and junior high schools to thirty-one (later thirty-two) locally elected community school boards. The high schools, however, remained under the jurisdiction of the central board of education. These community school boards had considerable powers to draw up zoning lines, appoint a superintendent, hire principals, and set education policy for each community.

In the beginning, Rogers and Norman Chung write in the 1983 sequel, *110 Livingston Street Revisited,* there was a sense of optimism that these school boards might succeed where the central board had failed. The first elected school boards had a "sense of mission," and their members "tended to be very dedicated, and they spent long hours on board affairs." Soon, however, parent-oriented community school board members were replaced by those supported by "the teachers' union, by political clubs, by parochial school groups and anti-poverty groups," and the boards "became more narrowly 'political' in the sense of looking out for these group interests." The unions wanted job security for their members and the political groups and antipoverty groups wanted patronage, while the religious groups worked to ensure that Roman Catholic and Jewish schools received their share of federal funds. Turnout at school board elections was consistently low, making it easy for small but well-organized groups to win seats.[4]

The fiscal crisis of the mid-1970s dealt a further blow to the prospects for viable parent and community engagement. With budgets slashed and thousands of teachers laid off, the New York school system struggled to maintain even minimal levels of service. Moreover, school boards, armed with the power to hire superintendents and principals, were plagued with reports of cronyism and patronage. Overall, it seemed, most parents had gained no more access or control over the schools than they had before. A 1987 report by the Public Education Association, a civic organization, notes that "the increase in parent and community involvement in education envisioned by proponents of decentralization failed to materialize." The report adds that parents found "many schools and districts continue to be inhospitable and unsympathetic to their concerns."[5]

In districts that included both middle-class and poverty areas, the middle class was generally overrepresented on the school boards. District 22, covering a large swath of Brooklyn from Mill Basin to Midwood, maintained an all-white board for many years, even as black and Hispanic students became the majority of the school population. For more than a decade, Ronald Stewart, an African American school parent, ran unsuccessfully for election to a seat on the all-white school board in District 21, encompassing Bensonhurst and Coney Island in Brooklyn; each time he tried to run, he said, opponents successfully challenged his nominating petitions.

Nonetheless, in some districts the community boards served a useful function. The Public Education Association's 1987 report notes that "election to local boards afforded minority groups a degree of political representation that was previously unavailable in the school system." The association maintained that "poor, minority, low-achieving school populations have achieved dramatic gains" in at least three districts: District 4 in East Harlem, District 1 on the Lower East Side, and District 13 in northern Brooklyn.[6]

Some districts, particularly those serving the middle class, flourished under local control. District 26 in northeast Queens maintained consistently highly regarded schools. Beginning in the late 1980s, District 2 on Manhattan's East Side became a national model for excellent public education, drawing on a national pool of talented teachers who flocked to the district, even taking pay cuts from suburban jobs, to be part of an exciting experiment.

Local control meant districts could experiment, and starting in the 1970s some, including District 4 in East Harlem, used their autonomy to create well-regarded alternative schools, such as Central Park East. A number of school boards, responding to parent pressure, opened alternative schools where parents were welcomed in the classroom, including the Bronx New School in District 10, the Brooklyn New School in District 15 in Park Slope, the Muscota School in District 6 in upper Manhattan, and the Manhattan School for Children in District 3 on the Upper West Side. District 1 on the Lower East Side created a network of parent-friendly progressive schools that were racially integrated and served a range of families of different income levels. District 3 on the Upper West Side and District 22 in Brooklyn responded to the concerns of parents of high-achieving children by creating gifted-and-talented programs in neighborhood schools. Although some complained that these programs created racial or class divisions within schools, others defended them because they kept middle-class families in the school system.[7]

These modest examples of school boards' responsiveness to parents' concerns did not dominate the headlines in the late 1980s and early 1990s. Rather, news coverage of the schools centered on the "culture wars" that raged as school boards debated sex education and the board of education's so-called Children of the Rainbow curriculum that promoted tolerance toward gays and lesbians (and included in a bibliography of recommended readings the book *Heather Has Two Mommies*). Resisting mandates from the central board, some districts offered sex education that stressed abstinence and refused to teach tolerance toward homosexuals.[8]

Reports of nepotism and corruption in as many as one-third of the school districts also dominated the news coverage. School board members were

accused of hiring unqualified friends, relations, and political supporters—
sometimes in exchange for bribes. A 1989 *New York Times* article reported that
the superintendent of District 27 in southeast Queens, Coleman Genn, had
used a hidden tape recorder to record a school board member's demand that
Genn hire eleven friends and political supporters to unnecessary jobs as para-
professionals.[9] A principal in District 12 in the Bronx, forced to resign for
selling poor students junk food at a profit, tried to get her job back by paying
a $2,000 bribe to a school board member in 1993, according to the *New York
Times*.[10] An independent probe by a special investigator for the schools, Ed
Stancik, claimed that principals in the Bronx were required to pay homage to
the superintendent by selling tickets to political fund-raising parties; some
administrators were asked to plant flowers or install a chandelier at a school
board member's home.[11]

In District 21 in Brooklyn, relatives of board members and other elected
officials were routinely appointed to jobs, according to Stancik's reports. Principals, hired for their political connections, were protected, even if they had
had run-ins with the law, as had Stuart Possner, the principal of PS 100, who
was eventually convicted of stealing $20,000 in supplies and false work
claims.[12] The District 21 school board was said to reward friends and punish
enemies. "If they consider you an enemy, they take your kid and put him in
the slow class," the *Times* quoted a community activist as saying. "If you coop-
erate, they can hire your granny as a school aide."[13]

Law Limits Local Control in 1996

In 1996, largely in response to public outrage over the corruption scandals, the
state legislature passed a law that limited the powers of the school boards and
expanded the power of the schools' chancellor. Under the new law, the chancellor appointed superintendents, and the superintendents hired principals.

The chancellor, Rudolph Crew, who had been furious when district superintendents ignored his orders and even refused to come to meetings, now had
the clear authority to dismiss corrupt or ineffectual school boards and superintendents. School boards still had significant powers, but the chancellor could
now take action against boards that abused their power.

Although the new law reflected a swing of the pendulum back to central
control, it also made provisions for parent and community involvement. The
law gave the chancellor new powers, but it also called for the creation of par-
ent-teacher councils to draw up budgets and school policy, in concert with the
principal. These councils, set up in 1999 and known as school leadership

teams, were designed to ensure that parents and teachers had a voice in decisionmaking. The school leadership teams were supposed to serve as a check on the power of the principals. School boards were still elected and still had some authority, serving as another check on the administration.

For some public school parents, this arrangement ended the worst of the corruption while allowing for significant community involvement in school policy. Ronald Stewart, who had unsuccessfully run for the school board three times, was finally elected in 1996 as the first African American school board member in District 21. The district, which encompassed mostly white neighborhoods like Bensonhurst as well as African American neighborhoods like Coney Island, had a reputation as a place where blacks need not bother to apply for jobs. At Stewart's urging, the district superintendent, Don Weber, agreed to work with the board of education's centralized office of personnel to hold job fairs and to recruit nonwhite candidates. Stewart, together with community members, worked with Weber to ensure that black children had a fair chance of admission to Mark Twain, the district's middle school for gifted children. They also worked together to extend the school day for low-performing schools in poor neighborhoods.[14]

Julie Applebaum, a PS 150 parent in Manhattan's District 2, recalls that she regularly attended monthly school board meetings in the early years of the twenty-first century, where the superintendent was required by law to be present. Some of the meetings were dominated by unresolved debates over topics such as the district's progressive math curriculum, which district officials staunchly defended despite widespread opposition by parents who called it "fuzzy math." But the meetings also offered an effective problem-solving forum. "Here was a venue where a parent could go and have someone who was in a position of authority do something," Applebaum reports. "I could say, 'Our playground is falling apart,' and [superintendent] Shelley [Harwayne] would say, 'Let me take care of it.' She was there to listen, and [district special counsel] Roy [Moskowitz] was there to help make it happen. They made you feel as if they knew you as a person. It really felt like a community."[15]

District 2 parents pressed for better high school options, and the district opened the well-regarded Eleanor Roosevelt High School and Millennium High School. In District 10 in the Riverdale section of the Bronx, parents who were reluctant to send their children to the massive and unruly John F. Kennedy High School agitated for a small, neighborhood high school closer to home, and the Riverdale-Kingsbridge Academy, serving students in grades 6–12, was opened in 1999. The school was zoned to exclude many poor blacks and Hispanics, and, though its population is now only 28 percent white, many poor parents felt the school board favored middle-class Riverdale parents. Protests by parents who were left out led eventually to the construction of a new, $80 million school, MS/HS 368, serving students in grades 6–12, in the more working-class neighborhood of Kingsbridge.[16]

Parents in Brooklyn's District 15 in Park Slope complained that middle schools were inadequate. In the late 1990s, the school board responded by closing large, unruly middle schools and creating a middle school choice program with a number of small themed schools. Although far from perfect, with the middle school choice program the board demonstrated that it was trying to be responsive to parents' concerns.[17]

Sadly, these were small signs of responsiveness in a school system that consistently failed to educate hundreds of thousands of children in large swaths of the city. Even in good districts like District 15, many schools in poor and working-class neighborhoods were neglected. Moreover, a large number of districts proved incapable of providing students with even minimal standards of education. In 1997 the Public Education Association issued a report documenting systemic failure in fourteen of the city's thirty-two districts. In these districts, dubbed "dead zones," only 29 percent of youngsters were reading at grade level, compared with 48 percent in the city's other eighteen districts. High schools in those districts had graduation rates of between 25 and 35 percent; fewer than 5 percent of graduates in those districts received Regents' diplomas, the report stated. (Alas, Districts 1 and 4 in Manhattan, which the association had singled out as success stories ten years earlier, were now included in the dead zones.) Even if the 1996 law had been effective in ending local corruption and nepotism while giving parent and community members an effective voice, and even if many districts had some excellent schools, the dismal state of the school system overall could not be denied.[18]

Mayoral Control

Mayor Michael Bloomberg was elected in 2001 with a promise to make the fight for quality public education the civil rights struggle of our time. He persuaded the state legislature in 2002 to give him direct control over the schools—an unprecedented swing of the pendulum toward a highly centralized system. The mayor had long had control over the size of the education budget; under the new law he now also controlled how the money was spent. The mayor was granted the power to hire a schools chancellor, who had previously been appointed by the central board of education. The state legislature reconfigured the board, giving the mayor for the first time the power to appoint the majority of members. (The borough presidents still named the others.) The local community school boards were disbanded and replaced by new community district education councils, with much more limited powers.

The mayor's schools chancellor, Joel Klein, has made clear his belief that parent and community involvement in decisionmaking is part of the problem, not part of the solution. "In the end, it is my responsibility to say, 'I think that this is the right policy,'" Klein told a reporter for the *Nation*. "The mayor holds me accountable, and the city holds the mayor accountable. We should not have 'shared decision-making.' That's what marks all unsuccessful school reforms."[19]

Parent and community groups had retained some powers under the 2002 law, but Klein interpreted these powers in the narrowest possible way, effectively discouraging activists from working within the official structures for parent engagement. In Klein's view, previous experiments with parent and community control had failed poor children, particularly blacks and Hispanics. "We are enacting these reforms so we can make sure whatever your skin color, wherever you live, your kid will get the education he needs and deserves," the *Nation* quoted the chancellor as telling a group of parents in the Bronx.[20]

Klein's vision of parent involvement is quite different from that envisioned either by the 1969 legislation establishing community school boards or the 1996 legislation establishing school leadership teams or the 2002 law that created community district education councils. The state laws see parents as citizens who may use the political process to help make decisions about their children's education. The Klein administration, on the other hand, sees parents as consumers, entitled to a better level of customer service than previous administrations have offered but not in a position to make decisions about the delivery of those services, matters that are better left to the professionals. In his view, it is the job of the administration, not of parents or community activists, to ensure that teachers and principals are held accountable. In this view, principals and other professionals, not parents, should decide all aspects of school policy, such as how to assign children to various schools and how to spend the budget.

Klein presides over a complex web of organizations ostensibly designed to engage parents. Each of these organizations exists within a system that is heavily weighted toward central control and against parent and community decisionmaking; each suffers from this administration's determination to limit parent and community power as much as possible. Under the best of circumstances, these organizations have unclear roles, overlapping responsibilities, and an uneven record of success. In many cases, they appear to be mere vestiges of an earlier system that gave real power to community activists.

Parent Engagement at the School Level

At the school level, there are four avenues for parent engagement: the parents association, the school leadership team, the Title I parent advisory council, and the office of parent coordinator. The first three are made up of parent-volunteers (or near-volunteers: school leadership team members receive a small stipend) elected by their peers, who have the potential to influence how money is spent. The fourth, the parent coordinator, is a paid employee of the New York City Department of Education, part of the chancellor's vision of an apolitical body of professionals charged with the task of running the schools.

Under long-standing chancellor's regulations, each school is required to have a parent association, which is responsible for representing parents' interests.[21] The precise responsibilities of parent associations are not clear, but they generally serve primarily as fund-raising organizations. In wealthy neighborhoods, where a parent association may raise hundreds of thousands of dollars each year, it can wield considerable power. For example, some such groups are able to hire assistant teachers to effectively reduce the ratio of grown-ups to children in classes, playground assistants to better supervise recess, or art and music teachers. Parent associations may also organize workshops for parents on topics such as how to save money for college or how to get children to go to bed on time. In working-class neighborhoods, the associations might not raise a lot of money but may serve an important role in building a sense of community. Parents may organize a teacher appreciation lunch, for example, or a potluck supper at which parents can get to know one another and the school staff.

School leadership teams, established in 1999 in accordance with the 1996 governance law, are supposed to share decisionmaking and management in their school. Each school has a ten- to seventeen-member team that includes the principal, parents, teachers, and a representative of other staff such as cafeteria workers. By law, at least half the members of the team must be parents, elected by the membership of the parent association. These teams meet monthly and draw up the school's annual comprehensive education plan with curriculum goals for each year. Until recently, the teams were supposed to weigh decisions about budgets—determining, for example, whether it is more important to spend money on lab equipment or library books, or whether it is better to hire a music teacher or a guidance counselor. The teams are supposed to arrive at decisions by consensus.

The school leadership teams have had a mixed record of success; in some schools, they work effectively and collaboratively; in others, it has been impossible to recruit parents to serve. Some principals welcome the help in making decisions, while others see the teams as an unnecessary intrusion on their authority.

Klein has taken steps to rein in any power the school leadership teams might have. In December 2007 he issued a new regulation limiting the teams' authority.[22] Instead of helping shape the budget, the school leadership teams now "develop a Comprehensive Education Plan that is aligned with the school-based budget." Instead of making decisions jointly, "the principal makes the final determination of the [plan] and the school-based budget."[23]

A Department of Education official said these changes were necessary to align the regulation with the new powers and responsibilities the chancellor gave to principals in the summer of 2007. But some parents were angry. "He unilaterally changed the regulations on the [school leadership teams], which no longer have a say in the budget," said Leonie Haimson, executive director of the parent-advocacy group called Class Size Matters. "That takes real power away from the parents."[24]

Title I parent advisory councils provide representation for parents at high-poverty schools receiving federal funds under Title I of the Elementary and Secondary Education Act. The councils help decide how a portion of the money is spent. The Department of Education recommends that the councils prepare a budget and a plan for use of the funds for parent involvement and submit it to the school leadership team, according to a memo posted on the department's website. The members of these councils often overlap with members of the parents association. Like the parents associations, parent advisory councils exhibit a range of effectiveness. In some schools they exist only on paper, while in others they are encouraged to make real decisions about their budget.

The final avenue for parent engagement on the school level is the parent coordinator. A new position created by Klein, the parent coordinator, named by the principal, is supposed to serve as a problem solver and source of information for parents. The parent coordinator may recruit volunteers to go on field trips or work with the parent association to plan events. Many of the parent coordinators are former parent association presidents who take on this paid, full-time job after their children graduate; many of them are bilingual and serve as a link to the school for parents who do not speak English.

At PS 43 in the South Bronx, one effective parent coordinator, Lourdes Rodriguez, has recruited fifteen parent volunteers to work in the classrooms, the library, the schoolyard, and the cafeteria:

> Rodriguez offers math and literacy workshops for parents on Saturdays, as well as fun "bonding" activities like parent-child art workshops. She passes out subway maps to encourage parents—many of whom rarely leave the neighborhood—to visit places like Central Park in Manhattan. She draws up lists of free and low-cost activities that can also be educational, such as collecting leaves in the park. She takes parents on walking tours of their neighborhood, showing new immigrants, many of whom speak Spanish, everything from the local supermarket to the public library. "If the parent doesn't know where the library is the child will never go," she said. And she has a good relationship with parents precisely because of her position in the school. "I'm not a threat to them because I'm not a teacher and I'm not the administration," she said.[25]

The parent coordinator may answer simple questions, such as "When is the next PTA meeting?" or "When may prospective parents tour the school?" He or she may solve simple problems, helping a child find a lost coat or arranging for an older student to accompany a child who is too young to walk home alone. But the parent coordinator is not in a position to resolve disputes a parent may have with the principal or to solve serious, schoolwide problems such as a climate of violence, ineffectual teachers, inadequate supplies, or inappropriate placements for children in special education. As an employee of the principal, the parent coordinator does not serve as an ombudsman or an advocate for parents so much as a liaison with the administration.

Forms of District-Wide Parent Engagement

Each parent body at the school level has a counterpart at the district level: the presidents council (made up of parent association presidents), the district leadership team (which, like the school leadership team, helps formulate budgets), and the district Title I parent advisory council (which helps allocate federal antipoverty funds). In addition, each district has an eleven-member community district education council, nine parents elected by the parent association officers of each school, and two members appointed by the borough presidents. The community district education councils were created by the state legislature under the 2002 law that disbanded community school boards. Each of these organizations could potentially offer a check on the power of the central administration. However, each has been ineffectual under the current administration. (Two additional citywide parent councils exist, one for parents of students in special education and one for parents of high school students.)

These structures were organized at a time when the school districts still had considerable power and when each superintendent had authority over the running of the schools in his or her district. However, the Bloomberg administration has all but dismantled the school districts and sharply curtailed the superintendents' authority. The district-wide forms of parent engagement were designed to complement an administrative structure that no longer exists.

Bloomberg's Reorganizations

Bloomberg, who took office with the firm belief that the decentralized system had failed poor black and Hispanic children, set about to radically reorganize the schools. At first, he consolidated the thirty-two districts into ten regions (combining historically strong, middle-class districts, like District 2 on Manhattan's Upper East Side, with historically weak districts serving poor children, like District 4 in East Harlem and District 7 in the South Bronx). After state legislators protested that he had overstepped his legal authority, he agreed to leave the districts in place, at least formally. However, most decisionmaking authority was shifted to the regions and to the ten regional superintendents.

In the summer of 2007, Bloomberg reorganized the school system once again, dismantling the regions and investing most decisionmaking power in individual principals. District superintendents still exist, at least on paper. But they no longer supervise principals on a day-to-day basis or even visit schools in their districts regularly. Instead, they have been given the additional role and title of senior achievement facilitator, assigned to judge the effectiveness of schools based on data such as test scores. These supervisors report to the chief accountability officer, at present Jim Liebman, a Columbia University law professor who was hired by Klein to assess schools' progress as measured by standardized tests.

The role of the community councils, which was vague enough in the statute, has become even murkier. "The [community district education councils] were designed to hold the superintendents' feet to the fire," said David Bloomfield, a former head of the citywide parents council for high schools, an advisory body created by the chancellor. "In this system, the superintendent has no feet."[26]

Under state law, the community district education councils may draw up zoning lines, evaluate the superintendent, comment on the capital plan, hold monthly meetings to give voice to the public, and review the district's educational programs. Klein, by issuing a new chancellor's regulation, sought to restrict even these limited powers, narrowly interpreting the definition of "zoning lines."[27] In the past, districts had interpreted "zoning" to include all forms of student placement, including assignment to gifted-and-talented programs or other types of school choice; Klein, however, determined that the central Department of Education—not the districts—had the authority to assign children to particular schools. Local control, he asserted, had led to a system of haves and have-nots, and only central control could ensure equity.[28]

Accomplishments of Community District Education Councils

Nonetheless, some of the community district education councils, despite their limited powers, have served as a bully pulpit for school improvement and problem solving. The citywide council on high schools, for example, has effectively raised issues of concern to high school parents.

In District 15 in Brooklyn, the community district education council organized a task force on middle school "articulation to help resolve what had one year been a chaotic middle school admissions process. The council set up a middle school fair, inviting principals to present information about their schools to parents learning about school choice. On another occasion, the council set up a "share fair" at which parent association presidents shared tips on topics such as fund-raising and setting up parent e-mail lists.

Community District Education Council 23 in Brooklyn's Ocean Hill–Brownsville held a public forum on gangs and school safety. Police, housing authority representatives, and school officials used the forum to work together to create "safe corridors" for children at dismissal time.

A number of councils have exercised their power to comment on the capital budget. The District 15 Community District Education Council in Brooklyn, for example, persuaded the School Construction Authority to create a barrier-free playground (for children in wheelchairs) at PS 10 in Park Slope.

In District 2 in Manhattan, the community council is "as effective as we could be given the limited amount of authority in our hands," Michael A. Propper, who served as council president for three years, wrote in a letter to constituents. "When we learned of a school with inadequate power supply and unacceptable wiring, we were able to communicate with the [Department of Education] and remedy the situation. When we learned of a school's gym in such disrepair that children were injuring themselves, [we] were instrumental in getting the repairs done the very next break." Propper also reported that the community district education council in his district had achieved some modification of the progressive math curriculum that had long vexed parents; it is possible that the low-key and conciliatory approach his council took was more effective than the high-volume complaints that parents had previously made to the old school board.[29]

Drawbacks of Community District Education Councils

But overall, the community councils have been ineffectual. The *New York Post* has reported that fewer than 25 percent of the councils are fully staffed. The councils of District 9 in the Bronx and District 16 in Brooklyn were unable to conduct any business for several months because they had not filled the six seats needed for a quorum.[30] "Nobody wants to be on these councils," said a Department of Education official. "What do they do? Why would I want to spend one evening a month with people who argue?"

Robert Caloras, the president of the community council for District 26 in Bayside, Queens, called his council "a drop above completely ineffective." Lisa Donlan, the president of Manhattan's District 1 council, dismayed that the Department of Education failed to consult with the council on important matters such as the opening and closing of schools, said, "I don't know how you could make [community district education councils] effective at this point. . . . It's a badly written law. It should not be so open to interpretation that everything is a turf war."[31]

Class differences account for some of the varying effectiveness of the community councils. The most effective councils have highly educated parents who bring a sense of entitlement that allows them to make demands, the skills necessary to navigate an opaque bureaucracy, and the enormous amount of free time needed for meetings and committee work. Mary-Powel Thomas, a former president of the council for District 15 and a former magazine editor, said it was easier for her to set up the middle school task force than it might have been for a working-class parent. "If you are a home health aide, you're not going to feel confident calling principals and saying, 'Will you be on my task force?'" she said.[32]

Moreover, the 2002 law has effectively prevented some of the most active parents—parent association leaders—and many of the people with the time to volunteer, such as retirees, from serving on the community district education councils. In the past, anyone who lived in the district could run for the school board. Now, council members must be public school parents and may not also serve in the leadership of the parent association—effectively eliminating the most involved parents. That is particularly a problem in poor and working-class neighborhoods, where there may be only a handful of parents able to serve as volunteers. And although the old school boards sometimes had members who were more interested in patronage than education, they also included older people whose children had graduated from the public schools. "We don't have these wonderful retirees who have everyone over for coffee and who run down to make photocopies and hand out fliers," said Lisa Donlan of District 1's council. Now, the ranks of the community councils are limited to parents of school-age children, most of whom have full-time jobs and substantial family responsibilities. "Having volunteer parents is just not the way to go. I can't think of a less able body to take on this work than working parents," Donlan said.[33]

The old school board elections had long been criticized for low turnout, but elections for the community district education councils have even less participation. In the past, all registered voters as well as all parents (including noncitizens) were eligible to vote for school boards. Now, the right to vote in these elections is limited to the top three parent association officers in each school. In the past, school board elections attracted thousands of voters in each district; now the number is limited to about two hundred.

By and large, the community district education councils are not seen as an effective forum for problem solving. Parents who once attended school board meetings were able to raise their concerns directly with a district superintendent, who had the power to address their issues. Superintendents are still required to attend the meetings. But they no longer have control over budgets or curriculum and have only nominal power to supervise principals.

Citywide Parent Engagement

There are several bodies designed to represent parents citywide. However, these too have limited powers and effectiveness. The 2002 state law reduced the power of the New York City Board of Education, which the mayor renamed the Panel for Educational Policy. By statute, the panel still has some powers: it may approve education policies and certain contracts and litigation settlements, and it can serve as an appeal board for students or staff challenging the chancellor's decision on disciplinary matters. However, the Bloomberg administration has taken steps to ensure that the board's role is tightly circumscribed.

Under the old law, members served for a fixed term. Under the new law, they serve at the pleasure of the mayor or borough president who appoints them. When it became known that a majority of members opposed the mayor's promotion policy—which he called a plan to eliminate "social promotion" and which opponents said relied excessively on the results of one standardized test—he fired them rather than yielding to their recommendations. Now the panel is known mostly as a rubber stamp for administration policies.

The Chancellor's Parent Advisory Panel is made up of parent leaders from each of the thirty-two districts. Each district's presidents council elects a representative to the panel, which meets monthly at the Department of Education headquarters. Relations between the panel and the chancellor have been frosty, with the advisory group complaining that its recommendations are routinely ignored.[34]

Office of Family Engagement and Advocacy

The chancellor responded to long-standing charges that he was unresponsive to parents by appointing Martine Guerrier, a Brooklyn parent who had served on the Panel for Educational Policy, as chief family engagement officer in February 2007. In keeping with his philosophy that schools should be run by professionals—not elected parent representatives, who may be tainted by politics—the chancellor set up an alternative structure for parent engagement in the summer of 2007, called the Office of Family Engagement and Advocacy. A parent who has a problem that is not resolved at the school level may contact the new district family advocate, part of that office. It is not clear, however, whether this office has any power to solve problems. Advocates for Children of New York gives this description:

> Say you want to complain that your child is being bullied by a classmate and are unable to resolve it with your teacher or principal, or you need to know which school bus your child is supposed to be on. You can go to speak to a [district family advocate] in your district office. Will he or she be able to fix the problem? The answer is "maybe." The [district family advocates] can make phone calls on your behalf and help you fill out paperwork, but they don't have authority over principals. If they are unable to resolve your problem, they should be able to direct you to someone who can.[35]

Some people in the field are even less optimistic that the offices of district family advocate will solve parents' problems. Under the organization of summer 2007, district superintendents no longer supervise principals on a day-to-day basis. Principals have been empowered to make decisions independently as chief executive officers of their buildings. That means no one in the district office has the authority to tell a principal what to do. "Other than giving out a phone number, how do [district family advocates] fix something?" said a Department of Education employee. "In the old days, if a principal got off track, the district superintendent could step in. Now, we live in a world where the principals are kings and queens."[36]

Some of the blunders of the Bloomberg administration—the midyear change in bus routes that left children on freezing street corners waiting for buses that never came, the alienation of thousands of parents over the ban on student cell phones, the midyear change in the length of the school day, which left parents scrambling to change child care arrangements—could have been avoided had the mayor submitted to a political process that required him to seek out support for his policies rather than impose them unilaterally.[37] "What the mayor has tried to do is take community opposition and racial politics off the table and make rational decisions," said Anne Mackinnon, who served as a school board member for District 22 in Brooklyn from 1993 until the board was disbanded in 2003. "I don't think there is anything wrong with [that idea], except solving these problems is more complicated than it appears."[38]

The mayor has made so little effort to persuade people that his policies are correct that he has alienated many parents who could be his allies. While a Quinnipiac University poll taken in July 2007 found that 51 percent of New Yorkers surveyed thought Bloomberg's takeover of schools was a success, only 28 percent said that parents have enough say in how schools are run. Only 28 percent believed the next mayor should retain complete control of schools, while 51 percent said the mayor should share control with an independent board. Whatever the achievements of this administration may be, the mayor and chancellor have failed to win public support for their limited vision of parent and community engagement.[39]

Notes

In the preparation of this chapter I conducted interviews with several education professionals. At the request of some, their names have been withheld.

1. On the conflicts over school reform, see Bernie Bookbinder, *City of the World: New York and Its People* (New York: Abrams, 1989), p. 132.

2. David Rogers, *110 Livingston Street: Politics and Bureaucracy in the New York City School System* (New York: Random House, 1968). On the 1968 strike, also see Jerald

Podair, *The Strike That Changed New York: Blacks, Whites, and the Ocean Hill–Brownsville Crisis* (Yale University Press, 2002).

3. Rogers, *110 Livingston Street*, p. 371.

4. David Rogers and Norman H. Chung, *110 Livingston Street Revisited: Decentralization in Action* (New York University Press, 1983).

5. Nancy M. Lederman and others, *Governing the New York City Schools: Roles and Relationships in the Decentralized System; A Report of the Board of Trustees of the Public Education Association* (New York: Public Education Association, 1987), p. 10.

6. Ibid., p. 3.

7. Clara Hemphill, *New York City's Best Public Elementary Schools: A Parents' Guide* (Teachers College Press, 2002).

8. Josh Barbanel, "Under 'Rainbow,' a War: When Politics, Morals, and Learning Mix," *New York Times,* December 27, 1992 (http://query.nytimes.com/gst/fullpage. html?res=9E0CE3D81731F934A15751C1A964958260&scp=1&sq=Josh%20Barbanel %20Under%20%91Rainbow&st=cse).

9. Joseph Berger, "Schools and Politics: Channels of Power," *New York Times,* December 11, 1989 (http://query.nytimes.com/gst/fullpage.html?res=950DE1DB1430 F932A25751C1A96F948260&sec=&spon=&&scp=1&sq=Joe%20Berger%20Channels %20Power&st=cse).

10. Josh Barbanel, "Bribery and Patronage Cited at School District in Bronx," *New York Times,* April 30, 1993 (http://query.nytimes.com/gst/fullpage.html?res= 9F0CE7DB143DF933A05757C0A965958260).

11. Ibid.

12. *New York Times,* "Ex-Principal Pleads Guilty to School Theft," April 24, 1996 (http://query.nytimes.com/gst/fullpage.html?res=940CE6D61F39F937A15757C0A960 958260&scp=3&sq=stuart%20possner%20convicted&st=cse).

13. Sam Dillon, "In District 21, Schools Plus Politics Equal Gain," *New York Times,* April 26, 1993 (http://query.nytimes.com/gst/fullpage.html?res=9F0CE0DA1E3CF935 A15757C0A965958260&sec=&spon=&pagewanted=2).

14. Ronald Stewart, interview by author, December 10, 2007.

15. Julie Applebaum, interview by author, December 11, 2007.

16. Clara Hemphill, *New York City's Best Public High Schools: A Parents' Guide* (Teachers College Press, 2007).

17. Clara Hemphill, *New York City's Best Public Middle Schools: A Parents' Guide* (Teachers College Press, 2004).

18. Parents Organized to Win Education Reform, *Futures Denied: Concentrated Failure in the New York City Public School System,* report prepared for the Industrial Areas Foundation-Metro New York (New York: Public Education Association, March 1997).

19. LyNell Hancock, "School's Out," *Nation,* July 9, 2007 (www.thenation.com/ doc/20070709/hancock).

20. Ibid.

21. New York City Department of Education, Regulation of the Chancellor A-660 (docs.nycenet.edu/docushare/dsweb/Get/Document-31/A-660.pdf).

22. Ibid.

23. New York City Department of Education, Regulation of the Chancellor A-655 (docs.nycenet.edu/docushare/dsweb/Get/Document-30/A-655.pdf).

24. Leonie Haimson, interview by author, December 15, 2007.

25. Advocates for Children of New York, "Review," *Insideschools.org, School Profile, PS 43* (www.insideschools.org/fs/school_profile.php?id=182).

26. David Bloomfield, interview by author, December 5, 2007.

27. New York City Department of Education, Regulation of the Chancellor A-185 (schools.nyc.gov/NR/rdonlyres/EB063CC7-8CB9-4FB0-B071-9442F73F4C7D/6991/A185Regulation.pdf).

28. David M. Herszenhorn, "Parent Councils Poised for Fight over Schools and Zoning," *New York Times,* January 15, 2005 (www.nytimes.com/2005/01/15/nyregion/15school.html?_r=1&scp=1&sq=David M. Herszenhorn Parent Councils&st=cse&oref=slogin).

29. These examples are gathered from various interviews of council members by the author.

30. Yoav Gonen, "Skeleton School Councils," *New York Post,* December 10, 2007 (www.nypost.com/seven/12102007/news/regionalnews/skeleton_school_councils_560907.htm).

31. Interview with author, December 17, 2007.

32. Interview with author, December 18, 2007.

33. Interview with author, December 9, 2007.

34. David Herszenhorn, "Parents Seek Greater Voice in Schools from Chancellor," *New York Times,* December 12, 2005 (www.nytimes.com/2005/12/12/nyregion/12schools.html?scp=2&sq=David%20M.%20Herszenhorn%20Parents%20seek&st=cse).

35. Advocates for Children of New York, "'Parent Support' Becomes 'Family Engagement and Advocacy,'" News and Views (www.insideschools.org/nv/NV_DOE_reorg_oct07.php?hp)

36. Interview with author, December 10, 2007. The employee asked not to be identified.

37. See David M. Herszenhorn, "New Tutoring Schedules in Schools Lead to Confusion," *New York Times,* February 7, 2006 (www.nytimes.com/2006/02/07/nyregion/07schools.html?scp=2&sq=David%20M.%20Herszenhorn%20new%20tutoring&st=cse); Elissa Gootman, "September in January: School Bus Changes Sow Confusion," *New York Times,* January 30, 2007 (www.nytimes.com/2007/01/30/nyregion/30buses.html?scp=4&sq=Elissa%20Gootman%20%20September%20January&st=cse).

38. Interview with author, December 7, 2007.

39. Perhaps for the future we should consider who defines the term *parent engagement.* Is it the mayor, the parents themselves, or the community? The definition seems to change depending on who is in power.

JOSEPH P. VITERITTI

10

New York: Past, Present, Future

If there is a New York political culture that can be gleaned from studying its unique history, traditions, and practices, it is a culture of paradox. From the birth of the consolidated city in 1898, New York mayors have been powerful figures. Yet within a municipal structure that was highly centralized there was always an appreciation for community that was reflected over the years in various forms of political decentralization.[1] Since Greater New York was the product of a merger that occurred when the original municipality in Manhattan and the Bronx was joined with the independent city of Brooklyn and dozens of towns sprawled across Staten Island and Queens, the borough connection has always been a significant consideration in how people identify themselves.[2] Within each of the five boroughs, the neighborhoods—defined by race, religion, ethnicity, class, and even sexual orientation—also figured largely in the political and social life of New York.[3] When all is said and done, New Yorkers see themselves as citizens of the city, residents of a borough, and members of a community. The hierarchy of power may reside at city hall, but the rhythms of daily life pulsate from the neighborhoods. While centralization was a response to reformers' desire to get things done and clean things up, political decentralization was a necessary by-product of size, geography, and diversity. This is New York.

From the Beginning

The government that originated in 1898 ostensibly had three centers of power: the mayor, the New York City Board of Estimate and Apportionment, and the local legislature. In reality, New York City was effectively controlled by the mayor. The board had authority to prepare the city budget and to approve franchises, debts, taxes, and assessments. It was composed of the mayor, the president of the Department of Taxes and Assessments for the City of New York, the corporation counsel, the comptroller, and the president of the city council. Since only the comptroller and the council president were elected independently of the mayor (who appointed the other two), the board functioned to supplement the mayor's power, making him statutorily one of the most powerful local executives in the history of American government. The mayor also appointed the city chamberlain, who served as treasurer, and chose a majority of the New York City Board of Public Improvements, assuring his dominance over public works and planning.[4] The city comptroller headed the city's finance department, which collected revenues and oversaw city contracts.

The bicameral Municipal Assembly of the City of New York was composed of a twenty-nine-member upper house called the city council and a sixty-member lower house called the board of aldermen. As a general rule, the size of the local legislature in New York was inversely related to its prestige and power.[5] The bigger it got, the more unwieldy it became and the more challenging it was to attract high-quality candidates for the office. The municipal assembly of 1898 had no power to increase the city budget, and the final budget had to be approved by the board of estimate and apportionment. The legislature needed a five-sixths majority to override a mayoral veto.

The first charter of the consolidated city, still reeling from effects of the corrupt Tweed years, took the reformist model of a strong mayor–weak legislature to an extreme; for all practical purposes, it had no system of checks and balances.[6] Albany Republicans had hoped that by electing one of their own to an enhanced mayoralty, they would be able to establish a stronger political foothold in the city. Two years before consolidation, the trustee system that had put education largely in the hands of patronage-driven local school boards was eliminated. As Diane Ravitch notes in chapter 8 of this volume, the appointment of William Maxwell as superintendent of schools by a board of education chosen entirely by the mayor ushered in a new era of professionalism and reform in the schools. Except for the appointment of school board members by the mayor and the board's reliance on city officials for local revenues, however, the school system was administered separately from the municipal government.

Even with this highly centralized municipal arrangement in place, the notion of community was apparent in the new government. The charter created twenty-two local improvement districts overseen by local boards. The boundaries of these districts corresponded to the boundaries of legislative districts in the upper house of the municipal assembly, which were also coterminous with state senatorial districts. (Districts in the lower house were coterminous with state assembly districts). The local boards were chaired by the borough presidents and composed of local legislators. They were allowed to consider (but not to approve) proposals for local improvements before they went to the board of public improvements or the municipal assembly.

Boss Tweed had died a horrible death in the Ludlow Street jail on April 12, 1878.[7] His huge corpse was taken to Brooklyn and buried in Green-Wood Cemetery; yet his spirit lived on for decades in the Tammany organization he entrenched in Manhattan. Eventually, Tammany not only controlled politics in New York County, but it also enjoyed a disproportionate share of power in the newly consolidated city. A confluence of forces came together in 1900 when Republicans and Brooklyn Democrats teamed up to demand a newly structured government. Governor Theodore Roosevelt, alarmed by lingering corruption unearthed in the administration of Mayor Robert Van Wyck, appointed a charter commission chaired by George Rieves.

Experts were divided over the proper course to take.[8] Putting so much power in the hands of a single chief executive had obviously created irresistible temptations for incumbent officeholders, especially when Tammany got to choose the mayor. Some reformers argued for a stronger rehabilitated city council, but they were soon reminded by others that the strong-mayor plan was a measure to undo the influence of a legislative body that had once been known as the Forty Thieves. In the end, resentment of Manhattan leaders by politicians in the four other boroughs won out. The charter recommended by the Rieves Commission in 1901 vested more power in the borough presidents through a restructured board of estimate and apportionment. It removed the mayor's appointees from the board and added the borough presidents. The city comptroller and the president of the restructured board of aldermen (both still elected citywide) remained, but the terms of office of all three citywide officials were reduced from four years to two. Under a system of weighted voting, the mayor held only three of the sixteen votes on the board.

The mayor's power was further reduced by the elimination of the board of public improvements. In 1905 the power to grant franchises was switched from the mayor to the board of estimate and apportionment. In 1916 the board was granted authority to regulate zoning. The borough presidents were also given substantial administrative authority over the construction and maintenance of public works. They continued to preside over local community boards, whose powers were enhanced by the elimination of the board of public improvements once controlled by the mayor. The unicameral board of aldermen that came into existence in 1901 was composed of sixty-five members. The new body needed a three-fourths majority vote (rather than the previous five-sixths) to override a mayoral veto, still leaving it in a weak position. In 1924, with the addition of a Home Rule Amendment to the state constitution allowing the municipality more discretion in the formation of its own government, the board of estimate and apportionment was formally designated the upper house of the municipal assembly.

Local abuses continued to attract Albany's attention through the early years of the twentieth century right up to the New Deal.[9] Mayor James "Jimmy" Walker fled to Europe as Governor Franklin D. Roosevelt launched another investigation into municipal corruption. Then in 1935 Mayor Fiorello LaGuardia, promising to uproot Tammany's influence over local affairs, appointed a charter commission that began to shift authority back to the chief executive.[10] Under the new charter, the mayor assumed power from the board of estimate and apportionment to prepare the executive budget, and his term was extended from two to four years. He also appointed six of seven members to the newly created New York City Planning Commission, which prepared a capital budget, passed on all zoning changes, and was responsible for drafting a master plan for the city, all of which were reviewed by the newly named New York City Board of Estimate. In 1936 local boards were given the authority to process assessable improvements that did not exceed $10,000; larger projects needed approval by the board of estimate, the planning commission, and the city council.

No longer considered a legislative body, the board of estimate functioned as a municipal board of directors. It was legally granted the residual powers of the city, which encompassed any powers that had not been assigned specifically to another governmental body. To enhance the prestige of the city council and the quality of its membership, the size of the legislature was reduced, linking it to the volume of voter turnout. The term in office for members remained two years until 1945, when it was increased to four. By the end of LaGuardia's tenure, the power of the mayoralty had been pitched on an upward trajectory that would continue through to the twenty-first century. The most significant check on that power, at least for a while, was found in the board of estimate, where the borough presidents held a good deal of sway.

From Decentralization to Recentralization

While the idea of community government had been planted in the municipal structure of New York from the outset, it did not begin to reach fruition until after World War II, as the population grew in the outer boroughs. In 1947 the Citizens Union published a report criticizing the city's crazy quilt of service districts that varied from department to department and proposed a plan for "small town governments" that would require the city planning commission to draw up district boundaries reflecting historic communities in order to better integrate services.[11] The commission, then under the chairmanship of Robert F. Wagner Jr., responded by drawing a map that identified sixty-six districts throughout the five boroughs. In 1951, after being elected borough president of Manhattan, Wagner established twelve community planning councils in the borough, an arrangement that would eventually become a model for the rest of the city.

Wagner continued his efforts on behalf of community government after his election as mayor, but not before appointing a charter commission, chaired by Judge John Cahill, that would begin to take power away from the borough presidents and put it into his own office. In 1961 the Cahill Commission developed a plan that transferred most of the administrative responsibilities of the borough presidents, then primarily in the area of public works, to the mayor. In addition, the mayor was authorized to choose the chair of the city planning commission, was put in control of personnel matters that had once belonged to the board of estimate, was empowered to reorganize the administrative structure of the municipal government, and was given all residual powers of the city.

Under the Cahill charter, the city planning commission was officially required to set the boundaries for the operation of community planning boards. The borough presidents appointed the members of the boards. Although members of the city council continued to sit on these local bodies, the new arrangement marked a shift from the original structure of community government by moving the center of gravity from the local legislature to the borough presidents. From then on, local council members played a more peripheral role. In 1963 the community planning boards were authorized to advise the borough presidents and the city planning commission on local matters. This was a modest first step in the true decentralization of the city government.

In 1965 John Lindsay was elected mayor as an Upper East Side Republican in a city where the political machinery of the Democratic Party was closely aligned with the administrative apparatus of service agencies and the union workers they employed, most of whom lived in the outer boroughs. As the city grew more diverse racially and President Lyndon Johnson's Great Society programs sought to funnel more federal monies directly into poor urban neighborhoods, Lindsay saw decentralization as a way to establish political roots in newly constructed community institutions.[12] He responded aggressively to the community action and model city programs that emerged from Washington by giving neighborhood leaders direct control over federal resources. He developed his own decentralized apparatus of service delivery by creating an Office of Neighborhood Government and opening neighborhood city halls staffed by his political appointees. Attentive to demands from minority activists for real power in the schools their children attended, he also encouraged the state legislature to institute community school boards in 1969.[13] That same year, the city council formally created community planning boards.

In 1972 the state legislature appointed a charter commission, chaired by state senator Roy Goodman, designed to "encourage genuine citizen participation in local government."[14] The city charter that was eventually adopted in 1975 specified the discrete powers that would apply to the newly named community boards. These could be broken down into three areas: land use, budgeting, and service delivery. Under the Uniform Land-Use Review Procedure, local boards were given a voice in zoning and land use decisions that affected their geographic districts. They were also given the opportunity to have input on the executive and capital budgets pertaining to their neighborhoods. The new charter required that the administrative boundaries of service districts in city agencies be made to coincide with the boundaries of community boards. This would allow the boards, through newly appointed district managers and staffs, to monitor and integrate city services at the neighborhood level. The boards were also authorized to hold public hearings in their areas of jurisdiction.

The fifty-nine coterminous service districts did not coincide with the boundaries of the thirty-two school districts created under the Decentralization Law of 1969. Nor did they match the boundaries of the thirty-five electoral districts represented on the city council. In this sense, government at the community level was left trifurcated. And despite the more specific delineation of authority that was granted to the community boards under the 1975 charter, the power of these local bodies remained advisory. Final discretion on land use, zoning, and the capital budget would lie with the city planning commission and the board of estimate; final discretion on the expense budget would remain with the board of estimate, the city council, and the mayor. At no point would the authority exercised by community boards ever measure up to that of community school boards, which were elected rather than appointed and had the power to hire key school personnel and manage school budgets.

A new set of public priorities would begin to take hold in 1975 that overshadowed the movement toward decentralized government. The fiscal crisis that put the city on the brink of bankruptcy led the state to appoint oversight bodies that would compromise the ability of the city to determine its budget, enact labor agreements, and borrow money.[15] The question was no longer which branch of the city government would dominate the others; now the question was whether New York City would have the power to govern its own future so long as it was dependent on the state to put its fiscal house in order. Perhaps, some thought, having so many arenas of power in its pluralistic political framework was one of the factors that made New York "ungovernable." That being said, the new charter did reflect a realization that the mayor's office had been complicit in the irresponsible practices that led to fiscal calamity and that legal provisions were needed to check his power and make him more accountable.[16]

The 1975 charter required the mayor to submit a preliminary executive budget to the board of estimate and the city council for extensive review, and it demanded that the budget be balanced. As a member of the board of estimate, the mayor was no longer permitted to vote on the budget. Nor could he veto reductions made by the board or the council. The mayor was also required to submit a management report to the two bodies, outlining the operational goals and assessing the performance of city agencies. The city council president was given new duties as the citywide ombudsman. The city comptroller was required to establish a uniform system of accounts designed by the state comptroller, and his audit responsibilities were substantially increased.

In 1986 a federal court in Manhattan ruled that the practice of giving each borough president one vote on the board of estimate, regardless of the population size in the boroughs that elected them, violated the one person–one vote legal standard required by the equal protection clause of the Constitution—five times as many people lived in Brooklyn as in Staten Island. After an appeals court affirmed the ruling, it was upheld by the United States Supreme Court in 1989.[17] Soon after the trial court decision was handed down, Mayor Edward I. Koch appointed a charter commission headed by Richard Ravitch to review the entire structure of the city government.[18] When Ravitch's term expired in 1989, he was succeeded by Frederick A. O. Schwarz Jr. The city charter that the voters of New York approved in November of 1989 brought about the most significant realignment in governance since 1901, when the Rieves Commission took power away from the mayor and gave it to the borough presidents.

The most dramatic change in the 1989 charter was the elimination of the board of estimate.[19] The big losers in the new governance arrangement were the borough presidents, who had relied on the board as their most significant lever of influence.[20] The big winner, supposedly, was the city council, which was expanded from thirty-five to fifty-one members to allow it to represent the increasingly diverse communities that were reshaping the city. The big question that emerged in 1989 was whether the city council, on its own, could serve as an ample check on the power of the mayor. History was not encouraging on that prospect; but this was the first time the council did not have a board of estimate to compete with in the stakes of local politics.

Under the 1989 charter, a legislative office of budget review was created, but it only lasted for one year. In 1996, at the demand of local reformers, an Independent Budget Office of the City of New York was established, which had ties to neither the city council nor the mayor's office. Moreover, the council took over the land use powers previously held by the board of estimate, which meant that it would approve all such decisions made by the city planning commission as well as the capital budget. The planning commission was expanded to thirteen members, seven of whom, including the chair, were appointed by the mayor, one by each of the five borough presidents, and one by the independently elected president of the city council. The mayor may veto any land use provision of the council, which can be overturned only by a two-thirds majority vote of the council. Under its legislative power, the council must approve a detailed contract budget. Agencies must adhere to a new contract review procedure that ultimately requires review and approval by a five-person procurement policy board, on which three seats are controlled by the mayor and two by the city comptroller.

The city comptroller also lost a significant seat in the governance structure with the demise of the board of estimate. The comptroller, nonetheless, remains the chief fiscal officer of the city, who conducts financial and performance audits, prepares reports on the city economy and finances, and has the power to stop agencies from entering into contracts if there is reason to believe corrupt practices were involved in their procurement. The last office to lose status with the elimination of the board of estimate was the president of the city council, an office that in 1993 was renamed the Public Advocate of the City of New York. One of three officials elected citywide, the public advocate presides over the city council when it is in full session and has the authority to break a tie vote. As the chief ombudsman of the city, she serves as a watch-dog and prepares reports on the functioning of the city agencies.

In the final analysis, the most significant institutional check on the mayor within the current municipal structure remains the city council. No longer having to share legislative, budget, or land use powers with the board of estimate, the city council is arguably the most potent local legislature in the history of the city. It also has authority to hold hearings and conduct investigations. But there remain several institutional factors that undermine its power. In the early history of the city, council members dominated local community boards; now these boards are controlled by the borough presidents, who also appoint borough-wide boards with advisory powers similar to their counterparts at the neighborhood level. And while council members sit on these neighborhood boards, their district boundaries remain unaligned with the boundaries of both community districts and school districts. Community government in New York City remains trifurcated, a far cry from the "small town governments" called for by the Citizens Union in 1947.

History tells us that a larger, more diverse body is more difficult to discipline, undermining its capability to act as a strong check on the mayor. More significant, perhaps, was the adoption of term limits by a popular referendum in 1993, which limited the tenure of council members to two consecutive four-year terms. The measure was affirmed in a 1996 referendum. The same limits were imposed on citywide officials (the mayor, comptroller, and public advocate), but they would take a larger toll on the functioning of the council. A mayor can draw on a wealth of knowledge and experience contained within the agencies he manages. Legislative bodies build expertise through a committee structure based on seniority. This process works most effectively when individuals who choose legislative careers become familiar with issues over time and use that expertise to counter the expertise of the executive. In 2008, at the urging of Mayor Bloomberg, the city council passed a resolution that suspended the term limits law and permitted all incumbents to stand for reelection for another term.[21]

While the elimination of the board of estimate served to enhance the power of the city council, it did at least as much for the mayor. We must also be reminded that, even in jurisdictions that follow a tradition of home rule, the most important legislation affecting local government gets written in the state legislature, not at city hall. New York is no exception. The primary function of municipal government is to provide essential services to the people who live in, work in, play in, and visit the city. On any given day in New York, that service population can exceed 20 million people. As chief executive of the city, it is the mayor who is expected to get all this done efficiently and effectively. He is the most visible public official. It is his job to oversee the agencies that deliver services at the street level. Therefore, for all practical purposes he runs the city.

And the Schools Too

By the time Michael Bloomberg took office as mayor in January 2002, neither the central board of education nor the thirty-two community school boards that administered elementary and middle schools in New York enjoyed much public credibility.[22] The central board was one of the last vestiges of power for the borough presidents, who collectively controlled five of its seven votes. As noted above, community school board elections attracted low turnout, and over the years many of the elected boards had drawn headlines in the local press for escapades involving incompetence, patronage, and petty corruption, although some had functioned quite well. When Bloomberg ran for election in 2001, polls consistently showed that education was the number one issue on the voters' minds. He promised to take over the school system and make it better and challenged the electorate to judge him on the basis of that promise.

In some ways Bloomberg fit the profile of Progressive Era reformers as a businessman-turned-mayor who had never worked in government or participated in politics. He is certainly independent; but it could hardly be said that he is not political. No individual could run for, get elected, and serve as mayor of New York without being political.[23] Bloomberg, however, has always played his own style of politics. Before running for election, Bloomberg switched his political party affiliation from Democratic to Republican to avoid a hotly contested Democratic primary, which more often than not determines who the mayor of New York will be. A self-made billionaire, Bloomberg financed his own $69 million election campaign, spending far more ($92.60 per vote) than any previous mayor had spent to get elected.[24]

After his second election in 2005, which he won handily, Bloomberg withdrew from the Republican Party and declared himself an independent. As he approached the last year of his second term, Bloomberg changed his previous position on term limits and announced that he would seek a third term, urging the city council to overturn a term limits law that had been adopted by two popular referenda. Before the announcement, Bloomberg courted the publishers of the city's major newspapers and leaders in the business community to rally support as polls showed that nine of ten voters opposed overturning the law by legislative fiat. An aide to the mayor was quoted as saying that

Bloomberg "does not care what it costs" to get reelected.[25] As the sunset of the state's school governance law approached, Bloomberg helped establish a $20 million campaign fund to prevent any changes in the law that might reduce or check the power of the mayor.[26]

Bloomberg continues to use his own personal resources to support political candidates from either party both locally and nationally. In addition to investing money in campaigns, he has filmed television ads for candidates and actually deployed his own political advisers to help United States senator Joseph Lieberman of Connecticut, a Democrat turned independent, win reelection.[27] In 2008 Bloomberg irritated Democratic leaders in the state legislature when he spent money to help Republicans maintain control of the state senate, where the GOP held the majority by only two seats. The intervention was rather bold for an incumbent mayor who would need Democratic leaders in Albany to support his legislative agenda. Resentment would fester through the remaining years of his administration.

During the 2008 presidential campaign, Bloomberg went to Florida to chide a Jewish audience for a "whispering campaign" that associated Democratic presidential candidate Barack Obama with Islamic extremists; in the same speech, he praised Republican candidate John McCain for not capitalizing on such innuendo.[28] In the spring of 2008, Bloomberg was rumored to be a possible candidate for the vice presidency, but even the most astute political analysts had difficulty figuring out on which ticket he was more likely to appear. So far as party affiliation was concerned, Bloomberg considered himself neither; political pundits could consider him either.

New York had never seen the likes of a Bloomberg in the office that once belonged to LaGuardia, and the new mayor seemed to relish that.[29] After being elected, Bloomberg took it upon himself to relocate the seat of power from the esteemed chamber at City Hall once occupied by the Little Flower to the refashioned quarters of the defunct board of estimate. The bull pen–style arrangement of the mayor's new office was designed to look more like the corporate headquarters that Bloomberg had left behind in the private sector than the seat of government for a municipality. Rather than take up residence in the mayor's official home at Gracie Mansion, Bloomberg chose to live in his own Upper East Side townhouse and let the mansion be used for official ceremonies. These were all subtle indications that change was in the air, that this mayor was operating from a different playbook.

Apart from his governmental role, Bloomberg's philanthropic activities make him one of the most influential figures in New York society. The year before he ran for reelection he was reported to have donated $140 million in gifts to more than 800 institutions, many of them in New York City.[30] At the beginning of his second term, Bloomberg announced that after leaving office he would set up his own foundation in an elaborate townhouse on the Upper East Side, not far from his home, where he would devote much of his time to doling out money to his favored charities. In June of 2008, it was reported that since taking office, Bloomberg had given away $175 million to organizations in New York, and he announced that he would award an additional $60 million over the next two years to 542 organizations in the city.[31] When Bloomberg's controversial plan to ease term limits came before the city council, leaders of charitable institutions that had benefited from his contributions reported that they were pressured to testify in his favor.[32]

Bloomberg was powerful and independent. He owed nothing to anyone and was accustomed to being his own boss. He lacked patience with the bureaucratic ways of city government and seemed to resent the limited checks on his power that remained in the city charter. Accustomed to working in the private sector, where things moved more quickly, Bloomberg found the institutions of government incongruous with the ambitious agenda for change that he had promised the voters, especially where education was concerned.

Bloomberg was a newcomer to city hall in 2002, but so were many officials serving in the other branches of the municipal government, who ordinarily might have functioned to check his power. Thanks to term limits, two-thirds of the seats on the city council were held by new members, not to mention four new borough presidents, the city comptroller, and the public advocate, who were sworn in on the same day as the new mayor. If the city council were to function as a serious constraint on the power of the mayor, it would not happen during the Bloomberg years. Council speaker Christine Quinn, a key legislative player chosen by the membership, has been one of the mayor's strongest political allies; and it was widely speculated that Bloomberg might eventually use his wealth to support her candidacy to succeed him as mayor when (or if) he was retired from the office by term limits.

Robert Jackson, the outspoken chair of the city council's education committee, did not hesitate to be critical of the administration or the chancellor when he saw fit, and he would consistently question policies at committee hearings. Even with its power to approve the budget, however, the council never seemed to match the might of a willful chief executive. As Jackson stated in his testimony to the Commission on School Governance, "I am frustrated by how little direct control we have over the budget process or operational oversight. [The Department of Education] is not the most forthcoming of agencies. We do not work together in a spirit of cooperation. We do not get accurate facts or data from [the department] to make informed decisions."[33]

A man with a penchant for surprises, Bloomberg's most unorthodox act as mayor came with his appointment of a schools chancellor. Joel Klein had been a federal prosecutor. He had no background in education and no experience in New York City government. He had never run an organization as large as the Department of Education, which at the time he took office had 120,000 employees and a $12 billion operating budget, serving 1.1 million students in twelve hundred schools. Klein had little regard for the archaic school head-quarters at 110 Livingston Street in Brooklyn, everybody's favorite metaphor for hidebound bureaucracy.[34] In another symbolic use of real estate, Bloomberg and Klein moved the school headquarters across the river to the old Tweed Court House, located right behind City Hall. When he was the mayor, Rudolph Giuliani used to talk about blowing up the school headquarters. Bloomberg and Klein just let it bleed to death by gradually removing personnel and resources and then moved the remains of the corpus to the smaller Tweed Building.[35] In the process, they lost many experienced educators.

It appeared that Bloomberg and Klein not only wanted to turn the system around; they wanted to turn it upside down and inside out. In creating Children First, their key instructional initiative, they reorganized the system into ten regions, all but closing the thirty-two district offices that had been left in place by the legislature when it eliminated elected school boards.[36] Legislative leaders protested that the reorganization violated the terms of the new governance law, contending that while appointed community district education committees did not have the power to appoint superintendents and principals (a power removed from elected boards in 1999), they still functioned as a community resource where parents could go to get information or express concerns about what was happening in their schools.[37] As Clara Hemphill explains in more detail in chapter 9, the reorganization that eliminated the regions in 2007 and returned some functions to poorly staffed district offices seemed to sow more confusion at the community level. This was exacerbated by the fact that the role of district superintendents, now also called senior achievement facilitators, was not entirely clear and the schools that the administrators were assigned to were not necessarily located in their geographic districts.

Bloomberg and Klein presided over a regime of change that was unprecedented in the history of the school system. They took it upon themselves to rename the central board of education the Panel for Educational Policy and to rename the citywide school district the Department of Education, making it sound more like a municipal agency. Among the changes the chancellor is proud to point to are the elimination of social promotion in the fifth, seventh, and eighth grades; new programmatic requirements in reading and math; the creation of 200 small secondary schools; growth in the number of charter schools from seventeen to eighty; devolution of power to school principals, granting them greater budgetary discretion and the ability to choose from a range of organizations for support services; a revised system of school funding designed to foster greater equity; implementation of school report cards grading schools from A to F; and contract revisions that reward principals and teachers on the basis of performance.[38] This is an impressive scorecard of innovation by any measure.

Many critics warned, however, that there were too many opportunities for the mayor and chancellor to have their way without sufficient accountability. Bloomberg's firing of two recalcitrant appointees on the central education panel while engineering the removal of a third by a borough president—the night before they were supposed to vote on his controversial plan to end social promotion—has been etched in the collective memory of school people as an abuse of power enabled by mayoral control.[39] The citywide reading program adopted under the Children First initiative was initially rejected by the U.S. Department of Education for not being research based. Klein's delegation of a controversial school accountability system to a former law professor seemed indicative of a larger turnover of pedagogical authority from professional educators to lawyers and business professionals who had no experience in schools. These criticisms were sounded repeatedly by individuals who appeared before the Commission on School Governance.[40]

Klein saw things differently. In his testimony before the commission, he argued that many disadvantaged students had nobody to represent their interests in the school system. Citing the landmark *Brown* v. *Board of Education* decision of 1954 and the unresolved academic achievement gap between the races, he declared that it was his job to meet the needs of those students in a system that works against them.[41] He noted that fixing the school system would require bold leadership and that he was prepared to accept the resentment it was sure to cause.

Assessing Mayoral Control

Because the Bloomberg-Klein administration was the only one in the city ever to operate under mayoral control, most New Yorkers' assessment of the governance model reflected their assessment of the administration. Among the attentive public—people who were directly involved in education or the schools—these viewpoints were rarely ambiguous. Their preoccupation with the incumbents presented a problem for the Commission on School Governance, since its mandate was to make recommendations for a governance plan that would outlast the existing administration. A new mayor and schools chancellor might handle mayoral control in an entirely different manner from the way Bloomberg and Klein had. Although the commission kept emphasizing that it was not appointed to evaluate the performance of Bloomberg and Klein, people who came before it wanted to discuss Bloomberg and Klein. That was understandable but not always helpful.

The commission made a strategic decision to avoid the test score debate, resisting the natural inclination to look at the proverbial bottom line of academic performance as a barometer for evaluating mayoral control. To do so would have invited well-deserved criticism. While Ken Wong has assembled an impressive body of evidence in chapter 4 to find a correlation between mayoral control and student performance in cities across the country, Jeff Henig's sobering analysis of data from the National Assessment of Educational Progress in chapter 2 suggests that there is no reliable relationship between school governance and education outcomes. To make claims of such an association on the basis of scores in one city for one administration would have been wholly irresponsible.

There had been notable gains in state reading and math scores during the Bloomberg-Klein years, but gains were also recorded in other cities around the state that did not have mayoral control.[42] Perhaps the recorded improvements were the result of a long-term effort by state officials—the state commissioner of education and the New York State Board of Regents, in particular—to implement more rigorous standards. Perhaps the statewide rise in the scores was a sign that the tests had become easier. While state test scores rose in New York City, National Assessment of Educational Progress scores for the city remained largely flat. Many critics of standardized tests were quick to point out that such scores are an inadequate measure of instructional quality. Even if one were to accept the state test scores as a valid measure of educational improvement, there was no sure way to link this improvement to governance. One observer might claim that progress was the result of bold leadership exercised by the incumbent administration; another might point to a significant increase in spending that occurred during the Bloomberg-Klein years, some 42 percent in the operating budget of the school system.[43] Either of these factors could be related to mayoral control. To make a direct connection between governance and student achievement, however, would be problematic.

The New York state legislature has three options to choose from when the school governance law that installed mayoral control sunsets in June of 2009: it can renew the 2002 legislation as it was originally written, it can institute an amended form of mayoral control, or it can return to the status quo ante. Although many of the more than one hundred individuals who appeared before the commission were critical of the way the schools were run, there was no strong outcry to eliminate mayoral control, and only a few wanted to return to the former system. When asked whether they supported mayoral control, most people who testified gave a "Yes, but" response. This general pattern was corroborated by a Quinnipiac University poll released in July 2008. When asked, 54 percent of the respondents said that Mayor Bloomberg's takeover of the schools had been a success, yet 55 percent said that the mayor should share control of the schools.[44]

There are tangible benefits that can be associated with mayoral control in New York. Most commentators agree that putting the mayor in charge of education is preferable to the former system that divided authority among six different officials who appointed the members of a seven-member central school board, only two of whom were chosen by the mayor. While much of the 42 percent increase in spending (from $11.9 billion to $16.9 billion) that occurred between 2002 and 2008 resulted from the infusion of state funds required by the settlement of a school finance suit, local spending in this fiscally dependent school district increased 48 percent (from $4.8 billion to $7.1 billion).[45] In his appearance before the commission, Dennis Walcott, the deputy mayor for education and community development, testified that being directly responsible for education gave the mayor an institutional incentive to invest more resources in the public schools.[46]

Other than representatives of the Bloomberg administration itself, perhaps the strongest advocate for preserving the 2002 governance law unchanged was Kathryn Wylde, the president and chief operating officer of the Partnership for New York City, a coalition of business leaders that had been founded by David Rockefeller. Wylde had lobbied Albany to pass the legislation and was a close ally of the mayor. When she spoke before the commission, she emphasized education's importance to business leaders and cited surveys indicating that "the depth, quality, and diversity of the talent pool is the most important consideration for business and job location decisions."[47] She stated that "the progress made in the schools under mayoral control is demonstrable and compelling." She argued that school improvement is reversing middle-class flight. She estimated that philanthropic giving to the public schools had risen since 2002 from $2 million annually to more than $100 million.

In drafting its findings, the Commission on School Governance acknowledged that "from 2002 to the present, the New York City school system has undergone more change than it has in any similar period in its history."[48] While the commission refrained from judging the desirability or effects of these changes, it linked them directly to mayoral control, which had replaced a governance arrangement that "was institutionally resistant to change and innovation." Focusing on the capacity for change, the commission concluded that "this could be the single most important and measurable advantage of mayoral control when the current governance arrangement is compared to the one that preceded it." "Although change is not synonymous with progress," it continued, "it is a prerequisite to progress."

In the same breath, however, the commission found that "more centralized power in the hands of a single office also introduces risks." The idea of mayoral control was strongly endorsed by a wide range of groups and individuals across the city, but many of the same raised concerns about the lack of effective checks on the power of the mayor. For example, Randi Weingarten, the president of the United Federation of Teachers (and since elected president of the American Federation of Teachers), testified that though mayoral control has made education a "higher priority in the city," there is a "lack of checks and balances, transparency, and public deliberation" with regard to policy.[49] Former congressman Herman Badillo, a friend of Bloomberg's and supporter of mayoral control, insisted, "The mayor should not be able to remove a board member simply because they disagree on a particular issue."[50]

The concerns raised by Weingarten and Badillo—along with numerous other community leaders, former legislators, local officials, and public school parents—are poignant when school governance in New York is considered within the larger institutional context of the municipal government. Historically, New York City mayors have had a strong hand in local government and politics. The enactment of mayoral control in the schools followed a long pattern of measures—solidified in the 1989 city charter—that enhanced the power of the mayor in relation to other institutional actors. Coupled with the fact that the position of mayor of New York tends to attract strong personalities, it has never been easy to curb their power once they have set their sights on a particular set of objectives, at least insofar as local decisionmaking is concerned. Mayoral control would certainly enable the mayor to hold the schools more directly accountable for their performance, as had never been so in the past. The big question to many observers was whether it would be possible to hold the mayor accountable.

There was much discussion among the interested parties as to whether the purported lack of effective checks on the power of the mayor and his chancellor were a function of the law itself or the way Bloomberg and Klein dealt with the law. Joel Klein, after all, was a practiced litigator. He read laws strategically. He viewed the boundaries set on his own power as encumbrances that would get in the way of changes that were needed in a hidebound system. He would work around them. Steven Sanders, the former chair of the New York State Assembly Education Committee that wrote the law, believes that Bloomberg and Klein violated the intent of the law. He asserted that it was never designed to equip the mayor and the chancellor with unfettered power. That being said, the law, he argued, needed revision and fine-tuning, some tightening. That is why it included a sunset provision. Looking ahead, he advised the commission that "the powers, duties, and responsibilities of the Governance Law are too important to be left to the creative desires or whims of any Mayor or Chancellor no matter how well-meaning they may (or may not) be."[51]

The mayor had already demonstrated, with dramatic effect, that he could literally dismiss central school board members who disagreed with his policies. Another major flaw in the law concerned financial audits. The law did not specify whether it was the state comptroller or the city comptroller who had primary responsibility for auditing the Department of Education. According to testimony offered by the city comptroller William Thompson, Klein sometimes acted as though neither agency did.[52] Functioning as though it was neither a city nor a state agency, the Department of Education had also failed to comply with procedures outlined in the city charter for the procurement of contracts. Thompson presented data indicating that the value of noncompetitive bids grew from $15 million to $45 million from 2001 and 2003; in 2003 they were valued at $25 million, and by 2007 the amount had quadrupled, to $100 million.[53]

One of the more notorious of these contracts, mentioned by numerous witnesses who came before the commission, went to the firm of Alvarez & Marsal. According to the city comptroller, the firm was paid $16 million over seventeen months to make recommendations that would cut operating costs in the Department of Education. It was their rerouting of the school buses that, without warning, left thousands of children stranded on street corners on a cold winter day. The fiasco incensed parents and became the grist for heart-wrenching stories in the local media. In his testimony, Thompson also mentioned two consecutive no-bid contracts that were given to a firm called Platform Learning for tutoring services. While the initial two contracts were valued at $7.5 million, costs eventually soared to $62 million. According to Thompson, the Office of the Special Commissioner of Investigation later found that the firm had used enticements, such as gift certificates, to persuade schools to use their services.

Finally, the city comptroller spoke about the difficulty in monitoring spending owing to unusually large units of appropriation within the Department of

Education budget. One unit of appropriation amounted to $5.6 billion. Since agencies are permitted wide discretion in spending within units of appropriation, this practice undermines serious attempts to guarantee fiscal transparency. In separate testimony along the same lines, Ronnie Lowenstein, director of the Independent Budget Office of the City of New York, alluded to a $6.2 billion unit of appropriation.[54] Lowenstein also mentioned that because the financial management system used by the Department of Education is different from the system used by other city agencies, it is more difficult to track budget and spending data for schools.

What about Democracy?

The second major feature of the new governance law—the elimination of thirty-two elected community school boards and their replacement by local councils chosen by parent association officers—created more anxiety. While there was no groundswell of support for returning to elected school boards in New York, the demise of the boards became part of a larger picture developing in the minds of community activists.[55] A powerful mayoralty, enhanced by a schools takeover, occupied by an ambitious billionaire who had installed an aggressive chancellor, in a system with few checks on his power, made many people feel left out of policymaking. Even under the best of circumstances, democracy has a way of eluding the poorest of the poor, who are most dependent on government for essential services. Under mayoral control in New York, it was not the people systematically disenfranchised from politics who were complaining the most. Discontent was apparent among public officials, established advocate groups, and well-organized parents.

Joel Klein would dismiss such criticism as sour grapes from many of the same operatives who had stood in the way of meaningful reform before mayoral control was adopted.[56] Supporters of the administration contended that the malaise resulted from a basic disagreement over priorities suffered by those who were on the losing side of political disputes. As James Merriman of the Center for Charter School Excellence stated, "It is important that we do not confuse the fact that certain parent groups with certain views may feel left out because the present administration does not share their views."[57] Merriman argued that the administration was acting in the better interests of public school children who are not sufficiently represented in school politics. There is some truth to the latter claim; however, the level of dissatisfaction that had emerged under mayoral control was too widespread to be ignored.

Merrill Tisch, a member of the state board of regents who supports mayoral control, told the commission, "The public feels that it has lost its voice."[58] Manhattan borough president Scott Stringer, a former state legislator who had voted for mayoral control, testified that the governance law needed to be revised, with one primary goal in mind: "ensuring that the establishment of strong executive leadership for our schools does not result in the sanctioning of authoritarianism."[59] John Englert of the Citywide Council on Special Education remarked, "The current school governance structure operates as a dysfunctional corporation that does not seek input from the most important stakeholders, the parents of [New York City] school children."[60]

While witnesses who came before the commission criticized the law itself, they also alluded to a management style that disregarded the public and requirements within the law. Parent advocate Leonie Haimson, a frequent critic of the administration and its policies, alleged that "there is no transparency, no serious attempt to listen to the concerns of stakeholders, and a heedless and arrogant abuse of power."[61] Other individuals who testified spoke of an expansion in the size of the press office in the Department of Education, its role in disseminating performance-related data, and its association with city hall under a regime of mayoral control.[62] As one longtime observer of the city schools and supporter of mayoral control put it, "The temptation to put the best face on school data is political catnip."[63]

Although the community district education councils that replaced elected school boards did not have the authority to appoint local school administrators—a power revoked from the elected boards before 2002—they were meant to serve as forums for parent and community consultation at the neighborhood level. There was a strong feeling among council members that their role was treated in a perfunctory manner. Their frustration was palpable as they recounted their experience with the new arrangement. Council member Christopher Spinelli complained, "The [Department of Education] has done a very complete job tying the hands of the [community district education councils] while keeping them busy running back and forth to meetings at Tweed."[64] Several council members recalled attending meetings with school officials to discuss issues only to discover a day or two later that a decision had already been reached before the meeting occurred. Others spoke about the exclusion of parents from decisionmaking at the school level. School leadership teams that had been created to involve parents and teachers in the development of comprehensive education plans aligned with school budgets had been disbanded or became nonfunctional. Training that was supposed to prepare parents for involvement at the community and school levels was provided only sporadically, if at all.

One cannot overlook community government in New York. It is encoded in the institutional DNA of the city. It was never a perfect vehicle for democracy, but it has always been there in one form or another. Fifty-nine appointed community boards that were created in the city charter of 1975 have served as a credible voice for community concerns regarding land use, budgeting, and municipal service delivery, but they do not deal with schools. A school system composed of fifteen hundred schools serving 1.1 million students needs some form of administrative decentralization. While there was talk about redrawing school district boundaries to align with the fifty-nine service districts in the municipal government, the fact is that since 1969 the existing thirty-two school districts determined how New Yorkers defined community when it came to education. Under mayoral control, district offices depleted of staff were no longer functioning as places where parents could go to get information on schools or register complaints when they saw a problem.

Community school district governance involved two basic questions. How would local boards be selected? What powers would they have? The questions are related. The more confident the architects of a governance arrangement can be about the representative nature of the institutions they create, the more justified they can be in assigning these institutions public authority. The level of public participation in local school districts had always been uneven, both between districts and within districts. Structure could never serve as a remedy to undo the social characteristics that leave many people on the sidelines of democracy. There need to be adequate channels for participation by those parent and community groups who choose to and are capable of being involved, but one cannot assume that those who are involved entirely represent those who are not.

The parents who testified before the commission were smart, articulate, public spirited, and constructive. They also tended to come from middle-class neighborhoods. They frequently and sincerely addressed the concerns of their less fortunate neighbors; but on relatively few occasions, despite efforts to engage them in a variety of forums, did the less fortunate appear before the commission to speak for themselves. Democracy can be ineffective in reaching the truly disadvantaged. On this point, the logic of mayoral control is relevant, if not entirely satisfying. Mayoral control puts power in the hands of the most visible public figure chosen by the largest percentage of eligible voters who participate in the electoral process. Relatively few New Yorkers would argue that school board elections were a better vehicle for democracy than mayoral elections.[65] Since there was not a strong demand to return to elected school boards, there was a rationale for maintaining school councils and letting the chancellor appoint district administrators (superintendents). The superintendents would, in turn, appoint school principals. This thinking, however, is only part of the governance puzzle.

The logic of mayoral control also demands that the mayor be held accountable. Democracy demands that communities and parents have a voice in governance. The size of the city demands that meaningful points of access exist at the community level. Many observers believed that mayoral elections held once every four years to assess the city's chief executive on a variety of issues were not sufficient for making the mayor accountable. They felt that if local representatives had no say in the selection and retention of district superintendents and principals, then there was no reason to expect that these administrators would take parents seriously.

The Future

The Commission on School Governance released its report in an exclusive to the *New York Times* on September 4, 2008.[66] In accord with its findings, the thrust of the commission's recommendations was twofold: check the power of the mayor without substantially diluting it and create meaningful opportunities for public input into policy without encumbering the capacity of the school system to move ahead. As stated in the chapter 1, good governance requires balance. An urban school district needs strong leadership, but it must also be democratic. It must be representative, transparent, and accountable. Under the commission's proposed plan, the mayor would continue to appoint the chancellor and a majority (eight of thirteen seats) of the central school board, but the members would serve for fixed terms and not be easily removed except for cause. The chancellor would continue to appoint district superintendents who appoint principals in their respective districts; but rather than chair the central school board, the chancellor would serve only as an ex officio member, without a vote.

This structure would establish the independence of the central school board and reinforce the dual reporting relationship that the chancellor has to the board and the mayor. That being said, one needs to be careful not to overstate the duality of the arrangement. Unlike plans that exist in other cities, the authority of the mayor to appoint both the school chief and a majority of the central school board would remain absolute, without review by a screening panel or confirmation by another governmental body. The plan would require the mayor and the chancellor to explain their actions and seek approval from a body dominated by appointees of the same mayor. A capable chancellor with sound policies should have no difficulty doing that.

The commission also explored ways to clarify lines of accountability already existing within the municipality that could better check the power of the mayor on education matters. Given the structure of the municipal government and its empowerment of the mayor's office, the practical options here are limited. Several witnesses suggested assigning a more substantial role in education to the city council, which under the city charter already must approve local funding and has the power to hold hearings and conduct investigations. As the commission was in the process of hearing testimony, however, the city council became embroiled in a scandal when it was discovered that its leadership had been funneling public funds to "phantom organizations" that had been created on fake budget lines.[67] An investigation of the council was under way as the commission was preparing its report.

Following another path, the commission recommended that the city comptroller be granted primary responsibility for auditing the accounts of the school department and that the department be required to follow the procedures required of all city agencies in awarding contracts. The latter provisions are meant to create more fiscal transparency and to curb the extension of no-bid contracts. The state comptroller would retain authority to audit school accounts as provided by state law. Given that the New York City school system has a combined capital and expense budget in excess of $30 billion, there is hardly a danger that the department might be overaudited. The commission also recommended that the Independent Budget Office of the City of New York be given a formal role in evaluating the performance of the school department. Since its creation in 1996, the office has developed a reputation as a reliable and objective source of data on the performance of city agencies. Granting it an explicit role in education makes the public less reliant on the Department of Education or the mayor's office for information needed to assess the progress of schools.

In 2007, following the resolution of a major school finance suit, the New York state legislature passed the Budget and Reform Act of 2007. The objective of the law is to ensure meaningful public input on how new monies coming into the city schools as a result of the court decision are spent and to guarantee transparency once funds have been committed. The law, which requires public notice, information, and deliberation in a variety of forums throughout the city, could serve as a general model for democratic decision-making in the formation of education policy. Before this can occur, however, existing education institutions must be better equipped to carry out their duties openly.

An independent central school board that creates mechanisms for public input is a necessary first step, but it is not sufficient. In a system as large as New York's, school administrators at the neighborhood level must be required to consult with constituents about budgets, policies, and practices that affect their children. While the chancellor should appoint district superintendents, local school councils must have an advisory role in the selection process and should evaluate the local superintendent on an annual basis. While principals should have authority to run their schools effectively, school leadership teams should be established so that parents can work with principals, teachers, and other school personnel to develop a comprehensive education plan tied to the school budget.

Fostering democracy in a diverse and sprawling urban school district is difficult. Whatever the state legislature chooses to do when the current governance law sunsets in June 2009, making and refining laws can take us only so far. To reach the least powerful members of the school community and give them a say in the education of their children, those with the most power must embrace the values of democratic government and make a commitment to abide by its principles. Public officials must follow both the spirit and letter of the law to establish a governing relationship between the rulers and the ruled that advances these principles without compromise.

Notes

1. For a delightful short history of the city, see Joanne Reitano, *The Restless City: A Short History of New York from Colonial Times to the Present* (New York: Routledge, 2006). For a summary institutional history, see Joseph P. Viteritti, "The Tradition of Municipal Reform: Charter Revision in Historical Context," in *Restructuring the New York City Government: The Reemergence of Municipal Reform,* edited by Frank J. Mauro and Gerald Benjamin (New York: Academy of Political Science, 1989), pp. 16–30.

2. David C. Hammack, *Power and Society: Greater New York at the Turn of the Century* (New York: Russell Sage Foundation, 1982), pp. 185–229.

3. Robert W. Bailey, *Gay Politics, Urban Politics: Identity and Economics in the Urban Setting* (Columbia University Press, 1998), pp. 215–48. In 1990 the districting committee for the newly composed city council actually carved out a district in Chelsea that was identified as "gay winnable."

4. It was the responsibility of the city chamberlain to manage the city bank accounts. Peter Sweeny pledged to reform the office in 1866 when he publicly announced that he would not keep the interest on the city accounts for himself, as was

customary during the Tweed years. Kenneth D. Ackerman, *Boss Tweed: The Rise and Fall of the Corrupt Pol Who Conceived the Soul of Modern New York* (New York: Carroll & Graf, 2005), p. 72.

5. Frederick Shaw, *History of the New York City Legislature* (Columbia University Press, 1954).

6. Theodore J. Lowi, *At the Pleasure of the Mayor: Patronage and Power in New York City, 1898–1958* (Glencoe, N.Y.: Free Press, 1962).

7. There is an extensive and entertaining literature on Tweed and his Tammany organization. See Seymour J. Mandelbaum, *Boss Tweed's New York* (New York: John Wiley and Sons, 1965); Alexander Callow, *The Tweed Ring* (Oxford University Press, 1965); Jerome Mushkat, *Tammany: The Evolution of a Political Machine, 1789–1865* (Syracuse University Press); Ackerman, *Boss Tweed*.

8. See Frank J. Goodnow, *City Government in the United States* (New York: Century Company, 1910), pp. 147–48; Edward Dana Durand, "Council Government versus Mayor Government," *Political Science Quarterly* 15 (December 1900): 675–709.

9. For portraits of Tammany's legacy in New York politics, see Warren Moscow, *What Have You Done for Me Lately? The Ins and Outs of New York City Politics* (Englewood Cliffs, N.J.: Prentice-Hall, 1967); Edward N. Costikyan, *Behind Closed Doors: Politics in the Public Interest* (New York: Harcourt Brace Jovanovich, 1966).

10. On LaGuardia's reforms, see Thomas Kessler, *Fiorello H. LaGuardia and the Making of Modern New York* (New York: McGraw-Hill, 1989).

11. Citizens Union, "Home Town in a Great City," *Searchlight* 37 (1947). See also Citizens Union, "Community Administration within New York City: Home Town in the Big City" (Citizens Union Research Foundation, 1962). I am indebted to my late former colleague and friend Dick Netzer for bringing these historical materials to my attention.

12. Robert F. Pecorella, *Community Power in a Postreform City: Politics in New York City* (Armonk, N.Y.: M. E. Sharpe, 1994), pp. 82–197; Joseph P. Viteritti, *Bureaucracy and Social Justice* (Port Washington, N.Y.: Kennikat Press, 1979), pp. 59–88.

13. Diane Ravitch, *The Great School Wars: A History of the New York City Public Schools* (Johns Hopkins University Press, 2000), pp. 287–406.

14. Statutes of the State of New York, chapter 634, May 26, 1972.

15. Robert W. Bailey, *The Crisis Regime: The MAC, the EFCB, and the Political Impact of the New York City Financial Crisis* (State University of New York Press, 1984); Martin Shefter, *Political Crisis/Fiscal Crisis: The Collapse and Revival of New York City* (New York: Basic Books, 1985).

16. See *The City in Transition: Prospects and Policies for New York; The Final Report of the Temporary Commission on City Finances* (New York: Arno Press, 1978), outlining the causes of the fiscal crisis.

17. *Board of Estimate of the City of New York* v. *Morris*, 489 U.S. 688 (1989). Between 1901 and 1958, the board of estimate had a weighted voting scheme for the borough representatives based on population.

18. See, generally, Mauro and Benjamin, *Restructuring the New York City Government.*

19. Joseph. P. Viteritti, "The New Charter: Will It Make a Difference?" in *Urban Politics, New York Style,* edited by Jewel Bellush and Dick Netzer (Armonk, N.Y.: M. E. Sharpe, 1990), pp. 413–28.

20. Because its representation was reduced to three seats in an expanded fifty-one member city council, Staten Island, feeling vulnerable, sought to secede from the city. See Joseph P. Viteritti, "Municipal Home Rule and the Conditions of Justifiable Secession," *Fordham Urban Law Journal* 23 (1995): 1–68.

21. David W. Chen and Michael Barbaro, "Mayor's Bid for Third Term Backed by City Council," *New York Times,* October 24, 2008, p. A1.

22. Diane Ravitch and Joseph Viteritti, "New York: The Obsolete Factory," in *New Schools for a New Century: The Redesign of Urban Education,* edited by Diane Ravitch and Joseph Viteritti (Yale University Press, 1996), pp. 17–36.

23. See Chris McNickle, *To Be Mayor of New York: Ethnic Politics in the City* (Columbia University Press, 1993); Vincent Cannato, *The Ungovernable City: John Lindsay's New York and the Crisis of Liberalism* (New York: Basic Books, 2001); John Hull Mollenkoph, *A Phoenix in the Ashes: The Rise and Fall of the Koch Coalition in New York City Politics* (Princeton University Press, 1992); Michael Goodwin, ed., *New York Comes Back: The Mayoralty of Edward I. Koch* (New York: PowerHouse Books, 2005); Wilbur C. Rich, *David Dinkins and New York City Politics: Race, Images, and the Media* (State University of New York Press, 2007); Fred Siegel, *The Prince of the City: Giuliani, New York, and the Genius of American Life* (San Francisco: Encounter Books, 2005).

24. Michael Cooper, "At $92.60 a Vote, Bloomberg Shatters an Election Record," *New York Times,* December 4, 2001, p. A1.

25. Michael Barbaro and David W. Chen, "Mayor Expected to Seek 3rd Term, Rejecting Limits," *New York Times,* October, 1, 2008, p. A1. See also Clyde Haberman, "The Bloomberg Test of the Democratic Process," *New York Times,* October 3, 2008, p. B1.

26. Jennifer Medina and Elissa Gootman, "A New Campaign to Keep Schools under the Mayor's Thumb," *New York Times,* September 2, 2008, p. B1.

27. Diane Caldwell, "Bloomberg, Seeing a Soul Mate, Sends Troops to Help Lieberman," *New York Times,* October 28, 2006, p. A1; Jill Gardiner, "Mayor Intensifies Fund-Raising for Candidates Near and Far," *New York Sun,* October 25, 2006 (www.nysun. com/article/42206).

28. Michael Barbaro, "Bloomberg in Florida Blasts Rumor on Obama," *New York Times,* June 21, 2008, p. B1.

29. This is not to say that the marriage of money and power is a recent development in New York. See Sven Beckert, *The Monied Metropolis: New York City and the Consolidation of the American Bourgeois* (Cambridge University Press, 2003).

30. Sam Roberts and Jim Rutenberg, "With More Private Giving, Bloomberg Forges Ties," *New York Times,* May 23, 2005, p. A1.

31. Diane Caldwell, "Bloomberg to Give Out $60 Million," *New York Times,* June 13, 2008, p. B4.

32. Michael Barbaro and David W. Chen, "Mayor Enlists His Charities in Bid to Stay," *New York Times,* October 18, 2008, p. A1.

33. Robert Jackson, Testimony before the Commission on School Governance, November 29, 2007, in *Final Report of the Commission on School Governance, Volume II: Written Testimony Submitted to the Commission,* prepared for Betsey Gotbaum, Public Advocate for the City of New York (Commission on School Governance, September 4, 2008). (Note that this reference applies for all subsequent citations of testimony to the Commission.)

34. David Rogers, *110 Livingston Street* (New York: Random House, 1968); Joseph P. Viteritti, *Across the River: Politics and Education in the City* (New York: Holmes & Meier, 1983), pp. xi–xv, 3–23.

35. Abby Goodnough, "Senior Officials Sent Packing in Overhaul of City's Schools," *New York Times,* January 29, 2003, p. B1.

36. Michael R. Bloomberg, "Major Address on Education," New York Urban League's Dr. Martin Luther King Jr. Symposium, January 15, 2003; Joel Klein, Testimony to the City Council Education Committee Regarding Children First, March 3, 2003.

37. David M. Herszenhorn, "Albany Attacks Bloomberg's School Plan," *New York Times,* April 23, 2003, p. B1.

38. Joel Klein, "Children First and Mayoral Control: Creating a System of Successful NYC Public Schools," New York City Department of Education, n.d.; Joel Klein, remarks on mayoral control, Manhattan Institute, New York, March 25, 2008.

39. David M. Herszenhorn, "Bloomberg Wins on School Tests after Firing Foes," *New York Times,* March 16, 2004, p. A1; Jennifer Steinhauer, "Mayor's Move to Hardball," *New York Times,* March 16, 2004, p. A1.

40. See also Norm Fruchter, "'*Plus ça Change . . .* ': Mayoral Control in New York City," in *The Transformation of Great American School Districts: How Big Cities Are Reshaping Public Education,* edited by William Low Boyd, Charles Taylor Kerchner, and Mark Blyth (Harvard Education Press, 2008), pp. 85–112.

41. Joel Klein, Testimony before the Commission on School Governance, April, 17, 2008.

42. Jennifer Medina, "Scores in Reading and Math Rise Sharply," *New York Times,* June 24, 2008, p. A1.

43. Between 2002 and 2008, the operating budget of the Department of Education grew from $11,883,216,000 to $16,875,522,000. Data supplied to the author by the Independent Budget Office of the City of New York, July 16, 2008.

44. Quinnipiac poll, July 16, 2008 (www.quinnipiac.edu/x1302.xml?ReleaseID= 1193).

45. Data supplied to the author by the Independent Budget Office of the City of New York, July 16, 2008.

46. Dennis Walcott, Testimony before the Commission on School Governance, April 17, 2008.

47. Kathryn Wylde, Testimony before the Commission on School Governance, December 20, 2007.

48. Commission on School Governance, *Final Report of the Commission on School Governance, Volume I: Findings and Recommendatons,* prepared for Betsey Gotbaum, Public Advocate for the City of New York (September 4, 2008), p. 13.

49. Randi Weingarten, Testimony before the Commission on School Governance, November 29, 2007.

50. Herman Badillo, Testimony before the Commission on School Governance, April 8, 2008.

51. Steven Sanders, Testimony before the Commission on School Governance, January 24, 2008.

52. William C. Thompson, Testimony before the Commission on School Governance, December 13, 2007.

53. See also David Herszenhorn, "No-Bid Contracts Draw City Council's Ire," *New York Times,* November 22, 2006, p. B1.

54. Ronnie Lowenstein, Testimony before the Commission on School Governance, March 27, 2008.

55. Abby Goodnough, "Some Parents Fear Weaker Role in Centralized Schools," *New York Times,* January 17, 2003, p. B3.

56. Joel Klein, Testimony before the Commission on School Governance, April 17, 2008.

57. James Merriman, Testimony before the Commission on School Governance, December 20, 2007.

58. Merrill Tisch, Testimony before the Commission on School Governance, November 29, 2007.

59. Scott Stringer, Testimony before the Commission on School Governance, March 6, 2007.

60. John Englert, Testimony before the Commission on School Governance, January 31, 2008.

61. Leonie Haimson, Testimony before the Commission on School Governance, February 21, 2008.

62. Sol Stern, Testimony before the Commission on School Governance, January 3, 2008.

63. David Bloomfield, Testimony before the Commission on School Governance, January 10, 2008.

64. Christopher Spinelli, Testimony before the Commission on School Governance, February 28, 2008.

65. One might argue that turnout in school board elections could have been improved in New York if the confusing system of proportional voting were changed

and elections were held in November. Because New York is a dependent school district, however, residents do not vote on a school budget or school taxes, issues that tend to drive turnout in other districts.

66. Jennifer Medina, "Panel Backs Leaving Schools under the Mayor," *New York Times,* September 4, 2008, p. B1. See also *New York Times,* "Preserving New York's Schools," editorial, September 10, 2008, p. A24. See also Michael R. Bloomberg, letter to the editor, *New York Times,* September 16, 2008, p. A28.

67. Diane Caldwell, "Longtime Practice of City Council Financing Lands on Speaker's Shoulders," *New York Times,* May 11, 2008, p. 29.

Editor's Postscript

As a political scientist who has given careful attention to the issue, I feel obligated to make a few closing remarks about the study of school governance in general and mayoral control of the schools in particular. Since you have read this far in the book, you know already that governance is more about politics than science. So be it. If there were ever a wellspring of wisdom on the subject to erupt from American soil, it was more likely to flow from Independence Hall in Philadelphia than from the Harvard Business School in Cambridge. Sure, management is important; but governance is first and foremost about the perpetuation of democracy. A governance plan that undermines leadership is weak; a governance plan that undermines the public is intolerable. With mayoral control, accountability must proceed on two levels: the schools are directly answerable to the mayor, and the mayor is ultimately answerable to the people.

If I had to summarize my advice to fellow researchers in one short sentence, I would say, "Be careful with what you look at; it might distract you from what you need to see." The adoption of mayoral control is a symptom of a general frustration with the progress of urban schools. Most people of good will want to see these schools improve so that the schools can enrich the lives of the children who attend them. If the reform of a governance structure does not advance the education agenda, then it cannot be deemed a success. That being said, it would be an enormous miscalculation to judge the success of a governance plan largely on the basis of student or school performance, however it is measured. As we have found in New York, there are too many intervening variables to draw a direct line between institutional structure and education outcomes. Governance is really an enabler. It enables public officials to better "take charge" of a situation, as much as any individual or institution can or should take charge in government.

The most significant attribute that mayoral control can bestow on a large urban school district is that of agility, which might be defined as ease of movement. Such facility is welcome in systems that historically have been inert, but quickness of action also generates risk. For one thing, it increases the probability of error. More important, it can disrupt the balance of power. Our founders purposely made government cumbersome because they feared that concentrating too much power in a single office could threaten democracy. If local governments and school districts become too cumbersome, however, they remain stagnant. The operative rule, once again, is balance. Cities and school districts have a stronger managerial imperative than the federal or state governments, yet local government belongs to the people.

When mayors take charge of education, schools are only one part of the governance puzzle. The power of a particular mayor is dependent on the institutional architecture of the municipal government, as well as the way we organize schools. The interlocking structures and processes that exist between cities and schools need to be assessed as part of a larger whole, even though we can only repair them in a piecemeal fashion. In a system that permits an individual to spend an unlimited amount of money to get elected mayor, tinkering with the fine points of school governance sometimes felt like putting a new latch on the barn door after the barn had collapsed.

Unfortunately, different players shape the various pieces of the governance puzzle, within several decisionmaking arenas in the political process. The state legislature generally has more to say across the board than any other deliberative body in a given jurisdiction. Legislators, however, have a more personal stake in election laws than they have in school policy, and the advocates who try to reform the campaign finance process do not necessarily overlap with school constituencies. City charters that arrange the structure of the municipality usually get written at the local level altogether. And whatever is done to fix the structures, processes, and laws pertaining to governance, those who most rely on the public schools to improve their lives will continue to dwell on the outskirts of power.

So when the governance puzzle finally gets assembled, the pieces do not quite fit as well as they should. This is why well-designed constitutions contain an amendment process. Similarly, a well-conceived school governance plan that veers from the traditional model should include a sunset provision. The job is never quite done. We need to keep working at it as the times, circumstances, and players change. In the process we must listen to as many people as we can and insist that our chosen leaders do the same.

About the Authors

CLARA HEMPHILL is with the Center for New York City Affairs at the New School University. A former reporter and editorial writer for *New York Newsday*, she shared a Pulitzer Prize for local reporting. The *New York Times* has called her series of books "the most definitive guides" to the best public schools in New York. She is also the founding editor of the Insideschools.org website.

JEFFREY R. HENIG is professor of political science and education at Teachers College, Columbia University. His most recent book is *Spin Cycle: How Research Is Used in Policy Debates* (Russell Sage and The Century Foundation, 2008). He is coeditor of *Mayors in the Middle: Politics, Race, and Mayoral Control of Urban Schools* (Princeton, 2004); coauthor of *Building Civic Capacity: The Politics of Reforming Urban Schools* (University Press of Kansas, 2001) and *The Color of School Reform: Race, Politics, and the Challenge of Urban Education* (Princeton University Press, 1999); and author of *Rethinking School Choice: The Limits of the Market Metaphor* (Princeton University Press, 1994).

MICHAEL W. KIRST is emeritus professor of education and business administration at Stanford University. He is the author of ten books, including *The Political Dynamics of Education* (McCutchan, 2005) and *From High School to College* (Jossey-Bass, 2004). He served as a member of the California State Board of Education from 1975 to 1982.

JOHN PORTZ is professor and chair of the Political Science Department at Northeastern University. He is the coauthor of *City Schools and City Politics: Institutions and Leadership in Pittsburgh, Boston, and St. Louis* (University Press of Kansas, 1999). He has served as an elected member of the town council and the school committee in Watertown, Massachusetts.

DIANE RAVITCH is a research professor in the Steinhardt School of Education at New York University and a senior fellow at the Brookings Institution and Stanford University. Among her many books are *The Great School Wars: A History of the New York City Public Schools* (John Hopkins University Press, 2000), *Left Back: A Century of Battles over School Reform* (Simon and Schuster, 2000), and *The Troubled Crusade: American Education, 1945–1980* (Basic Books, 1983). She has served as assistant secretary of education (appointed by President George H. W. Bush) and as a member of the National Assessment Governing Board (appointed by President Bill Clinton).

WILBUR C. RICH is the Walter J. Kenan Jr. Professor of Political Science at Wellesley College. He is coeditor of *Mayors in the Middle: Politics, Race, and Mayoral Control of Urban Schools* (Princeton University Press, 2004). Among the books he has written are *Black Mayors and School Politics* (Routledge, 1996) and *David Dinkins and New York City Politics: Race, Images, and the Media* (State University of New York Press, 2007).

ROBERT SCHWARTZ is academic dean and Bloomberg Professor of Practice at the Harvard Graduate School of Education. He has served as the first president of Achieve, Incorporated, and directed education grant making at the Pew Charitable Trusts. He has been an education policy adviser to both the mayor of Boston and the governor of Massachusetts and has served as special assistant to the president of the University of Massachusetts and executive director of the Boston Compact.

DOROTHY SHIPPS is associate professor of public affairs and education at Baruch College, City University of New York. She served as managing director of the Consortium on Chicago School Research from 1996 to 1999. She is the author of *School Reform, Corporate Style: Chicago, 1880–2000* (University Press of Kansas, 2006) and coeditor of *Reconstructing the Common Good in Education: Coping with Intractable American Dilemmas* (Stanford University Press, 2000).

JOSEPH P. VITERITTI is the Blanche D. Blank Professor of Public Policy and chair of the Department of Urban Affairs and Planning at Hunter College, City University of New York. Among nine other books, he is the author of *The Last Freedom: Religion from the Public School to the Public Square* (Princeton University Press, 2007), *Choosing Equality: School Choice, the Constitution, and Civil Society* (Brookings, 1999), and *Across the River: Politics and Education in the City* (Holmes and Meier, 1983); and he has edited (with Diane Ravitch) *City Schools: Lessons from New York* (Johns Hopkins University Press,

2000) and *New Schools for a New Century: The Redesign of Urban Education* (Yale University Press, 1997). He has served as special assistant to the chancellor of schools in New York and as a senior adviser to the school superintendents in Boston and San Francisco.

KENNETH K. WONG is Walter and Leonore Annenberg Professor in Education Policy at Brown University, where he is director of the Urban Education Policy program. He is the coauthor of *The Education Mayor: Improving America's Schools* (Georgetown University Press, 2007) and the author of *Funding Public Schools: Politics and Policy* (University Press of Kansas, 1999).

Index

Academic performance. *See* Performance assessment

Accountability: in Boston public schools, 92–93, 95, 106, 110; and capacity building, 80; in Chicago public schools, 54, 76, 118, 121; for education, 67, 79, 86; and fiscal discipline, 83; and governance, 62; and mass media, 4; of mayors, 6–7, 27, 47, 52, 65, 227; of parents, 127; and policy decisions, 132; and public speeches, 26; of school districts, 227; and test scores, 32; in top-down model, 51

Achievement gaps, 2, 37, 56, 65, 72–73, 75, 107

Achievement inequality ratios, 73–77

Ackerman, Arlene, 28

ACT scores, 152

Adamany, David, 154–55, 162, 163

Advocates for Children of New York, 202

African Americans: achievement and test scores for, 70, 78, 107, 129; in Boston, 51, 98; in Chicago, 5, 119, 120, 121, 129; and community control, 194; and decentralization, 198; and desegregation, 187–88; in Detroit, 149–50,

152–53, 164; graduation rates for, 129; and learning gap, 2; and lowest-performing schools, 71; and mayoral relations, 7–8; promotion and retention for, 127, 130; and public school systems, 30; and Riverdale-Kingsbridge Academy, 192–93; on school boards, 161, 189, 192

African Free School (New York City), 172, 173

AFSCME (American Federation of State, County, and Municipal Employees), 158

After-school programs, 111, 139

Aguirre, Pam, 154

Aiello, Steve, 10

Alabama, civil rights in, 48

Albuquerque, 26, 46

Aldermen. *See* Board of aldermen

Alvarez & Marsal (firm), 223

American Federation of State, County, and Municipal Employees (AFSCME), 158

American Federation of Teachers, 125

American School Board Journal, 157

Anagnostopoulos, Dorothea, 65

Annenberg Foundation, 103, 105